Ray Didinger

Finished Business

My Fifty Years of Headlines, Heroes, and Heartaches

TEMPLE UNIVERSITY PRESS

Philadelphia • *Rome* • *Tokyo*

TEMPLE UNIVERSITY PRESS
Philadelphia, Pennsylvania 19122
tupress.temple.edu

Library of Congress Cataloging-in-Publication Data

Names: Didinger, Ray, author.
Title: Finished business : my fifty years of headlines, heroes, and heartaches
  / Ray Didinger.
Description: Philadelphia : Temple University Press, 2021. | Includes index.
  | Summary: "The memoirs of Philadelphia sportswriter Ray Didinger,
  including his time covering the Eagles, Flyers, 76ers, and Phillies"—Provided
  by publisher.
Identifiers: LCCN 2020029894 | ISBN 9781439920602 (cloth)
Subjects: LCSH: Didinger, Ray. | Sportscasters—Pennsylvania—Philadelphia—
  Biography. | Sports—Pennsylvania—Philadelphia—Anecdotes.
Classification: LCC GV742.42 .D52 2021 | DDC 796.092/274811—dc23
LC record available at https://lccn.loc.gov/2020029894

♾ The paper used in this publication meets the requirements of the American
National Standard for Information Sciences—Permanence of Paper for Printed
Library Materials, ANSI Z39.48–1992

Printed in the United States of America

9 8 7 6 5 4 3 2

Praise for Ray Didinger
and *Finished Business*

"**W**HEN IT COMES TO THE CONSCIENCE of Philly sports, there's only one voice I want to hear—Ray's voice. There is no one better to take us through the last five decades covering the city's biggest moments and largest characters. I couldn't put the book down. You will laugh. You will cry. You will shake your head in disbelief. You will understand why I feel Ray is the most respected Philly sports journalist of my lifetime."
    —**KEVIN NEGANDHI,** ESPN SportsCenter anchor
    and Philadelphia native

"**F**OR LONGER than most Philadelphians have been rooting for the Eagles, Ray Didinger has been writing about them better than anyone else. He knows football, but his interest goes well beyond the game. It's the people he loves, the ever-changing cast of characters in the locker room, those whose paths lead to crushing failure as much as those who achieve brilliant success. In his work, football becomes a metaphor for life."
    —**MARK BOWDEN,** best-selling author of *Black Hawk Down*

"**I**T IS SAFE TO SAY NO SPORTSWRITER is or has been in a better position to chronicle the last 50 years of Philadelphia sports history than Ray Didinger. His literary skills combined with his integrity, due diligence, and work ethic opened the door for him to enter any and all sports sanctuaries. . . . It takes a long time to earn real credibility in the sports writing community. Ray has done that."
    —**DICK VERMEIL,** Eagles Hall of Fame coach and
    Super Bowl–winning coach with the St. Louis Rams

"**N**O JOURNALIST I CAN THINK OF has supplied more information with less ostentation than Ray Didinger. Over the years, Ray has passed so seamlessly from reporter to columnist to broadcaster that I think of him as only one way—communicator. This city has produced a small army of talented sports journalists, all of whom could (and would) argue about who's the best. But in my mind, Ray would be on that Mount Rushmore for sure."
    —**JACK MCCALLUM,** *Sports Illustrated*

"**T**HIS BOOK IS A MUST-READ for any Eagles fan, but even for average Philadelphians who don't care about pro football, because Ray Didinger, perhaps the greatest Philadelphia sportswriter of all time, writes a book that will delight Eagles fans with its football lore. But at the same time, he captures what the city of Philadelphia is about and how our grittiness and toughness, which make us special, were reflected in the Eagles Super Bowl championship team."
—**EDWARD G. RENDELL,** former Governor of Pennsylvania

"**R**AY DIDINGER is a treasure to all of those who have read, listened to, or watched him over the past half-century in Philadelphia. This book reflects all of his many gifts—painting a picture with the brushstrokes of a wordsmith, inviting the reader inside every locker room and smoke-filled room, and answering the toughest questions with boldness and precision. Ray has been a guest on my radio show for 30 years now, and his every appearance leaves me in awe. This book will have the same effect on you."
—**ANGELO CATALDI**, 94WIP Sports Radio

"**R**AY DIDINGER has been more than a chronicler of Philadelphia sports over the years—he's been a rich character in the unfolding dramas and comedies that make this city so special. Ray's retelling of his life on the scene will make you laugh, holler, applaud—and ultimately want to read this book all over again."
—**GLEN MACNOW,** 94WIP Sports Radio

"**F**OR OUR SAKE, let's hope Ray Didinger's business is never finished. His insight, analysis, warmth, and—above all—sheer storytelling prowess make this book another must-read."
—**MICHAEL BARKANN,** NBC Sports Philadelphia anchor

"**F**OR THE LONGEST TIME, I wanted to marry Ray Didinger. It's not like I even knew him. I tease him about it whenever I see him these days. As a high schooler who longed to be a journalist, I was smitten with his stories in the *Delaware County Daily Times*, especially one about a haberdashery in Chester, my hometown. The accompanying photos were of Ray wearing—what else?—a hat. Cowboy, straw, and a soft felt number, among others. I thought he was so brave! As it turns out, Ray is indeed a man of many hats. Playwright, producer, filmmaker, sports-writer, screenwriter, radio host, TV analyst, and author. *Finished Business*, his memoir of 50 years covering the Philadelphia sports market, is meant to be slowly sipped and savored. So, kick back, let his words wash over you, and enjoy. Hats off to you, Ray."

—**TERRY TAYLOR**, Associated Press Sports Editor (1992–2014)

"**F**ROM EAGLES BEAT WRITER to NFL Films producer to Eagles host for NBC Sports Philadelphia to award-winning playwright, Ray Didinger shares his journey with each and every one of us. His memoir had me laughing, crying, and taking an introspection deep into my soul."

—**BRIAN BALDINGER**, NFL Network analyst

"**I**T'S HARD FOR ME TO BELIEVE that I have known Ray Didinger for over 40 years, but our start goes way back, without knowing it, to our youth football days when the likes of Tommy McDonald, Pete Retzlaff, and Chuck Bednarik hoisted the NFL Championship Trophy for the world to see. We were dreamers then, opponents on opposites sides of the ball, but we shared the same passion . . . our beloved Philadelphia Eagles.

Our paths would cross again in 1976 when my Eagles dream was fulfilled and when Ray's intellect and insight vaulted him to stardom in the Philly press corps. It was in 1976 when Ray dubbed me as *Invincible* Vince Papale, and Disney picked up on it 30 years later, . . . with Ray ironically appearing in one of the scenes.

Pro sports I found is a family, based on trust, and there are plenty of hugs of joy and anguish that go with the range of emotions associated with winning and losing. So, Ray's story of hugging his son is so reminiscent of me hugging my Dad when I made the Eagles and hugging as a family in the stadium when Brady's 'Hail Mary' thankfully fell to the turf. Eagles fans hugging with tears of joy, all over the world. A moment in time never to be forgotten . . . like, where were you when the Eagles won the Super Bowl?

So, *Finished Business* is all about the hugs, and the emotions and recollections of the most trusted and witty sports journalist that we will ever see. Ever! Social distancing or not, if Ray were here with me right now, I would give Ray a huge hug. He is the example of what being Invincible is all about!"

—**VINCE PAPALE**, former Philadelphia Eagle
and the inspiration for the film *Invincible*

Acknowledgments

WRITING THIS BOOK and looking back over fifty years in sports media made me realize just how many people I have to thank.

I have to start with my parents and grandparents for encouraging me every step of the way. Their love of sports was something they passed on to me during our Sunday bus rides to Franklin Field and our trips to Eagles training camp.

My best friends growing up, John Zappacosta and Bob McCauley, knew what they wanted to be. John wanted to be a teacher. Bob wanted to be an architect. I wanted to be a writer. Guess what? John became a teacher, Bob became an architect, and I became a writer. I think we inspired each other. I know they inspired me. I cherish our friendship to this day.

Sister Clare Ursula, S.S.J., my fifth-grade teacher, and Donald Bell and John Mooney, my English teachers at St. James High School, encouraged me to develop my writing skills. Doug Perry, John Praksta, Lew Klein, and John Roberts brought real-life experience to their classes at Temple University. It was so cool to see Mr. Roberts anchor the late news on Channel 6 and walk into our classroom the next morning.

Growing up in Philadelphia, I had many role models in the local media. Reading Sandy Grady and George Kiseda in the *Philadelphia Bulletin* and Stan Hochman in the *Philadelphia Daily News* was an education in sports writing. Listening to Bill Campbell call the Eagles and

Phillies games on the radio made me appreciate the power of the spoken word. To hear Bill describe a Richie Allen home run on a warm summer night was like sweet music to my ears.

I was fortunate to have editors like Arthur Mayhew of the *Delaware County Daily Times*, Jack Wilson of the *Philadelphia Bulletin*, and Mike Rathet of the *Philadelphia Daily News*. I worked with many talented journalists, including Alan Richman, Jim Barniak, Nick Nagurny, Bob Vetrone, and Mark Whicker at the *Bulletin*; and Dick Weiss, Dick Jerardi, Paul Domowitch, Mike Kern, Jay Greenberg, Bill Fleishman, Marcus Hayes, Mark Kram, Les Bowen, and Rich Hofmann at the *Daily News*.

Steve Sabol welcomed me into his NFL Films family and gave me the opportunity to work with true artists, including Phil Tuckett, Chris Barlow, Steve Seidman, Dave Plaut, Keith Cossrow, Ken Rodgers, Vince Caputo, Dave Robidoux, Mike Adams, Kevin Mattice, Peter Frank, and Jeff Hillegass. Thanks for letting me be part of the one NFL team that never has a bad season.

Randy Covington and Tom Stathakes gave me a chance to work in television at KYW (Channel 3) during the 1985 newspaper strike; that part-time job opened the door to a whole new career. Today, at NBC Sports Philadelphia, I share the *Eagles Post-Game Live* set with Michael Barkann, Seth Joyner, and Barrett Brooks. Doing the show after Super Bowl LII will always be a special memory.

It is hard to believe, but I have now worked in radio longer than I worked in newspapers. Glen Macnow, my co-host, and I have been together for almost twenty years at 94WIP Sports Radio. We're part of a lineup that includes Angelo Cataldi, Al Morganti, Rhea Hughes, Joe DeCamara, Jon Ritchie, Keith Jones, Ike Reese, Jon Marks, Rob Ellis, Joe Gigilo, Joe Conklin, and Big Daddy Graham. They keep it real every day in the best sports town in America.

Thanks to Eagles coaches Dick Vermeil and Charlie Gauer, who took the time to teach me the pro game. I appreciate your wisdom and friendship. I also thank Ron Jaworski and Brian Baldinger, who left the office door open so I could watch film with them. Jim Murray, Leo Carlin, and Jim Gallagher, three true gentlemen, brought warmth and humor to the Eagles front office.

Jim Solano and Dave Frankel have been invaluable in handling my business affairs. Ray Kelly Jr., Paul Giordano, Jack McCaffery, Mike Sielski, Bob Ford, Jayson Stark, Bill Lyon, Reuben Frank, and Mark Eckel made the press box a fun place to hang out.

I owe a special thanks to Tommy McDonald for inspiring me with

Finished Business

• To Maria •

Contents

Photo gallery follows page 152

his friendship and allowing me to share in his Hall of Fame weekend. I never had a bigger thrill than standing next to Tommy in Canton, Ohio. Thanks to Joe Canuso, Deborah Block, and Bruce Graham for believing in the story of *Tommy and Me*. Thanks to the actors—Tom Teti, Matt Pfeiffer, Simon Kiley, Ned Pryce, and Frank Nardi Jr.—for bringing Tommy's story to life.

The staff at Temple University Press—in particular, director Mary Rose Muccie, editor-in-chief Aaron Javsicas, production editor Ashley Petrucci, and art director Kate Nichols—worked overtime to keep the book on schedule through the COVID-19 pandemic. Thanks to Heather Wilcox of Second Glance Editorial, who fine-tuned the manuscript.

Pat McLoone, managing editor for sports at the *Philadelphia Inquirer*, helped acquire material for the book. Bob Laramie, Brad Nau, and Ed Mahan dug through their archives to find some great photos.

Most of all, I want to thank my wonderful wife, Maria; our children, David and Kathleen; their spouses, Christine and Scott; and our grandchildren, Haley, Kaitlyn, Emmet, and George. They provide the best home-field advantage imaginable.

Finished Business

Introduction

I WAS STANDING at the baggage carousel, listening to chants of "E-A-G-L-E-S" echo through the airport. It was the morning of February 5, 2018, the first morning to dawn with Philadelphia wearing the crown of Super Bowl champions. The celebration had been going on all night, and judging by the looks on people's faces, no one had slept very much.

I had just stepped off a plane from Minneapolis, where I had watched the Eagles defeat the New England Patriots, 41–33, in a breathtaking title game that went down to the final play, a Hail Mary pass from Tom Brady that fell incomplete. It was a moment that seemed frozen in time, that felt dreamlike, leaving you to wonder in that instant, "Is this really happening?"

Then the confetti began to fall from the ceiling of the U.S. Bank Stadium. You looked closely. Yes, it was green and silver confetti. The Eagles logo was flashing on the scoreboard under the words "Super Bowl Champions." Doug Pederson and Nick Foles were celebrating on the field, and Tom Brady was trudging, head down, toward the tunnel.

That's when it hit you: The Eagles had done it. They finally had won the Super Bowl, and they had done it with a stunning victory over the Patriots. They had done it as underdogs, which seemed altogether appropriate for a team from Philadelphia, the city where people still run in the footsteps of Rocky Balboa.

Watching the trophy presentation on the field, I could only imagine what was happening on the streets of Philadelphia. The city had waited fifty-two years for this moment, waiting for the Eagles to finally win the big one and wash away the heartache of all those bitter losses. I almost wondered whether the city would still be standing when we landed at Philadelphia International Airport on Monday.

Thankfully, it was.

I was in the baggage area, waiting for my suitcase, when an airport worker approached.

"That must have been quite a flight," he said, pointing to the other passengers, all of whom were dressed in Eagles green and still aglow from a long night of partying.

"I think they could've flown home without the plane," I said.

The man smiled and said, "I have to tell you something."

He paused, trying to find the words.

"That moment with your son, the hug," he said.

He paused again. He looked like he was about to cry.

"That was beautiful," he said.

He was a big man with a raspy voice and the thick, calloused hands of a blue-collar worker. He seemed embarrassed by his show of emotion.

"Next to the 'Philly Special,' that was the highlight of the night," he said, referencing the outrageous trick play the Eagles used to score a touchdown, with Trey Burton lobbing the ball to a wide-open Foles in the end zone. "When you and your son hugged, it was like you were hugging for the whole city. That's the damn truth."

He laughed, and then he hugged me too. I thanked him before he disappeared into the crowd. We had never met before, and we haven't met since, but that memory will stay with me. It made the Super Bowl victory personal in a way that surprised even me.

For one fan—and, as I would later discover, for many others—my son David and I had become avatars for Eagles fans everywhere. We didn't know it at the time, but when we put our arms around each other, we were putting our arms around the entire region.

The Hug. I still hear about it to this day.

I should explain how it happened. David is an Emmy Award–winning cameraman for NFL Films. He has worked at more than twenty Super Bowls, but this one was special because the Eagles were in it. He grew up around the team. Not only did I cover the Eagles as a newspaper reporter; his mother was once an Eagles cheerleader. The family album is full of pictures of David as a boy posing with the coaches and players. Veterans Stadium was like his personal Astroturf playground.

I had moved from newspapers to radio and TV by 2017, but I was still identified with the Eagles, serving as an analyst for NBC Sports Philadelphia. We knew we would be in the stadium for the Super Bowl postgame show, but we didn't know where exactly.

David vowed that if the Eagles won the game, he would find me so we could celebrate. I said not to bother. It is total chaos at the end of a Super Bowl. It would be like trying to find someone in Times Square on New Year's Eve. He insisted.

"I'm gonna find you," he said, "and give you a hug."

We didn't know until the morning of the Super Bowl where we would be for the postgame show. As it turned out, it was a booth on the mezzanine level behind the end zone where Brady's final pass came down. It was located near a large contingent of Philadelphia fans, which made for a lively show after the Eagles' victory.

About forty minutes into the broadcast, I saw the door open and David appear. He had finished filming the postgame celebration and, as promised, found our location. I whispered to Michael Barkann, who was hosting the postgame show, "When's our next break?"

"Why? You need to use the bathroom?" he asked.

"No. David's here, and I promised him a hug," I said.

"That's great," Michael said. "Let's do it on camera."

My immediate reaction was to say no, not on camera, but it was too late. Michael was already letting the audience know we had "a special guest." With that, he introduced David, who walked onto the set, and we embraced.

Prior to that, I had held my emotions in check. I was happy the Eagles had won. I was happy for the city and the fans who had not celebrated an NFL championship since 1960. Now they could finally pop the cork on that musty bottle of champagne.

I felt the pride of every native Philadelphian and every fan who suffered through all those bleak, bone-chilling Sundays at Franklin Field. But as a reporter, I learned to suppress my emotions. I believed that it was my job to remain professional, even on the day the team pulled off the biggest win in franchise history.

But when I wrapped my arms around my son, objectivity collapsed under the weight of the moment. I thought about my own father and how much I wished he could be there. He talked all the time about how

4 • **Ray Didinger**

much he wanted to see the Eagles win a Super Bowl. He talked about it until the day he died in 2009.

When I hugged David, I said, "That was for Grandpop."

I started to cry, right there on camera.

Ed Rendell, the former mayor of Philadelphia and governor of Pennsylvania, was with us. A native of New York, he became an Eagles fan during his undergraduate days at the University of Pennsylvania. When the NBC Sports Philadelphia network was launched as Comcast SportsNet in 1996, he became part of the show.

In what other city does the mayor spend his Sundays talking football on TV? Only in Philadelphia.

When I returned to my seat, I felt embarrassed, not with the emotion itself—if we had hugged off camera, I would've been fine with it—but knowing it was broadcast to a huge TV audience back home made me uncomfortable. The governor said not to worry.

"That same thing is happening all over Philadelphia," he said. "They're Eagles fans. They'll get it."

As a politician, he understands such things. He understands television, and he understands messaging, but most of all, he understands Philadelphia. That understanding is what made him such an effective mayor. His finger is always on the pulse of the city. He knows what people are feeling, because he feels it himself.

When I returned home, my email inbox was overflowing with messages, many from total strangers saying exactly what the governor had said earlier.

"An amazing game and an amazing moment with you and David."

"I was very moved by your emotions on the postgame show. Seeing you celebrate with your son was one of the best moments of the night."

"I was watching when David came on the set, and I was moved to tears by your response."

"Your broadcast after the Super Bowl was so heartfelt. I wanted to let you know we were right there with you."

"To watch you and your son hug and share the joy was truly awesome."

"It made me think about my father and how I wish he was here to see this."

The messages poured in for days, all of them expressing the same sentiments. The Eagles' victory was about more than football—it was also about family. It was about how generations of fans invested their emotions in a team, how they built their lives around tailgate parties and road trips, how they shared it all as family.

When the Eagles won the Super Bowl, it was for all those people, even those who weren't here anymore. Our hug made it all seem real somehow.

One particular letter stood out. It was from a man named Mike, who described himself as a life-long Philly sports fan. He grew up watching ball games on the twelve-inch TV in his father's tailor shop. He rooted for his favorite player, Richie Allen, to hit one over the left-field roof at Connie Mack Stadium. Being a fan was something he and his father shared throughout their lives.

He hoped to have the same experience with his own son, but his son became addicted to heroin. He was in and out of rehab seven times. He was back in rehab when the Eagles won the Super Bowl, so Mike and his son were not able to watch the game together. When Mike saw David and me celebrate the victory, it made him think of his own son and how he wished he had the same opportunity.

"When I saw you hug your son and shed those tears, I cried right along with you," he wrote. "The only thing better than watching another Super Bowl win would be to enjoy it with my son at my side. God willing, we'll get to experience that."

It was while reading those messages that this book began to take shape. I was coming up on my fiftieth year in the sports-media business, all of it in Philadelphia, and to finally see the Eagles hoist the Lombardi Trophy brought me a feeling of closure, like it was OK now to reflect.

That's what this book is: a reflection of a life lived on deadline, images that remain vivid and precious—like a father and son hug—after all these years.

1

The Bottomless Well

THE ACTIVITIES ROOM at the Chestnut Hill Presbyterian Church was unusually crowded for a Wednesday afternoon. Most of the seats were already filled, and people were still filing in when I arrived.

"We're sending out for more chairs," the lady said. "I thought we had enough but. . . ."

It was September, it was football season, and people wanted to talk about the Eagles. There were finger sandwiches and sponge cake, but mostly there were questions about Doug Pederson, Carson Wentz, and where this NFL season was headed.

A white-haired lady in the back raised her hand.

"How long have you been covering the Eagles?" she asked.

I said I had been covering the team either as a newspaper columnist or TV analyst since 1970.

"Don't you get tired of writing about the same thing all the time?" she said.

I had been asked thousands of questions over the years, but that one was new. I could see her point, though—fifty years is a long time to do anything.

I explained that the job is not really the same thing every day. There are always new stories: another game to be played, a new face in the locker room. The beauty of sports is that it has no script. From week to week, you never know what will happen. So there's that.

There is also the adrenaline rush of game day: the strategy, the chess match between coaches, and the wonder of great athletes doing amazing things. But after fifty years as a reporter, there had to be something more, something deeper that still tethered me to the game.

As I thought about it, I realized that it was not the game itself—it was the people, the characters and personalities I encountered over the years. They kept me coming back.

To me, the Eagles' locker room is what the Mississippi River was to Mark Twain. It is a constant source of inspiration, an ever-changing, endlessly fascinating passage of eager faces, each with its own backstory. Some arrive with the fanfare of rock stars. Others show up with a backpack and little else, but they all want the same thing: They want to play pro football.

For a writer, it is a bottomless well of material. Even if the team isn't very good—and there have been many such seasons with the Eagles—the human side of it makes you care. Scores and statistics fade over time, but the people stay with you.

I covered my first Eagles training camp in the summer of 1970. The team was practicing at Albright College, a small school on the hilly outskirts of Reading. In that unlikely setting, John Carlos, the former Olympic sprinter, tried to build a career in pro football.

The Eagles selected Carlos in the fifteenth round of the NFL draft, hoping to develop the 6'4", 190-pound track star into a receiver. The Dallas Cowboys had done it successfully with Bob Hayes, but he had been a football star at Florida A&M before winning the 100-meter dash at the 1964 Olympics.

Carlos was an entirely different story. He never played organized football. He played touch football as a kid growing up in Harlem, but that was hardly the kind of preparation he would need to make an NFL roster, even one as depressed as the 1970 Eagles.

Carlos was two summers removed from the Mexico City Olympics, where he bowed his head and raised his gloved fist on the medal stand to protest racial injustice in the United States. Carlos, who won the bronze medal in the 200 meters, was joined by gold medalist Tommie Smith in the silent protest. They made headlines around the world, and the U.S. Olympic Committee sent the two sprinters home, where they were met by a storm of criticism.

Brent Musburger, then a columnist for the *Chicago American*, wrote: "Smith and Carlos looked like a couple of black-skinned storm troopers." He referred to their protest as "a juvenile gesture by a couple of athletes who should have known better."[1]

Smith and Carlos knew exactly what they were doing and why they were doing it.

"I made the statement because I felt injustices were taking place in society, before my time, during my time, and after my time," Carlos said. "Something needed to be done. Someone had to speak up."

There were repercussions. Sponsors backed away from him, and his track opportunities dried up, so when the Eagles took a flier on him near the bottom of the 1970 draft, he figured, "Why not?"

Initially, Carlos said he wanted $1 million to sign. It was laughable, considering that he was the 371st player selected in the draft. He wound up signing for $12,500 with a $500 bonus.

When Carlos reported to camp, he was shunned by many of his teammates. The Eagles were a predominantly white team in 1970, with a lot of older players from the South who disapproved of his politics.

On the first day of practice, I was leaving the locker room with Bill Shefski, who covered the team for the *Philadelphia Daily News*. We noticed Carlos standing by his locker, with his football equipment scattered around him. Most of the players were on the field, but Carlos was standing there in a T-shirt and socks.

"You got a problem?" Shefski asked.

"I don't know how to put this stuff on," he said.

"You're joking, right?" Shefski said.

"I wish I was," he replied.

Helping players dress for practice wasn't part of our job description, but we felt sorry for the guy. We offered to give him a hand. Only one player, safety Ed Hayes, stopped to help.

I put the thigh pads in his football pants. Shefski laced up his shoulder pads. Hayes giggled as he helped him into his hip pads. Carlos did not appreciate it. He was, after all, a world-class athlete and an Olympic medalist, not some dorky loser.

"You had someone help you when you did this for the first time," Carlos said.

"Yeah, but I wasn't twenty-six years old," Hayes said.

Carlos winced as he put on a helmet for the first time.

"This thing is heavy," he said.

"You'll get used to it," I said.

Out of eighty players in camp, Hayes was the only one who offered to help the rookie dress for his first practice. The others couldn't be bothered. He was a lonely figure that summer. So was I.

At twenty-three, I was a decade younger than the other writers in camp. I was only in my second year with the *Philadelphia Bulletin,* so I'm sure the other writers saw me as a clueless lightweight. At night when they went to the bar, I went back to the Holiday Inn and watched TV.

Since we didn't have anyone else to talk to, Carlos and I talked to each other. Most photographs after the Olympics showed Carlos with a sullen expression. He was commonly referred to as a militant and a member of the Black Panthers, which wasn't true. The guy I met in Reading was fun to be around. He was very bright and loved talking about music and politics.

We didn't talk much about Mexico City. I didn't mention it because I thought he was tired of talking about it. But one night, he brought it up himself. He said it didn't matter what he did in football or anything else—he would always be remembered for that moment on the medal stand.

"Does that bother you?" I asked.

"No, because I know why we did it," Carlos said. "We needed to get people's attention. There are people suffering, and nobody's doing anything about it. We knew some people wouldn't like it, but if it opened their eyes and got them thinking, maybe it would do some good.

"But here we are two years later, and I'm not seeing many changes, and that's what hurts."

Carlos was a competitor, and he was committed to playing football. It was not a publicity stunt, and it sure as hell wasn't for the money—he could have made more money selling snow cones in the parking lot.

I never saw him without his playbook. He was always studying it, puzzling over the Xs and Os. He didn't have a playbook in track; he just ran.

I found myself quietly rooting for him. If he had a good day at practice, I wrote about it. If he made a nice catch, I mentioned it. He worked hard, and even some teammates got behind him. You would see the occasional pat on the back or hear someone yell, "Nice grab, Los." I began to think that this experiment might work after all.

One day, I asked an assistant coach, Charlie Gauer, whether he thought Carlos had a future in the NFL. It was understood that we were talking off the record. He said that Carlos had no chance.

I asked why. He had the size. His speed was undeniable. He demonstrated a willingness to work at improving his skills. So why couldn't he make it?

"Watch the next time he runs a pattern," Gauer said. "See how he stutter-steps before he makes a cut? See how he stops when he changes direction? He needs three or four steps to get going again. By then, it's too late. It is the difference between stopwatch speed and football speed. Just because a guy runs fast doesn't mean he plays fast."

Unlike other coaches, Gauer didn't put much stock in forty-yard-dash times. How often, he would ask, do you see an NFL player run forty yards in a straight line? It rarely happens. The game is played in short, violent bursts, five or six yards of quick cuts and slashes, and that isn't something you can measure. Quick and fast are two different things.

"Carlos is a long strider, which is fine for track," he said, "but to do what he has to do here—stop, start, turn, cut—it takes that stride away."

Gauer shrugged.

"You wanted an honest opinion," he said.

The Eagles kept Carlos on the practice squad that season, hoping he could refine his skills. Head coach Jerry Williams gave him a ball of Silly Putty and told him to squeeze it every day. Williams said it would make his hands stronger. Carlos walked around all day, squeezing that ball of Silly Putty. It probably made his hands stronger, but it didn't make them any more reliable. He still dropped too many passes.

Carlos twisted his knee in practice one day and tore the ligament. He underwent surgery and worked hard in his rehab. He came to training camp the next summer ready to compete for a roster spot, but in that year's draft, the Eagles selected a 6'8" wide receiver from Southern University named Harold Carmichael.

He was a seventh-round pick, a long shot, but no one had ever seen anything like him. On the practice field, he looked like a giraffe running in a herd of buffalo. With his height and long arms, he was a target that even the Eagles' scattershot quarterbacks could hit now and then. I could see right away that this lanky kid had a chance.

In the final cut, it came down to a choice between Carmichael and Carlos. The coaches had invested a year in Carlos, and although he had improved, he still wasn't ready to play in the NFL. Carmichael was pretty raw himself, but he was more likely to see the field than Carlos was. The coaches chose Carmichael, which proved to be the right decision:

He developed into the most prolific pass receiver in Eagles history. He played for thirteen years and set franchise records for receptions (589), yards (8,978), and touchdowns (79). He was voted into the Pro Football Hall of Fame in 2020.

Carlos was released and became a footnote in the team's history. In announcing the decision, Williams said, "The determining factor was a lack of consistency in catching the ball." But the coach praised Carlos's toughness and noted how the track star willingly took part in the blocking drills and did not shy away from contact.

"There was no doubt about his courage and no doubt about his effort," Williams said. "He was a good team man, but we saw more potential in Carmichael."

Carlos was disappointed but not surprised.

"Pro football is a business," he said. "Produce or you're out. If I didn't get hurt, things might have been different, but I'm not blaming anybody. I'm not ashamed of anything. I gave it my best shot."

As he was leaving, Carlos shook my hand.

"You were always in my corner," he said. "I appreciate it."

No other NFL team claimed Carlos, so he signed with Montreal in the Canadian Football League. He was there just a short time before he was released again. That was the end of his football career. He went through some tough times. He worked as a manual laborer in Los Angeles for a while. Eventually, he became a youth counselor and track coach at Palm Springs High School.

In many ways, Carlos was ahead of his time. The stand that he and Tommie Smith took in 1968 was the same stand that San Francisco quarterback Colin Kaepernick took in 2016; the only difference was that they raised a fist, and Kaepernick took a knee. They made the same statement almost a half century apart. They were judged harshly for it and paid a heavy price. Kaepernick was just twenty-eight when he began his protest and was effectively banished from the NFL.

But today, especially after the 2020 death of George Floyd, with the global backlash and outrage that followed, people everywhere, regardless of their politics, see the call against racial injustice in a different light. They better understand what Carlos and the others were fighting for. Today, a statue of Carlos and Smith, fists raised, stands on the campus of San Jose State University.

"Thanks for the acknowledgment," Carlos said at the unveiling. "The fight goes on."[2]

TIM ROSSOVICH was also on that 1970 Eagles team. He was a first-round pick from the University of Southern California, an All-America defensive end on a national championship team. Six players from that team went in the first round of the draft, including two—O. J. Simpson and Ron Yary—who wound up in the Pro Football Hall of Fame.

Rossovich spent five seasons in the NFL but never played on a winning team. He started his career with the Eagles and was traded to the San Diego Chargers in 1972. The Eagles acquired a first-round pick, which they used to select tight end and future Pro Bowler Charles Young, so you have to say they got the better of the deal, but they were a duller team without Rossovich.

He was a one-of-a-kind free spirit, an uninhibited wild child of the 1960s. Deacon Jones played one season with Rossovich in San Diego and said, "I would not advise any normal human to party with this guy. He does things that are straight-up insane."[3]

In college, Rossovich took off all his clothes, slathered his body in shaving cream, and ran down the street past his fraternity house. There were stories about him eating light bulbs, biting the tops off beer bottles, and doing swan dives off balconies. I thought these tales were either wildly exaggerated or pure fiction. I learned otherwise.

My first day at training camp, I met Ron Medved, a defensive back who hung out with Rossovich. I told him I was curious.

"I heard a lot of stuff," I said.

"Believe it," Medved replied.

"I heard. . . ."

"He did it."

"The story about. . . ."

"He did it."

"You don't even know what I'm. . . ."

"Whatever you heard, he did it."

"What about the. . . ."

"Yeah, that too."

"The birthday cake. . . ."

"Yeah, he sat in it."

"And he was . . . ?"

"Naked, yeah."

"Really?"

"Whatever you hear," Medved said, "believe it."

At one team meeting, Rossovich raised his hand like he wanted to ask a question.

"Yes, Tim," the coach said.

Rossovich opened his mouth and a bird flew out.

"What kind of bird?" I asked.

"A sparrow, I think," Medved said. "Something small. I didn't get a good look. I was too busy laughing."

He talked about their latest prank, which involved Rossovich setting himself on fire. They would show up at a party, and when the host opened the door, Rossovich would be standing there in flames. People would scream. Occasionally, someone would faint.

Medved said the stunt was not nearly as dangerous as it appeared. Rossovich would wear two shirts. One was a tight T-shirt soaked in water. The outer shirt was loose and untucked. He sprayed the outer shirt with lighter fluid and put a match to it. The wet T-shirt provided insulation. Medved had a blanket to smother the flames. It was over in a matter of seconds, but people talked about it for weeks.

"Tim's moustache got singed a couple times, that's all," Medved said. "It was nothing, really, but once the media got a hold of it, it blew up big time."

Sports Illustrated did a twelve-page feature on Rossovich. The title was "He's Burning to Be a Success."

Give Rossovich credit: He knew how to attract attention. The color photograph that accompanied the story showed him dressed in a monk's cloak, staring at the camera like a bushy-haired Rasputin. In the story, he talked about a dream in which he won the Super Bowl and the game ended with his hitting the quarterback so hard that the quarterback's head exploded and oozed out of the ear holes in his helmet. It made the 6'4", 230-pound Rossovich sound like a combination of Dick Butkus and Hunter Thompson.

When we first met, Rossovich eyed me suspiciously.

"What happened to the old guy?" he asked.

He was referring to Hugh Brown, the reporter who had covered the team for three decades. I said Brown had retired, and I was taking over.

"What kind of writer are you?" he asked. "Are you gonna rip us?"

"Not if you win," I replied. "That's up to you."

"We'll see," he grumbled.

The trouble was that the team didn't win: It didn't win that season, it didn't win the next season, and, in fact, it didn't win for the next eight years. As a result, I wrote a lot of stories that irritated the players. I didn't make many friends, but I accepted it as part of the job. I was assigned to write what I saw, and what I saw was a hapless team that each week invented new ways to lose.

Most coaches and players claim they don't read the newspapers. Rossovich was different. He read every story, and he let you know what he thought. In those years, I flew on the team charter. Brown had done it, so the editor told me I might as well do it too. I soon realized it was a mistake. It was convenient, but I was uncomfortable traveling with the coaches and players, since I wasn't part of the team.

It was particularly awkward on the flight home from a game when I would open my portable typewriter and start writing. The clack, clack, clack of the keys annoyed the players, who were trying to sleep. Also, the team was usually flying home from a loss, which meant (a) the players were in a bad mood and (b) I was writing something unflattering.

Once, on a flight home from Dallas, Rossovich was leaning on the back of my seat as I wrote my story. I would type a line or two, and he would offer an editorial comment, such as:

"That's not what happened."

Or . . .

"Did you even watch the game?"

Or . . .

"Are you really gonna put that shit in the paper?"

Finally, I said, "Do you mind? I'm trying to work."

"Oh, you can watch us and criticize us," he said, "but you don't like it when someone does it to you."

He had a point. If I was going to criticize the players and coaches, I should be able to take some criticism in return. That was fair. But it also struck me that this arrangement wasn't a good thing. As a reporter, I should not be accepting the perks of a charter flight. Ethically, it was a problem. So that was my last charter. I flew commercial after that.

But the episode confirmed what I long suspected about Rossovich: that beneath the Dracula capes and tie-dyed shirts, he was pretty smart. A lot of the stuff—the Gregorian chants, the haunting "I'm gonna get you, man" stare—was done for effect. He was creating a character he could market, and it worked. He landed several lucrative advertising deals and starred in an NFL Films special titled *The New Breed*.

The show made Rossovich the face of a new generation of NFL stars, one with its roots in the turbulent '60s. He was shown making candles on the beach as he talked about sex, drugs, and rock-and-roll. The show connected with viewers, but it offended the NFL owners, who called it "subversive and immoral," according to NFL Films president Steve Sabol.[4]

The league office was alarmed when it learned Rossovich was sharing an apartment with Sabol. They were bachelors in their early twenties, living in Center City amid all sorts of temptations. The owners felt nothing good could come of that.

"We had a lot of fun, but it was all innocent," Sabol said. "We'd go to dinner, and Tim would slap a piece of lettuce on his forehead. He'd call the waiter over and say, 'Someone is throwing salad at me. What kind of an establishment are you running here?' Silly stuff like that."

Rossovich did not sleep in a bed. He slept face down on the floor, his head pointing due north. He said that allowed the earth's magnetic waves to pass through his body and energized him for the next day. Sabol said half the time, he couldn't tell whether his roommate was really asleep or unconscious.

Rossovich was an All-Rookie selection in 1968 and went to the Pro Bowl the next year, but his play declined after that. The coaches moved him from defensive end, his natural position, to middle linebacker. Also, the Eagles were losing, and that was something he had never experienced in college.

"It was so depressing, losing all the time," Rossovich said. "I'd go in the training room, and it was like a morgue. I felt like it was up to me to do something."

Rossovich would get a running start and dive head-first into the whirlpool. He would pop up and shake his head like an otter splashing around in the zoo. At training camp, Rossovich would sometimes crawl into a shoe store in downtown Reading and startle female customers by kissing their toes. He did it, he said, to relieve the boredom.

The coaches tried to convince the media that Rossovich was a regular guy. All these stories, they said, were overblown nonsense. One day, during training camp, a New York columnist came in to write a profile on Rossovich. A thunderstorm rolled through Reading and washed out practice, so the writer was interviewing Jerry Williams in his office.

"Don't believe those stories," Williams said. "Tim is a serious young man."

Just then, a shrieking Rossovich ran past the coach's window, carrying a table. He threw himself into the flooded street and rode the table like a surfboard through the rush-hour traffic. The writer said, "Isn't that . . . ?"

Yes, it was.

"Rossovich was one of those larger-than-life type athletes," said Larry Merchant, a former columnist with the *Philadelphia Daily News*, "one of those self-possessed, self-promoting wild men who comes along every once in a while. He was willing to market himself that way, like Dennis Rodman in basketball. With people like that, you always wonder, are they legitimately crazy? I think they have to be, at least a little bit. There has to be some basis of reality in their unreal antics."[5]

Rossovich was like other young people from the '60s; he was not afraid to push back against authority. He did not clash with Williams, an easy-going sort who didn't have very many rules. But when Williams was fired and replaced by Ed Khayat, a hard-nosed drill-sergeant type, Rossovich spoke out openly against the new coach and his methods. When Khayat ordered all players to shave and cut their hair, Rossovich was the first to challenge him, and this time he wasn't fooling around.

"He's wrong," Rossovich said. "He says it will help discipline. It will hurt discipline. Instead of concerning ourselves with [football] practice, everybody is talking about mustaches and sideburns. All I'm hearing is dress codes, wear socks with your sandals, shit like that. They worry about the little things. Why don't they worry about helping me develop as a middle linebacker? Nobody has helped me."

Khayat set a noon Wednesday deadline for all players to shave. Rossovich waited until 11:55 A.M. just to make his point. He considered *not* shaving, but the team was 0–3, and in his words, "I don't want to make the shit any deeper."

Rossovich lasted just one more year in Philadelphia before the trade to San Diego. He played two years with the Chargers and then returned to Philadelphia to play for the Bell in the World Football League. When the WFL went under in 1975, he signed with the Houston Oilers but played only one year. He was out of football at age thirty.

He moved back to California and found work as a stuntman in the movies. One night, I was watching *Charlie's Angels* and saw Rossovich get tossed through a window by Kate Jackson. I also saw him gunned down in a western, *The Long Riders*, and punched out by Ryan O'Neal in a boxing movie, *The Main Event*.

Gary Pettigrew, who played next to Rossovich on the Eagles defense, found it ironic that his former teammate was always cast as a heavy. "Timmy is really a gentle soul," Pettigrew said. "He just looks scary."[6]

In 1980, Rossovich was cast in a TV show called *When the Whistle Blows*. It was a lame comedy about five construction workers. Rossovich played a character named Hunk Kincaid. The series was canceled after ten episodes.

I did a piece on Rossovich for NFL Films. We talked about his wild days with the Eagles. He said he rarely thought about them. What he remembered most was the losing, which he said hurt more than he let on.

"I live to enjoy myself, and losing was no fun," he said. "It was miserable. A lot of the crazy shit I did, it was because I was bored.

"In high school, our team won all the time. In college, I won a national championship. Winning was all I knew. I came to the NFL, and it was the total opposite. We were losers. Worse than losers, we were a laughingstock. I hated it. I started doing the other stuff to take my mind off the losing."

I pointed out that he did the same crazy things in college, and he was winning then.

"I did things in the moment," he said. "I'd see a spider walking across a table. A girl would scream. I'd grab the spider and eat it just to see her reaction. If I was by myself, I probably wouldn't have done it. Steve [Sabol] always said I was a clown. Maybe I just never grew up."

Rossovich believed that his reputation intimidated some opponents. It probably worked to his advantage, although he didn't plan it that way. He laughed when I told him Oakland center Jim Otto thought he was certifiably insane.

"I definitely think some of them thought I was possessed," he said. "I'd stare at them and say, 'I'm coming to get you, man.' They'd look at me like, 'Oh shit.' The guys on our team thought it was the funniest thing in the world.

"I think it was a way to get attention and also cheer people up," Rossovich said. "I love to make people laugh. When people talk about me now, they laugh, right? If that's how I'm remembered, so be it."

———

THE MOST MEMORABLE EAGLES TEAM I've covered will surprise you. Most people would expect me to say the first Super Bowl team under Dick Vermeil, or the Andy Reid team that went to the Super Bowl with Donovan McNabb and Terrell Owens, or—the most obvious choice—the team that finally brought home the Vince Lombardi Trophy from Super Bowl LII.

Each was memorable in its own way, but for me, the most memorable team was one that didn't win anything: the Buddy Ryan team of the

1980s. That was a locker room with more characters per square inch than any other team I've been around. The 1993 "Macho Row" Phillies team comes close, but Ryan's Eagles were like a reality TV show.

It was actually two teams. The defense was Ryan's baby, and he treated it as such. He indulged the defensive players, allowing them to knock off early on hot summer days. The offense was largely an afterthought. He had inherited an outrageously talented quarterback in Randall Cunningham, but he did not build an adequate supporting cast around him.

Ryan believed that his defense was good enough to win games. If Cunningham provided two or three big plays with either his arm or his legs, that would be enough.

The divide between the defense and the offense was easy to see. There were fights on the practice field almost every day. Usually the defense started it with a late hit or a shove. When the punches started flying, Ryan stood off to the side, smiling and twirling his whistle.

It was a team of strong personalities: linebacker Seth Joyner, safety Wes Hopkins, receiver Mike Quick, tight end Keith Jackson, and, of course, Cunningham, who was featured on a *Sports Illustrated* cover as "The Ultimate Weapon." But I believe that Reggie White and Jerome Brown were the team's emotional core.

White and Brown were different personalities, yet they were closer than many brothers. White was a man of God, an ordained Baptist minister committed to saving souls when he wasn't sacking quarterbacks. He was the big brother. Brown was the rambunctious little brother: loud, profane, and quick to anger.

White would tell Brown to stop acting like a bully. Brown would give him a puzzled look and say, "What do you mean, Reggie?"

White was a great player, a first-ballot Hall of Famer. Brown had the talent to be great, but early in his career, he was lazy and undisciplined. White would become frustrated with Brown, because he saw the younger man's potential. They had adjoining lockers at Veterans Stadium.

White talked endlessly about his faith and his mission to help others. His nickname was "the Minister of Defense." He could also be playful and downright silly. He would sneak up on visitors and startle them by barking like a dog. He did impressions of Elvis Presley, Muhammad Ali, and Rodney Dangerfield. He was a fan of professional wrestling and enjoyed trying out Hulk Hogan's latest move on his teammates.

Brown was a boisterous loudmouth, ridiculously profane even by the X-rated standards of an NFL locker room. He enjoyed calling out reporters, usually after they wrote something critical of the team. He would berate the offender and threaten to stuff him in the nearest trash can. Then he would burst out laughing and walk away.

I once left a message on his answering machine. The next morning, the phone rang. It was Brown calling from his car. I could hardly hear him over the roar of his stereo system.

"Could you turn down the music?" I asked.

"I did turn it down," he said.

Oh.

Putting White and Brown side by side in the locker room seemed like someone's idea of a joke. White would be scheduling Bible study classes, and Brown would be on the stool next to him, talking about his latest adventure at a strip club. But there was an undeniable affection between the two, and there was also a sense that White was having a positive influence. Ryan noted it, saying, "Jerome's maturing some. I think Reggie is rubbing off on him."

White's good works in the community were well known. He believed that God had given him the ability to excel on the football field so that he could use his fame to spread the Gospel to a wider audience. He teamed with Herb Lusk, a former Eagle and the pastor of Greater Exodus Baptist Church in North Philadelphia. Every Friday after practice, White joined Lusk in the neighborhoods. They would start by distributing baskets of food, and once they had a crowd, they would begin preaching.

"It is really something to see this big old giant wading through a crowd of youngsters, talking to them about doing the right things, staying in school and off drugs," said Lusk, a running back drafted by Vermeil who walked away from pro football in 1978 to devote himself to full-time ministry. "Once, we were at this housing project, and there must have been two hundred kids around Reggie. Out of the crowd, Reggie saw three little boys. Their eyes were glazed over; their clothes were shabby. They were hurting, you could tell.

"Reggie put down the microphone and swept the boys up in his arms. If you could have seen their faces; they lit up like sunshine. The next week, he came back with toys for those youngsters. That's what makes Reggie special. He cares enough to get involved."

I asked White if I could go along on one of the visits to North Philadelphia. I wanted to write an article about it. He said, "You can come on one condition; that you *don't* write about it." He did not want anyone to think that what he was doing in the community was some kind of photo op. This was God's work.

I left my notebook at home and followed White through the poor neighborhood near Temple University. An elderly woman took his hand and said, "I've been praying for something like this." She had no idea who he was, but it didn't matter.

"So few people care," she said. "He cares."

Similarly, Brown became involved in civic projects in his hometown of Brooksville, Florida. He started a football camp that attracted more than three hundred youngsters to a week of workouts under the guidance of teammates Joyner, Hopkins, White, and Cunningham. Brown rented two Greyhound buses and took some two hundred youngsters to the NFL Football Clinic when the Super Bowl was held in Tampa.

Brown started a similar football camp in South Jersey, and the day ended with the 6'2", 300-pound Brown engulfed in a sea of shrieking youngsters, handing out Eagles T-shirts and wearily pleading, "Hold on. Y'all are gonna make me pass out."

White and Brown were crushed in January 1991, when team owner Norman Braman fired Ryan. The Eagles had been eliminated in the first round of the playoffs for the third year in a row, and Braman had seen enough. He canned Ryan and promoted offensive coordinator Rich Kotite to head coach.

The team's 0–3 playoff record was only part of it. Braman had a personal dislike for Ryan, who enjoyed making snide references to "the guy in France." It was Ryan's way of tweaking Braman, who was notoriously tight-fisted in dealing with his coaches and players but spared no expense in stocking the wine cellar in his Mediterranean villa, Les Falaises.

Ryan's irreverence endeared him to the players and greatly amused the blue-collar fans, but it infuriated Braman, and pissing off the boss inevitably had consequences.

White and Brown were fiercely loyal to Ryan and believed that Braman made a huge mistake in firing him. They were sure that the Eagles were close to being a Super Bowl team, but with Ryan gone and Kotite running things, they felt like they were starting over. White, who had feuded with Braman about his contract two years earlier, made no attempt to conceal his anger.

The Eagles adopted a "win it for Buddy" mindset in 1991, and even though Cunningham went down with a knee injury in the opener, the defense carried the team to ten wins and fell just short of the playoffs. Brown finally dedicated himself to football, dropped thirty pounds, and had an All-Pro season. The defense was dominant, finishing first against the run, first against the pass, and first overall. No NFL defense had done that since the 1975 Minnesota Vikings.

Tragically, Brown was killed in a car crash six months later. He was riding with his nephew Gus and lost control on a rain-slicked road in Brooksville. The car slammed into a tree. Both were killed instantly.

White had often talked to Brown about his driving. His teammates grew accustomed to the sight of his RV screeching around the hilly campus at West Chester University. He was the guy who once said, "I'm not the type of person you dare to do something. If you say, 'Don't do it,' it's done."

But the reckless driving worried White. He would shake his head when he saw Brown leave another patch of burning rubber in front of the dorms. "That ain't funny," he would say. "Somebody can get hurt."

On the morning of June 25, Brown's family called White with the awful news. If something like that happened today, word would spread quickly through social media. It was a different world in 1992. When White stepped to the podium that night at Veterans Stadium to speak at a Billy Graham rally, most of the capacity crowd had no idea what had happened earlier in the day.

"Today, I lost a great friend, and Philadelphia lost a great football player," White said. "Jerome Brown died today."

There was a loud gasp in the stadium and cries of "Oh no." White lowered his head and wiped away tears.

"I loved Jerome," White said. "He was like a brother to me."

The Eagles dedicated the 1992 season to Brown. They kept his locker intact and framed his no. 99 jersey. They took on a mission: Bring it home for Jerome. The goal was to win that elusive Super Bowl.

The team made it to the playoffs and won a postseason game, which they had never done under Ryan, upsetting the New Orleans Saints, 36–20. The equipment managers packed Brown's gear and set up a locker for him in the Superdome. It inspired the team, especially the defense, which intercepted Saints quarterback Bobby Hebert three times. White iced the game by sacking Hebert for a safety.

The next week, the Eagles lost in Dallas, 34–10, and the team started breaking up. White was the first to leave, signing a four-year, $17-million contract in Green Bay. The Eagles made no effort to keep him, even though three thousand fans turned out at city hall for a "Save

Reggie" rally. Braman was willing to let him go, claiming that the thirty-one-year-old White was in decline.

White proved otherwise, playing six seasons in Green Bay where, along with quarterback Brett Favre, he led the Packers to two Super Bowls. He set a Super Bowl record with three sacks in Green Bay's win over New England. He played a total of fifteen seasons in the NFL and retired with 198 sacks. He was voted Defensive Player of the Year three times.

In November 2004, I went to White's home near Charlotte to interview him for an NFL Films show on religion in football. I didn't know what to expect. I heard that his life had taken a new direction. He was not going to church anymore, and he was questioning his faith. It sounded very unlike the guy I had seen spreading hope in the mean streets of North Philadelphia.

White met me at the door with that familiar smile. We talked for three hours. It was true that he had gone through some profound changes. Since retiring from football, he had more time for reflection. He was no longer preaching. Rather, he was spending his time at home learning Hebrew. He wanted to study the Bible in its original text, believing that was the only way he could have a true understanding of God's word.

"I look back on all the years I was playing football and preaching," he said, "and I realize I was more of a motivational speaker than a teacher of the Word. People asked me to speak at their churches because I was a football player, not because I was a great theologian. They came to see Reggie White, but what was I really offering?

"I gave the perception that I understood what I was talking about, but I really didn't. All I was doing was preaching what somebody else wrote or quoting what somebody else said. Yet ministers kept inviting me to speak at their churches. As I got older, I got sick of it. I felt like I was being prostituted. I realized if I was going to find the Lord and do his work, I had to go find him for myself."

For White, that meant spending long hours in his den, studying Hebrew with the long-distance assistance of an Israeli scholar who coached him on the language.

"I feel like I've been in seclusion," he said. "I heard people are spreading rumors about me, that I've converted to Judaism, that I've become a Muslim, all sorts of crazy stuff. I've become an outcast among some people in the church. They don't understand."

White said he had begun rethinking his beliefs one year into retirement. He had been reading a book about the apostles. He always thought of himself as a modern-day apostle, but in reading the book, he saw a difference.

"They lived their doctrine," he said. "I was just some guy talking."

He felt the need to read the Old Testament in its original text, not some eighth-generation translation. He wanted to form his own conclusions about his faith. He did not turn his back on religion, as some people suggested—if anything, he was more committed than ever. He could not wait to get out among the people again and spread the message. But this time, he wanted it to be a message that he understood and believed.

"This is the hardest thing I've ever done, much harder than playing football," he said. "I was never disciplined when it came to reading. I hate reading. So to make myself sit here for ten hours a day and practice my Hebrew is hard, but I'm excited, because every day I get deeper into it. I understand so much more. I've never felt more at peace."

Looking back, White admitted that his views had changed. The idea that God wanted him to use his fame to preach the Gospel, he said, was silly.

"God doesn't need football to glorify his name," he said.

He also said that while he believed that God had given him certain signs about his career path, God had not actually told him to go to Green Bay in 1993. He had said as much at the time.

"A lot of things that I said God said, I realize now, he didn't say anything—that's what Reggie wanted to do," he said. "I never heard God's voice the way the prophets did. I'm hoping I will hear his voice now that I'm reading the original scripture."

"But Reggie," I said, "you helped a lot of people. What you did in Philadelphia, what you did in Tennessee, that was important. You know that, right?"

"I was doing the right things," he said, "but I feel like I was doing them for the wrong reasons. I'm going to change all that."

White walked me through his home, which resembled a castle on a lake. The walls were lined with photographs. There were highlights from his football career next to scenes of him and his wife, Sara, opening Hope's Place, a home for unwed mothers. There was an exercise room where he worked out every morning. He was still an imposing figure at 6'4" and 295 pounds.

"I don't want to get fat like some other guys," he said.

When we shook hands in the driveway, I said, "I'll see you in Canton." I was referring to his slam-dunk first-ballot induction into the Pro Football Hall of Fame. He gave me a big smile.

"It's a date," he said.

One month later, I got a call from my son David. It was Sunday morning, the day after Christmas. He was at Heinz Field for the Steelers game. He asked if I had heard the news about White.

"He died," David said. "They just announced it in the press box."

I couldn't believe it.

"I just saw him last month," I said. "Are you sure?"

"They think it was a heart attack," David said. "They rushed him to the hospital, but it was too late. I'm sorry, Dad. I know you were friends."

I sat alone at the kitchen table for a long time. I kept thinking about the last time White and I were together and how excited he was about the new path he hoped to pursue. He could not wait to get started. Now he was dead at age forty-three.

On August 4, 2006, he was inducted into the Pro Football Hall of Fame. Sara and their son, Jeremy, accepted the game's greatest honor on his behalf. I kept thinking about how great it would have been to see him on the stage in his gold blazer, calling out to Jerome Brown in the audience. I thought about the laugh they would have shared. How sad that both were gone.

I once promised him that I would not write about his work in North Philadelphia. I honored his request for years, but I feel like I have to write about it now. People need to know he was more than a great football player.

2

Ray's Tavern

MY GRANDFATHER named his bar Ray's Tavern. He could have gone for something catchier— the guy across the street named his place Pretzels—but my grandfather was Ray Didinger, so Ray's Tavern worked for him. He was plain-spoken that way.

He was an authority on all things sports. OK, he didn't care much about hockey. When I talked to him about the Philadelphia Ramblers, the minor league hockey team that played at the Arena, he only pretended to listen. When I told him the Ramblers beat the Clinton Comets, he would say, "That's great, Champ," but the conversation ended there.

If you wanted to talk about the other sports, well, that was a different story. My grandfather knew everything there was to know. Other taprooms kept record books behind the bar to settle arguments. There was no such need at Ray's. He had all the answers.

Whether it was how many yards Steve Van Buren gained in the 1949 NFL championship game (196) or how many complete games Robin Roberts pitched in 1953 (33), my grandfather knew it.

He was like Google, only better: Google will give you the answers, but it can't serve you a beer at the same time. At Ray's, you got it all: cold beer, sports news, and good old-fashioned common sense, all for a bargain price.

I helped my grandfather clean the bar in the morning. I held my breath when he opened the door, because I hated the smell of stale beer. I never had any desire to drink beer after that. Emptying all those ashtrays convinced me never to smoke. You might say working in the bar helped me lead a healthier life.

There was no shortage of bars on Woodland Avenue, but Ray's did the biggest business. The place was packed every day, and it was because of my grandfather. He was the best storyteller in town. He was the Garrison Keillor of Southwest Philadelphia.

My parents and I lived two blocks down on Woodland Avenue. We had a little apartment over a shoe store. We were on the same block as two movie theaters, the Benn and the Benson. Every night, the lights from the marquees filled my room. We didn't have a yard, so I spent most of my time at the bar, playing shuffleboard and listening to the men talk sports.

These gruff, blue-collar guys were fully invested in what happened on the field. If the Phillies blew a game in the ninth inning, the whole mood of the bar soured. The TV went dark, and the brooding began. Even as a kid, I understood that this stuff mattered.

My grandfather and grandmother drove to Florida every year for spring training. They spent most of their time in Clearwater, watching the Phillies. My grandmother always came home believing that it was the Phillies' year. My grandfather was more realistic. He wanted them to win, but he knew they were the Phillies. He bought World Series tickets in 1964, but when they blew the pennant, he shoved the tickets in a drawer and said, "I shoulda known."

My grandmother was a tough cookie. If you marry into the bar business, you have to be. She loved baseball, especially the Athletics. It broke her heart when they left town. She was particularly fond of a left-handed pitcher named Lou Brissie. He was badly wounded in World War II, when an artillery shell shattered his leg. The doctors wanted to amputate, but he pleaded with them to save his leg.

He underwent twenty-three surgeries, with the doctors finally replacing the bone with a metal rod. He was unable to bend his leg, but he could still throw a baseball. He spent three years working his way back. In 1947, he signed with the A's. He won fourteen games in 1948 and sixteen games in 1949. He was named to the American League All-Star team and won the Most Courageous Athlete award from the Philadelphia Sports Writers Association.

One night at Connie Mack Stadium, Brissie was mowing down the

New York Yankees, and Phil Rizzuto laid down a bunt. With his bad leg, Brissie couldn't get to the ball, and Rizzuto had a base hit. My grandmother was in the stands, and she hated Rizzuto for taking advantage of Brissie's disability.

"That louse," she called him.

The next spring when she went to Florida, she stood at the railing in the Yankees' camp, waiting for Rizzuto. When she saw him, she called him over. Rizzuto assumed that she wanted an autograph. He came over with a big smile on his face. He had no idea that he was about to experience my grandmother's Southwest Philly wrath.

"I was there the night you bunted on Lou Brissie," she hissed. "That was a rotten thing to do."

She stormed away, leaving Rizzuto speechless. My grandfather loved telling that story. He said, "It was like Peg hit him in the face with a whipped cream pie."

My parents and I went to Hershey each summer for Eagles training camp. We spent two weeks—Dad's entire vacation—watching practice. We went to the morning workout, grabbed some lunch, and then came back for the afternoon session. There were no fences or security guards in those days, so we could get up close and personal with the players.

Our family loved the Eagles. My parents went to every home game and brought the programs back to the apartment. I read them cover to cover. I knew the names and numbers of every player. I was the only six-year-old in America who could spell Alex Wojciechowicz.

I actually became a game in my grandfather's bar: The customers would bet beers on whether I could come up with a certain jersey number. Someone at the bar would call out a player's name, and I'd have to give his number.

It usually started with friendly bets and easy numbers—Pete Pihos, 35; Al Wistert, 70—but it wasn't long before the stakes were raised and the names became more obscure: Skippy Giancanelli, for example, or Maurice Nipp. Still, I had the answers. Giancanelli was number 27. Nipp wore 68. My grandfather says I never missed. I can't swear to that, but I know that I built up quite a reputation.

Guys would come in groups of four and five from General Electric. Soon, they would be whooping and cheering as I worked my way through the roster. I didn't understand what was going on, but I liked the attention. Sometimes a guy would drop a quarter in my hand just for knowing that Otis Douglas was number 71. It beat sitting at home and watching *Howdy Doody* on TV—nobody gave me a quarter for that.

Most of my grandfather's customers were season-ticket holders, and they bought their tickets through him so they could all sit together. At one time, more than two hundred season tickets were in his name. He had the biggest account on the Eagles' books. He was offered the chance to buy a piece of the team, but it was $3,000 a share, and that was more than he could afford at the time. His one regret was that he didn't buy a piece of the team when he had the chance. I know that he wouldn't have hired Joe Kuharich, that's for sure.

In the 1950s, the NFL had a twelve-game season with six home games. The tickets cost $3 per game, so you could buy a season ticket for $18. It doesn't sound like much, but it was a lot for the working men who came to Ray's. They paid him back on the installment plan. He kept a copy book behind the bar, and every payday, guys would give him a dollar or two. He would mark it down until the accounts were settled.

He chartered a bus to take his regulars to the home games. The bus would park on the curb next to the bar, and we would climb on board, with my grandparents, my parents, and me occupying the seats up front. We did it every Sunday, going from nine o'clock Mass to the bar and then to Franklin Field. I couldn't tell where the religion left off and the football began. Jim Murray of the *Los Angeles Times* once wrote, "There is no cult in the world like a busload of fans on their way to a home game." That was how it felt riding down Woodland Avenue on those crisp autumn Sundays, the air thick with cigar smoke and laughter.

The Eagles stumbled through the '50s, but our faith was rewarded in 1960. The team finally had a good coach in Buck Shaw and a great quarterback in Norm Van Brocklin. At thirty-five, Chuck Bednarik still was a fearsome presence at center, and when an injury sidelined linebacker Bob Pellegrini, Bednarik replaced him on defense. "Concrete Charlie," the oldest man on the team, played virtually every snap on the Eagles' drive to the NFL championship.

They defeated the New York Giants twice in two weeks to clinch first place in the Eastern Conference. Bednarik put a crushing hit on Frank Gifford, knocking him unconscious and forcing a fumble that ensured the victory. The image of Bednarik dancing over the motionless Gifford was spread across two pages in *Sports Illustrated* and linked the two men forever.

In the championship game, the Eagles met the Green Bay Packers, a young team playing under a then-unknown coach named Vince Lombardi. Eleven future Hall of Famers were on the Green Bay roster, but no one knew it then.

Christmas fell on a Sunday that year, and Pete Rozelle, in his first year as the NFL commissioner, did not want to play the championship game on a religious holiday. He scheduled the game for noon on Monday, December 26. Following the rules of the time, the telecast was blacked out in Philadelphia, setting off a mad scramble for fans to either rig up a homemade antenna to pull in a New York station or drive to a motel somewhere outside the ninety-mile blackout so they could see the game.

The Ray's Tavern regulars already had their tickets. The price more than doubled—the tickets in Section EE jumped from $3 to $8 for the title game—but no one complained. Our seats were in the lower deck, halfway up behind the end zone. My favorite player, Tommy McDonald, caught his touchdown pass right in front of us, and Bednarik tackled Green Bay's Jim Taylor as the final seconds ticked off the clock, with the Eagles winning, 17–13.

When the game ended, I gave my grandfather a hug, and I saw tears in his eyes. It was the first time I ever saw him cry. It made me realize what this meant and how important it was. I'm sure that is a part of what I was feeling when I hugged my own son after Super Bowl LII.

That was the most memorable Eagles game at Franklin Field, but there was another I won't forget any time soon. It was on November 24, 1963, two days after the assassination of President John F. Kennedy. Rozelle made the decision to play the NFL games that Sunday as scheduled.

It was the first time I awoke on a Sunday with no desire to head for Franklin Field. My parents felt the same way, but after forty-eight hours of living with the horrific TV images from Dallas, they hoped they could find some comfort in the familiar surroundings. We went to my grandfather's bar and found all the regulars there, although there was none of the usual laughter. The TV was on, with a somber Walter Cronkite delivering more news coverage.

When the bus arrived, we took our usual seats. My grandfather went back inside to turn off the TV and lock up. When he returned to the bus, he said, "Somebody just shot Oswald."

"That's not funny," my grandmother said.

"I'm not kidding," he said. "Somebody shot Oswald. It was live on TV."

That is how we learned that the president's assassin, Lee Harvey Oswald, had been gunned down in the basement of the Dallas police station. It was one more shock on top of all the grief we were feeling already. Hardly anyone spoke on the ride to Franklin Field. Even my grandfather, who normally stood for the whole ride, joking with the driver, sat quietly next to my grandmother, staring out the window.

More than sixty thousand fans showed up for the game, but it did not sound like the usual crowd. People filed through the gates quietly. Never has a stadium so big and so full felt so empty. Team president Frank McNamee was so angered by Rozelle's decision to play that he refused to attend. He went to a memorial service at Independence Hall instead.

Before the kickoff, the Eagles and the Redskins formed a circle at midfield. A bugler played "Taps." The public-address announcer asked those in attendance to sing the national anthem. There was no band, just the sound of sixty thousand voices. The game was a listless affair that ended with the Redskins winning, 13–10. Washington's Bobby Mitchell said he felt as though he had played "in slow motion."

After the game, King Hill, the Eagles quarterback, found his car vandalized. At first, he thought it was the fans taking out their frustrations for the loss. But why was his car the only one with its tires slashed? Then it dawned on him: His car was the only one with Texas license plates.

———

DURING THESE YEARS, I kept scrapbooks on all the Philadelphia teams. I clipped stories out of the sports section and read them over and over. I especially enjoyed the columns by Sandy Grady, whose writing often made me laugh but always made me think.

I began writing myself. I would come home from an Eagles game, go to my room, and write my own account of what had happened. I was an only child, which was a rarity in those baby boom years. I think it is one of the factors that led me to become a writer. I have found that a high percentage of people in the newspaper business—and writers in general—are only children.

I don't think it is a coincidence. Writing is a solitary pursuit, and an only child is likely to spend more time alone. There is more time for reading and reflection.

I know it was true for me. I was in my room writing all the time, but it wasn't until I was in the fifth grade that I thought it could become something meaningful. I was attending Our Lady of Peace grammar school in Milmont Park. One day, our teacher, Sister Clare Ursula, gave us an assignment: Write an essay about the person you most admire.

I wrote about my father, who also was named Ray Didinger. He had been a navigator on a B-24 bomber and had survived the horror of the air war over Europe. One day, I was looking for something in the closet and found a shoebox. It was full of medals my father won in the war. They were not framed and on display—they were at the bottom of the closet, buried under the snow boots and Christmas decorations.

I brought them to my mother. She told me to put them back.

"Your father doesn't like to talk about that," she said.

I didn't understand it then, but I understood it later when I read about my father's outfit, the Eighth Air Force. They flew daylight missions deep into Germany. Those missions crippled Hitler's war machine and turned the tide of the war, but at a terrible price. The Eighth Air Force lost more than forty-seven thousand men. At the height of the war, the life expectancy of a B-24 crewman was six missions; my father flew thirty. He had nightmares for years.

Today, we call it post-traumatic stress disorder (PTSD). I'm sure my father had it. I suspect most of the men who returned from the war had it to some degree. There was no term applied to it, and no one really talked about it. Men like my father just lived with it. Once, he was sleeping, and fireworks started going off nearby. He fell out of bed and woke up shaking. He thought it was anti-aircraft fire.

My middle name is Reede, which I couldn't understand. It was not a saint's name, and almost all Catholic boys were named after saints back then. Years later, I learned it was the name of my father's best friend during the war, a fellow navigator who was shot down over Berlin. My father never told me that; my mother did.

Most of the men who went off to war were just kids off the street corner. That was true of my father and his flight crew. He was nineteen when he flew his first mission. Of the nine men in the crew, five were still in their teens. The pilot was the old man at twenty-two.

My father saved dozens of letters written to him during the war. I found them after he died. Most of the letters were from my mother. Reading them offered a wonderful insight into their courtship. In one letter, my mother wrote, "Remember that day on the trolley? You were reading a book and I kept pulling it away from you? I loved to tease you." She also wrote, "I was just a dizzy, crazy, silly kid. I only lived to jitterbug but I'm through with that now. All I think about it is you. I pray that you come home to me. I love you." She signed off with hugs and kisses, three rows of them.

The thought of my mother jitterbugging was very amusing. I never saw her dance, not once, but the scene on the trolley sounded familiar.

She did enjoy teasing my father. After dinner, they would stand together at the sink, washing the dishes. She would scoop up the soap suds and rub them on my father's face. He would just keep drying the dishes. He was a quiet man, very different from his father, the bartender who could talk for hours.

When I was born, my father was working as an engineer at General Electric and taking classes at Drexel University at night. It was a grind, but he never complained. He played semipro football on weekends. At 6'3" and 215 pounds, he was one of the bigger men on the field. My mother would put me in a stroller, and we would watch from the sidelines. I didn't know what was going on, but I learned later that my father was a very good player, a split end with long arms and sure hands.

When my father came home from work, my mother's face lit up, and our boxer puppy danced around the kitchen, her nails tapping on the tile floor. My father brought the house to life just by opening the door. So when Sister Clare gave us the essay topic of the person I most admired, I thought of him immediately.

Some of my classmates wrote about President Eisenhower, and others wrote about the pope. One girl wrote about Elvis Presley. One boy wrote about Davy Crockett. I wrote about my father. The next day, Sister Clare came into the classroom and said, "I want to read you an essay written by one of your classmates."

She began reading, and I immediately recognized my essay. I stared straight ahead, not saying a word. When she finished, Sister Clare said, "That essay was written by Raymond Didinger."

"Mr. Didinger," she declared, "you should be a writer."

My friend Joe Cronin asked, "How did you do that?" I said, "I don't know." I'd say the same thing about every story I've ever written. Writing isn't like cooking a meal or fixing a car. It doesn't come with a how-to manual. You just do it. It comes from somewhere deep inside. That is the beauty of the written word, but also the challenge.

I had no idea how hard it would be. I had no idea how many hours I would labor over my columns. Self-doubt haunts every writer. I know. I've lived it. Yet nothing gives me as much pleasure as writing a piece that feels just right.

When I enrolled at St. James High School, an all-boys Catholic school in Chester, my English teachers Donald Bell and John Mooney saw promise in my writing. When the school held its essay contest, Mr. Bell made me enter. The topic—What St. James Means to Me—was not particularly inspiring, but Mr. Bell said, "You *will* enter this contest." So I did.

Two weeks later, the principal came on the loudspeaker to inform everyone that judging for the essay contest was completed: "The winner is Raymond Didinger." I was called to the stage at the next assembly and presented with a $25 savings bond, a record player, and a Bobby Darin album. Why Bobby Darin? I have no idea.

I later learned that only three students—in a student body of thirty-five hundred—had entered the contest. Mr. Bell broke the news to me at our twenty-fifth class reunion. It took a little luster off the honor, but at that point, I was already into my second decade as a journalist. There was no turning back.

In high school, no one shared my interest in writing. Even the guys who worked with me on the student newspaper had no desire to take it any further. Most of them wanted to be lawyers or teachers. Putting out a newspaper was just something to do after class.

The library had a series of books about careers—careers in accounting, careers in law, careers in medicine, and so forth. When I was a freshman, I found the book on journalism. I was surprised to see that no one else had checked it out. I looked at other books in the series; they had been checked out dozens of times, but no one had shown any interest in journalism. Odd, I thought.

When I was a senior, I had already made up my mind to enroll at Temple University to study journalism, but I wanted to read that book one more time. I took it off the shelf, turned to the back page, and found that I was *still* the only one to have checked it out. It gave me pause. I truly believed this was the career for me, but why did no one else share that interest? I mean, was there something wrong with *me?*

You can imagine how relieved I was in September 1964, when I walked into my first journalism class at Temple and found a roomful of people who shared my passion for writing.

My classmates included J Russell Peltz, who went on to become a Hall of Fame boxing promoter; Dick Weiss, who is now one of the most esteemed basketball writers in America; Ron Pollack, the son of Harvey Pollack, the National Basketball Association's foremost statistician; and Frank Bertucci, a fellow hockey fan who would later work with me at the *Bulletin* and the *Daily News.*

I joined the student-run *Temple News* and WRTI, the campus radio station. It was a thrill to sit on press row at the Palestra alongside reporters from the *Bulletin,* the *Inquirer,* and the *Daily News.*

In my sophomore year, I took a marketing class. For our term paper, we had to develop a strategy for a start-up business in Philadelphia. It could be a bank, a supermarket, anything—it just had to be a start-up.

It was the spring of 1966, and Philadelphia was one of six cities that had been awarded a National Hockey League expansion franchise. I picked that as my start-up.

I went to the team's offices, which were in Center City. Most people walked by without a second look. The average Philadelphian knew very little about hockey. They knew there was a league called the NHL, but outside of those six cities that already had teams—Montreal, Toronto, Boston, New York, Detroit, and Chicago—it wasn't something people talked about.

I loved hockey. I loved the minor league Ramblers, so naturally I was excited to learn that an NHL expansion franchise was coming to town, and I could parlay that interest into a term paper. I went to the office, hoping to get some publicity material and perhaps interview someone in the ticket department.

I walked in unannounced. I told the receptionist what I had in mind.

"Wait here," she said, leaving her desk and walking down the hall.

As I waited, I looked around the lobby. The walls were decorated with photographs of NHL stars: a smiling Bobby Hull, missing most of his teeth; the great Gordie Howe, scoring a goal on Glenn Hall; Maple Leaf captain George Armstrong hoisting the Stanley Cup. I read all the hockey magazines, so the profile of Montreal's Jean Beliveau was as familiar to me as that of Sandy Koufax or Johnny Unitas.

The Philadelphia team was little more than a letterhead. It didn't have any players—the expansion draft was months away—and it didn't have a name. There was a poster on the wall that read: The NHL Comes to Philadelphia. Below was a drawing of a hockey player in a red and gray uniform with a yellow Liberty Bell on the chest. I thought, "I hope that's not the uniform." The colors were dreary, and the Liberty Bell looked stupid on a hockey jersey.

The receptionist returned and said, "Follow me." She led me to a large corner office. There behind the desk was a distinguished-looking man I recognized as Bill Putnam, the team president. Before I could say a word, he smiled and waved me in.

"Have a seat," he said. "What can I do for you?"

I wasn't expecting this. A one on one with the team president? I stammered, "I have a class assignment. . . ."

"OK," Putnam said with an indulgent smile.

"It's a marketing course," I said, feeling underdressed in my Temple University sweatshirt and jeans.

I'm sure Putnam had better things to do than answer a lot of questions from some college kid who had wandered in off the street, but he rocked back in his chair and said, "What do you want to know?"

I explained the nature of the term paper. I said I had chosen the hockey team as my start-up because I was a hockey fan. I wanted to know how he intended to sell this sport in a city where 98 percent of the folks wouldn't know a hockey puck from a pumpkin.

"I ask myself the same question every day," he said.

Putnam wasn't from Philadelphia. He was born in Idaho and grew up in Texas. He wasn't really a sports guy, either. He had worked for Morgan Guaranty Trust in New York but crossed over to sports by brokering several franchise purchases, including the sale of the Eagles to Jerry Wolman in 1964. That is where he met Ed Snider, the Flyers' owner who was also the vice president of the Eagles. Snider brought him in to run the day-to-day operation when the NHL awarded the franchise to Philadelphia.

Putnam talked to me for almost an hour. It shows how grateful the team was for any notoriety that a college student could just appear and in a few minutes be face to face with the team president. Today, a wall of personal assistants, publicists, and security guards separates the public from the people who run the teams. In 1966, the Flyers' president was as accessible as a convenience store clerk.

I asked Putnam questions, but he asked me questions too. He wanted to know what I hoped to see in the new team. At the risk of appearing brash, I said I did not like the uniform on the poster.

"That's just a sketch," he said. "Our uniform won't look anything like that. I don't like it either."

Putnam said the plan was to have the fans name the team. They made it a contest, with fans mailing in their suggestions. Putnam and Snider would pick the winner. As it turned out, the name "Flyers" was first suggested by Snider's sister Phyllis. She mentioned it one night over dinner at a Howard Johnson's on the Jersey Turnpike. The family was on its way home from a Broadway show.[1]

Snider liked the name immediately, but he couldn't award the first prize—a twenty-one-inch color TV and two season tickets—to his own sister, so he went through all the entries until he found one from a nine-year-old boy in Narberth who suggested the name Flyers. The youngster was declared the winner, and Philadelphia's NHL franchise had a name. Putnam chose the colors orange and black in part because he was a University of Texas alum, so he was partial to orange.

What impressed me about Putnam was how confident he was that the NHL would succeed in Philadelphia. Many doubters, including some in the media, believed that the team would not survive.

"Hockey is a great sport, and Philadelphia is a great sports town," he said. "It's a perfect fit."

That quote was the theme of my term paper. The professor could not believe that I had scored a one-on-one interview with the team president. I didn't tell him how easy it had been. If he wanted to believe that I had fought my way through weeks of red tape, that was fine by me. I just know everything that Putnam said about the NHL and its future in Philadelphia came true.

———————

I GRADUATED IN JUNE 1968 and landed a job at the *Delaware County Daily Times*, which was then located in downtown Chester.

I was hired by executive editor Arthur Mayhew, a native Texan who walked through the newsroom smoking a pipe and projecting an air of quiet confidence. He had a slight drawl and answered his phone with a pleasant, "Mayhew. May I help you?"

A fellow Texan, Tom Schmidt, was the city editor. Tall, broad-shouldered, and as bald as Mr. Clean, he was an imposing figure. He ran the news desk, barking out orders on deadline.

I wanted to write sports, but there were no openings. The newspaper had a three-man sports staff with no budget to add a fourth, so Mayhew offered me a job on the news side. He said I might get to write an occasional sports story, but mostly I would be covering school board hearings, transit strikes, murder trials, bake sales, and whatever else was going on in the county.

"We can start you at $100.25 a week," Mayhew said.

He saw the disappointment in my face. I didn't expect to make a fortune but, geez. . . .

"That's where we start everyone," he said.

It was OK, I said. I was just happy to have the job.

When my father asked how much I was making, I said, "A hundred and a quarter," hoping he would think I meant $125. It still wasn't much, but at least it sounded better.

As it turned out, working on the news side was a good thing. It taught me how to dig for stories and find the facts in unfamiliar material. When I was assigned to the Media courthouse, I had to figure out what the news was and whom to talk to. Lawyers and politicians don't wear numbered jerseys. No one in a striped shirt is spelling out the rules. I had to learn the players, and quickly.

Luckily, the *Daily Times* had an excellent team of reporters. One of them, Arlene Notoro, had worked with me at the *Temple News.* Having her at a desk next to me helped a lot. The other reporters—Lou Antosh, Jack Hopkins, Kathy Begley, and Pamela Erbe—were experienced in covering local news.

The *Daily Times* wasn't a large paper, but it had a strong independent voice, and the bureaucrats of the county had to respect it. Almost every day, I would hear Arlene on the phone with some official, saying, "Don't give me that. That isn't what you said before." She would hang up and say, "Arthur, I've got the story." Often, it was the lead in the next day's paper.

As the new reporter, I was assigned to stop at Crozer-Chester Medical Center each morning on my way to the office. I went to the emergency ward and checked the overnight reports, looking for anything newsworthy. Shootings, stabbings, and car crashes were common in Chester. Unless it was fatal, it was usually not worth following up. I stopped at the Chester police station and went through their reports as well. I was amazed at how much violence was written off as routine.

Once in the office, I joined the other reporters in taking information from our various correspondents. Known as "stringers," they went to night events and phoned in the details the next morning. The *Daily Times* had one stringer in each borough. Schmidt would yell, "I have Marion Logue from Swarthmore, who's free?" A few minutes later, Barbara Ormsby would be calling from Ridley, and so on.

We took the information over the phone and wrote a story for that day's edition. The *Daily Times* was an afternoon newspaper, so the copy deadline was around noon. Our mornings were spent banging out those stories. Once the edition was put to bed—I loved the satisfying shudder of the presses rolling—we started working on our own pieces for the next day. Most were assigned by Mayhew or Schmidt, but we could generate our own ideas as well.

One time, I saw that Tom Hayden, the '60s activist and president of the Students for a Democratic Society (SDS), was scheduled to speak at Villanova. I told Schmidt I wanted to cover it.

"That's not really our area," he said, "but if you want to do it, OK."

I sat in the half-filled auditorium and listened to Hayden's talk. He appeared bored, perhaps disappointed by the turnout. It was small and sleepy. Lines that got standing ovations on more radical campuses fell flat at Villanova. His SDS manifesto did not resonate on the Main Line.

Hayden seemed to lose interest halfway through his talk. He ignored the few students who tried to ask questions. I approached Hayden as he left the stage, but he shook his head and kept walking. I wrote a column anyway.

The story everyone at the *Daily Times* dreaded writing was the Vietnam obituary. In 1968, the war was raging, and almost every week we learned that another soldier from Delaware County had been killed. A staff reporter would be sent to the soldier's home to interview the family and write a profile of the deceased.

You would knock on the door, introduce yourself, and ask, "Can I speak to you about your son?" It was one of the hardest things I've ever done. Each time, I fully expected the parents to slam the door in my face. I would not have blamed them if they had. Remarkably, that never happened, not once.

In every case, the parents would welcome me into their home, usually offer me something to eat or drink, and patiently answer my questions. Most welcomed the chance to talk about their son. They would say things like, "Make sure you tell people he was a great kid." They did not want their son to be just one more name etched on a wall and forgotten.

The hardest part was when I would ask for a photograph to run with the story. One of the parents—usually the mother—would take a photo off the mantle, gently remove it from its frame, and hand it to me with a request that it be returned. I assured them that I would return it personally, which I always did. If I had mailed it and somehow it was lost or damaged, I never would have forgiven myself.

I tried to tell myself that I was doing a good thing. I was telling the stories of these young men, many of them just out of high school, who had died in the service of their country. I wanted our readers to care about them: who they were, where they came from, and what they had done. I wrote every piece with that goal in mind. I hoped that in some small way, it brought comfort to the parents.

Sometimes people ask what it's like to walk into a losing locker room. They say, "That must be hard." It's not, really. A team lost a game, maybe a big game, but it is just a game. There will be other games, other seasons, and other chances. But when you look into the eyes of a parent who has lost a son or a daughter, there is a sadness that haunts you forever.

3

"That's for the Players"

THE VOICE ON THE PHONE was familiar.

"This is Jack Wilson. I told you that you'd be hearing from me. Remember?"

Remember? How could I forget?

Wilson was the sports editor of the *Philadelphia Bulletin*, the largest afternoon newspaper in America, with a circulation approaching seven hundred thousand. Its slogan—In Philadelphia, Nearly Everybody Reads the *Bulletin*—was true. The *Bulletin* was the paper of record.

I grew up reading the *Bulletin*. The bylines were as familiar to me as the Phillies' batting order. Ray Kelly covered baseball. Hugh Brown covered the Eagles. Bob Vetrone covered college basketball, and George Kiseda covered pro basketball. Jack Fried wrote about boxing, and columnist Sandy Grady wrote about everything.

When I began thinking about a career in journalism, I thought first of the *Bulletin*. To me, the *Bulletin* building was like Yankee Stadium: It represented the big time. If I was going to work in newspapers, I wanted to work *there*.

When I was a senior at Temple, Wilson came to campus for a career day. The line of students waiting to see him snaked down three flights of stairs. I was one of the last to see him. I handed him a few columns from the *Temple News*. He spread them out on the desk and started reading. When he finished, he gave me a grin.

"I see you're a Sandy Grady fan," he said.

"How did you know?" I asked.

"You're imitating his style," he said.

Wilson said that all writers are influenced by other writers much in the way that artists are influenced by other artists. It would be foolish not to learn from the masters, he said, and he certainly considered Grady a master. Over time, he said, a true writer develops a style and voice all his own.

"You'll get there," he said.

I told him my dream was to write sports at the *Bulletin*. He gave me the speech that coaches have been giving eager rookies for years: You aren't ready yet. You need experience. He told me to look for a job at a smaller paper.

"You'll be hearing from me," he said.

Now, here he was on the phone, calling to discuss a job at the *Bulletin*.

"Are you interested?" he asked.

I immediately said yes.

Two days later, I took the train to 30th Street station and walked across the street to the *Bulletin* building. I rode the escalator to the third floor. The teletype machines were clicking, reporters were pounding away on their typewriters, and editors were bellowing "Copy" as they summoned copy boys to the news desk.

I felt my pulse quicken as I walked into the room. It was a lot bigger and noisier than the newsroom at the *Daily Times*. I recognized the writers from the pictures that ran with their columns. They were as familiar to me as the faces on my baseball cards.

J. A. Livingston, the Pulitzer Prize–winning financial writer, was at his desk, deep in thought. Frank Brookhouser, who wrote the nightlife column, was doing an interview. Ernest Schier, the movie critic, was typing his next review.

The sports department was on the far side of the room. Kiseda was immediately recognizable, with his shock of gray hair. Wali Jones of the 76ers nicknamed him "the Silver Quill." Fried was immersed in the *New York Times* crossword puzzle. Grady was at his desk, puffing on a cigar. Wilson saw me and waved me over.

He got right to the point: He wanted me to take over the high school beat. The job paid $150 a week, a nice raise, but the money didn't matter as much as the opportunity. I enjoyed working at the *Daily Times*, but I wanted to write sports, and Wilson was offering me the chance to write sports for a great newspaper.

I couldn't say yes fast enough.

This was the job I wanted, the job I thought about every day while riding the subway to Temple. Writing sports for the *Philadelphia Bulletin*, the paper I had delivered as a kid, the paper my father read every night, the paper my grandfather kept under the bar. I never imagined it could happen this quickly. It was hard breaking the news to Mayhew, the man who hired me at the *Daily Times*, but he understood.

"If you ever get tired of sports and feel like going back to Media courthouse, give me a call," he said. He knew that wasn't happening.

On my first full day at the *Bulletin*, Wilson walked me to my desk: It was the desk next to Sandy Grady. I felt like a kid called up from the minor leagues and assigned the locker next to Babe Ruth. Grady smiled and shook my hand. I thought about telling him how much I admired him, but I thought it might sound too gushy. I settled for "Nice to meet you, Mr. Grady."

"Call me Sandy," he said.

I covered the 1969 high school football season, which meant writing about John Cappelletti, the future Penn State Heisman Trophy winner, who was a senior at Monsignor Bonner. Billy "White Shoes" Johnson was playing at Chichester High School. Haverford had an all-state passing combination in quarterback Steve Joachim and tight end Randy Grossman, who would go on to win four Super Bowl rings with the Pittsburgh Steelers.

As the season wound down, we learned that Hugh Brown was leaving the Eagles beat. He had covered the team since the Chuck Bednarik days, and he was ready to retire. Speculation began about who would replace him. Brown was a crusty character, born in Scotland, gruff and profane with a four-pack-a-day smoking habit, but his byline was synonymous with Eagles football. He would be a tough act to follow.

Wilson took me aside one day and said, "Let me buy you a soda." He didn't have an office, so when he wanted to have a private conversation, he took you to the cafeteria. That's where he told me that I would be taking over the Eagles beat. I was stunned.

"I've only been here one year," I said.

"I think it's a good fit," he said.

I knew that people would question Wilson's decision. It was a huge leap of faith to put a twenty-three-year-old on the Eagles beat. The other papers had veteran reporters covering the team: Bill Shefski and Jack McKinney at the *Daily News*, Gordon Forbes at the *Inquirer*, and a half dozen experienced writers at the suburban dailies. They knew the coaches and players; they had sources around the league. I would be coming in cold.

I arrived at the Albright College training camp in July 1970. The press room was in the basement of a dormitory near the practice field. All the writers shared one desk. I did my best to stay out of the way. I was so terrified of being scooped that I filed three or four stories a day. I kept cranking out copy, hoping to make up in volume what I lacked in experience and perspective.

Charlie Gauer approached me one day after practice. He had been around the game a long time. He had been an assistant coach on the 1960 championship team. He was the one who moved Tommy McDonald from halfback to flanker. He also moved Pete Retzlaff from fullback to split end. Gauer knew his stuff.

"You seem like a nice boy," he said, "and I can tell you're trying hard. But I read the stuff you're writing, and, well, you don't know much about football."

It was nothing personal, he said. He believed that most writers, even the older ones, didn't know the game.

"I can show you a few things if you're interested," he said.

Gauer watched film every night in his dorm room. He said his door was always open.

"It's up to you," he said.

I knew that Gauer was right. There was a lot that I didn't know about the game. I had followed football for years, played it, and talked about it endlessly, but it's a complex game, especially at the NFL level. To do the job right, I needed to know more.

Several times a week, I went to his room and watched film. He explained the pass routes, the reads and blocking assignments. It was a simpler game in 1970. Teams played mostly man-to-man coverage. It was nothing like the exotic zone concepts that teams use today. Still, there was enough to fool a novice like me.

In studying a touchdown pass, Gauer would ask, "Who's responsible?" I would usually point to the nearest defender. Wrong, he would say. The safety was responsible for that receiver, but he blew the assignment, so the cornerback—the player I would have blamed—was just chasing the safety's mistake.

"You put in the paper that the cornerback got beat, people read it and think that's what happened," Gauer said. "Next Sunday, they're booing the guy because you told them he screwed up. You guys make mistakes, and we have to live with them."

As good a coach as Gauer was, he couldn't do much with that Eagles team. They were two years removed from the Joe Kuharich era, during which Kuharich, as coach and general manager, ran the franchise into the ground.

The fans were so disgusted by the end of the 1968 season that they rented a plane to fly over Franklin Field, trailing a banner that read: "Joe Must Go." Street vendors sold buttons with the same message. My mother bought one and wore it into the final home game.

The owner, Jerry Wolman, lost his fortune on a failed construction project. He sold the team to Leonard Tose, a millionaire trucking executive from Bridgeport, a Philadelphia suburb. Tose fired Kuharich and hired Pete Retzlaff as general manager. Retzlaff hired Jerry Williams as head coach.

Retzlaff was one of the most revered sports figures in the city. He was a great receiver with the Eagles and a popular sports anchor on Channel 10. Handsome and articulate, he had enormous credibility. Williams was the defensive coordinator on the 1960 championship team and achieved success as a head coach in the Canadian Football League.

It made for a great photo: Tose, the dapper millionaire; Retzlaff, the broad-shouldered Adonis; and Williams, the bespectacled wizard with a championship ring. But behind the smiles, there was an inherent problem: Tose was a first-time owner, Retzlaff was a first-time general manager, and Williams was a first-time head coach in the NFL.

No one said much about it at the time—the city was just glad to be rid of Kuharich—but it became an issue in the day-to-day operations.

"We were all rookies," Tose said. "We didn't know what we were doing."

In 1970, they had a mess on their hands. The roster was a poorly constructed mix of aging journeymen and overmatched youngsters. Most of the veterans were castoffs from other losing organizations. The locker room felt like a bus station with a lot of strangers passing through. They shared the space but little else.

As a rookie reporter, I was an outsider. I was writing mostly negative stories, which didn't endear me to the coaches and players. I also didn't know training-camp etiquette. On one particularly hot afternoon, I was watching practice and reached for a cup of Gatorade. Someone behind me shouted, "That's for the players!"

I was so startled that I dropped the cup on my foot. I turned and saw tight end Gary Ballman glaring at me.

"I'm sorry, I didn't know," I said.

"Now you do," he barked.

Those words—"That's for the players"—were burned into my psyche. For the rest of that summer and every summer since, I haven't once touched the Gatorade. Every time I see it, I hear Ballman's voice.

Those Eagles did not roll out the red carpet for anyone. On winning teams, the veterans welcome the newcomers; the older players mentor the rookies. There is a sense of community. On losing teams, it is the opposite. There is a pervasive insecurity, because the veterans know the coaches are always looking to make changes. Every new face represents a threat. The 1970 Eagles were that kind of team.

A good example was the kicking situation. The incumbent was Sam Baker, acquired in one of Kuharich's worst trades, a swap of Tommy McDonald to Dallas for Baker and two mediocre linemen. Who trades for a kicker? Kuharich did, and in 1969, Baker made just 16 of 30 field-goal attempts. So, Retzlaff and Williams selected a kicker in the fourteenth round of the 1970 draft. His name was Mark Moseley.

Baker was popular with the other veterans. He was an easy-going thirty-eight-year-old with a wry sense of humor. He once used the term "dastardly" to describe an opponent. Who wouldn't love a football player who uses a word like that? Moseley was a nobody out of Stephen F. Austin. He was here for a cup of coffee, if that.

But Moseley outkicked Baker every day at training camp. On the final cut, the coaches waived Baker and kept Moseley. It was the right call but not a popular one. The veterans treated the rookie as if he had done something wrong. Moseley dressed in cowboy boots and jeans, so the veterans began calling him "Midnight Cowboy" after the dim bumpkin played by actor Jon Voight in the 1969 film.

When the team practiced, Moseley went to the other end of the field and practiced alone. A ball boy helped out occasionally, but most of the time, Moseley worked alone, kicking the ball, retrieving it, and kicking it again. Finally, I offered to shag for him. I would catch the ball and throw it back.

Most kickers kick before practice and then in the special teams' period after practice. The rest of the time, they watch from the sidelines. Moseley kicked for two hours straight. He didn't want the veterans to think he was goofing off.

Late in the season, his performance tailed off, and I was convinced it was because he had a tired leg. A few months later, the Eagles used a fourth-round pick to select James "Happy" Feller, a kicker from the University of Texas.

Feller made the team, and Moseley was released. He spent two years installing septic tanks, but in 1974, coach George Allen brought him to Washington, where he spent thirteen years with the Redskins. In 1982, he was 20 for 21 on field-goal attempts and won the NFL's Most Valuable Player award, the only kicker to be so honored.

In the sixteen years after they cut Moseley, the Eagles went through seven different kickers. If they had just stayed with Moseley, they would have been better off. The draft picks they used to select Tony Franklin and Paul McFadden could have been used to fill other positions. Also they would not have had a punter (Mike Michel) attempting a 34-yard field goal on the final play of a wild-card game. Michel missed wide right and never was heard from again.

By the time Moseley retired in 1986, the game had been taken over by soccer-style kickers, guys with names like Garo, Horst, and Uwe. He was the last of the straight-on kickers, guys from the old school who kicked the ball with their toes and not their insteps. Moseley retired as Washington's all-time leading scorer with 1,206 points. Feller did not even last one season in Philadelphia. He was released in October after missing 14 of 20 field-goal attempts.

The 1970 season was the Eagles' final year at Franklin Field. They had planned to move into Veterans Stadium that year, but construction delays forced them to stay at the old stadium on the Penn campus for one more season.

My favorite memory of that season came in Week 3, when Washington came to play at Franklin Field. I felt a tap on my shoulder at halftime. It was Jim Heffernan, then director of public relations for the NFL.

"The commissioner wants to meet you," Heffernan said.

"Yeah, sure he does," I replied.

Heffernan was a former *Bulletin* sportswriter and an old friend. I assumed he was kidding, but he wasn't.

"Pete likes to meet all the new beat guys," Heffernan said as he led me to the far end of the press box.

There, as promised, sat Pete Rozelle, dapper as always, extending his hand.

"Welcome to the NFL," he said.

I'll always remember that moment: the warmth of his smile, the ease in his manner. It wasn't at all what I expected from the man known as the czar of professional football.

He was eating a hot dog. His binoculars hung on a strap around his neck. He looked like a regular fan, and, in truth, that's what he was. His greatest pleasure was sitting back on a Sunday afternoon and watching a game, even if it involved two winless teams, which this one did.

I asked Rozelle why he came to see the 0–2 Eagles play the 0–2 Redskins. He said he thought it would be a good game, but, of course, it wasn't. The Redskins crushed the Eagles, 33–21. But Franklin Field was full, the October sun was shining, and to Rozelle, it was Camelot on the Schuylkill River.

Rozelle always saw the bigger picture, and 1970 was the dawn of a golden age for professional football. The NFL and the American Football League (AFL) had just merged. *Monday Night Football* had debuted to blockbuster ratings. The Super Bowl had vaulted to the top of America's sports marquee. The NFL was lifting off like a NASA rocket, and Rozelle had his hand firmly on the throttle. I was along for the ride.

We talked for about ten minutes. Rozelle asked about my background. At twenty-three, I was the youngest beat man in the league. He reminded me that he was only thirty-three when he became commissioner. He said, "I'll tell you the same thing the [club] owners told me: You'll grow into it."

Ironically, I was at Franklin Field in 1959 when Rozelle's predecessor, Bert Bell, suffered a fatal heart attack while watching an Eagles-Steelers game. From Section EE, we saw a flurry of activity behind the visitor's bench. We saw the ushers and security guards carrying a man down the steps and lifting him into an ambulance. We had no idea who it was.

After the game, the news came over the radio that Bell had died in the stands at age sixty-five. It was so ironic that Bell died in the stadium where he had played as a Penn undergrad, watching two teams, the Eagles and Steelers, he once owned. It seemed almost fitting in a way. The owners picked Rozelle, who was general manager of the Los Angeles Rams, to succeed him.

In 1971, the Eagles moved into the Vet. Everyone was excited about the new stadium, which cost $52 million to build. It was similar in design to the other cookie-cutter stadiums of the day: Riverfront in Cincinnati, Three Rivers in Pittsburgh, and Busch Stadium in St. Louis. The multipurpose stadium built to serve football and baseball was considered the wave of the future.

Two major problems quickly became apparent. For one thing, the circular shape made it a lousy place to watch a game. Fans were too far away from the action, especially for football, where a 50-yard-line seat was farther away from the field than a seat in the end zone. The problem for baseball was that the stadiums were too big. You could fill sixty-five thousand seats for football, but the typical baseball crowd was less than half of that, so most nights, the place felt empty.

The other problem was the artificial turf, which was like a thin layer of outdoor carpet stretched across asphalt. It was bad for baseball and worse for football. I could not imagine being tackled and falling on that surface. It was so hard.

The Vet was owned and operated by the city of Philadelphia, so it was maintained by city workers, not the teams. They installed the baseball field with cutouts for home plate, the pitcher's mound, and the bases. When it was time for football, they filled the cutout areas with dirt, but seams and gaps remained around the cutouts and potholes where one wrong step could end a career.

The night before the Eagles played their first game at the Vet—an August preseason affair against Buffalo—the team worked out at the new stadium. It was the first time the field was converted from baseball to football. The Eagles had been assured that the switch would not be a problem. They found that was not the case.

Retzlaff came storming off the field, heading straight toward me.

"Come with me," he said. "I want you to see something."

There were bumps and lumps everywhere. At the cutouts around the bases, the wooden frame was raised several inches. A player could easily trip and fall.

Retzlaff walked me to the 15-yard line.

"Look at this," he said.

He put his foot down, and his brown loafer dropped out of sight.

"It's like stepping in a gopher hole," he said. "It isn't safe to play on a field like this."

Retzlaff raised hell with the stadium workers, walking them from one trouble spot to another, insisting that they repair it. The workers rolled back the turf and shoveled in more dirt, but Retzlaff was still unhappy. He went off to find Tose, who was upstairs showing guests around the new offices.

Retzlaff pulled Tose aside, still fuming.

"It's a disgrace," he said. "I'm embarrassed. I'm not sure we can play on this."

"Slow down, Pete," Tose said. "What are you saying?"

"The field is unplayable," Retzlaff said. "We might have to cancel the game."

Cancel the first game in the new stadium? With all the buildup, all the excitement? The owner made it clear that wasn't happening.

"The game's not for another twenty-four hours," he said. "Tell them to work all night if they have to. But goddamn it, we're playing tomorrow night."

The field wasn't the only problem. Jim Gallagher, the public relations director, came upstairs to inform Tose that the air-conditioning wasn't working in the Eagles' locker room. It was so unbearably hot that the players were changing their clothes in the corridor. Yes, naked men were roaming the halls.

"What the hell's going on?" Tose asked. "Do we have to go back to Franklin Field? This is unbelievable."

They repaired the air-conditioning, but the playing surface remained a concern forever. In 2001, the Eagles had to cancel a preseason game because the field was deemed unsafe. Player reps for both teams—the Eagles and the Baltimore Ravens—conferred with the officials and made the ruling. It was a national story, one more chapter in the Vet's troubled history.

Initially, everyone was excited about the new stadium. When the media toured the place in the spring of 1971, the reviews were effusive. The locker room was enormous, more than twice the size of the locker room at Franklin Field. The training room was a spacious suite. There was a weight room, a sauna, and a racquetball court. The term "state of the art" appeared in almost every story.

But over time, as other stadiums were built and teams began moving away from the multipurpose model, the Vet became an object of scorn. The artificial turf claimed more victims every year, and the fans in the 700 level earned the reputation as the most unruly in sports.

A court was created in the basement, with Judge Seamus McCaffery dispensing justice. In the past, a drunken fan was simply ejected from the stadium; now he was handcuffed and taken before Judge McCaffery, who issued a stiff fine. If the offender couldn't pay, he was sent to jail.

In 1971, however, the stadium and the fans weren't as embarrassing as the product on the field. The Eagles were a pitiful team. In the first regular-season game at the Vet, they lost to Dallas, 42–7, as Pete Liske threw 6 interceptions. They were outscored 110–24 in the first three games. Tose fired Williams and replaced him with Ed Khayat, the defensive-line coach.

Khayat, another veteran of the 1960 title team, was new to the role of head coach. He had worked as an assistant coach with several teams but had never been the man in change until Tose gave him the job on an interim basis. Khayat believed in military discipline. One of his first acts was to insist that all players cut their hair and shave their mustaches.

I wrote a column mocking the new rules. Would cutting their hair and shaving their mustaches make them better players? No. It was the '70s. Most players looked like roadies for a rock band. So what? If a guy can play, who cares? The Eagles' problem was that they had too many guys who *couldn't* play.

I wrote that Khayat's pregame speech should be "Win one for the Clipper." Tose sought me out the next day and accused me of taking a cheap shot at the coach. He should have consulted the players: They thought Khayat's rules were ridiculous. Rossovich was the most outspoken, but he wasn't alone. Even some assistant coaches—who also were forced to shave—thought the edict was stupid.

Cornerback Nate Ramsey said he didn't even recognize himself when he looked in the mirror.

"I had my mustache since seventh grade," he said. "Ridge Avenue Elementary School in Neptune, New Jersey. I had it before I got into this game. It was as much a part of me as my eyes and nose. I'm thirty years old. Why should somebody else tell me how to look after all these years?"

Rossovich had his mustache when he won a national championship at Southern Cal, and he had it when the Eagles drafted him in 1969. He could not understand why, suddenly, it was an issue. Rossovich also was involved in several advertising campaigns for which his face appeared in commercials and on billboards. Now, without his familiar Fu Manchu, he looked completely different.

"Why doesn't [Khayat] tell Tose to trim his eyebrows?" Rossovich asked. "I mean, why not? It is a team thing, right?"

All the players were ordered to shave by noon on Wednesday, and everyone, even Rossovich, complied. When the team went out to practice, linebacker Billy Hobbs walked past the media throng—which was larger than usual because of the shaving edict—and announced, "I have no comment except to say I love being a prisoner of war. My name is Hobbs, and my serial number is 0056."

The Eagles took advantage of a soft schedule to win six of their last nine games, including a 41–28 rout of the Giants in the final week. It was fool's gold, all of it, but Tose embraced it happily. He gave Khayat a two-year contract extension and declared, "I think we can bring a championship to Philadelphia next season."

The team face-planted in 1972, and most embarrassing was a 62–10 loss to the Giants at Yankee Stadium. Earlier in the week, Tose had gone on record, guaranteeing the Eagles would win that game; instead, they suffered their most lopsided loss in forty years. They finished the season with a 2–11–1 record, and both wins were by 1 point. They were winless at home (0–6–1) and scored just 12 touchdowns all season. But give them this: They were clean-shaven.

The lone bright spot was Bill Bradley, the All-Pro safety. He was the first player in NFL history to lead the league in interceptions in consecutive years, quite a feat when you consider that most players who rank high in interceptions play for winning teams. Opponents are forced to play catch up, which means that they throw more passes. For Bradley to have 20 interceptions in two seasons while playing for a team that won just eight games is remarkable.

We were the same age and had similar tastes in movies and music. We became friends, which wasn't a great idea, since I was covering the team and had to maintain my objectivity. We were standing in line at the Main Point one night, waiting to see the Allman Brothers, and I said, "You know, if you mess up on the field, I have to write about it."

"Then I won't mess up," he said in his Texas twang. "Problem solved."

Bradley lived in the Benjamin Franklin Hotel downtown. He enjoyed painting. His style was similar to that of Peter Max, an artist who was popular at the time. Bradley's work was impressionistic with bright colors and bold images. His art was very good, but he asked me not to write about it.

"People don't want to read that shit when the team's losing," he said, and he was probably right.

Bradley had never experienced losing prior to coming to the Eagles. He was a legend in Texas, where he led his high school team to the state championship, earning the nickname "Super Bill." He was recruited by every major college but chose to play at the University of Texas. He was a Playboy All-American as a quarterback and for a time dated a coed named Farrah Fawcett.

Bradley played in the Southwest Conference at a time when it was almost lily white. It bothered him, because he hadn't been raised that way. His father worked for the railroad, and the family lived in a racially mixed area. When he was selected to play in a Texas high school all-star game, he roomed with Jerry LeVais, a star running back from Beaumont. It was the first time a white player and a black player in the game were roommates.

"The lady at the desk asked, 'Are you sure you want that room? You'll be with a Negro boy,'" Bradley said. "I told her, 'No, ma'am, I'll be with my teammate.'"

The story of Bradley and LeVais rooming together was such big news that author Jim Dent turned it into a best-selling book, *The Kids Got It Right: How the Texas All-Stars Kicked Down Racial Walls*. Bradley carried himself with a breezy self-confidence that allowed him to make friends with everyone, black or white.

In 1972, Bradley held out for a new contract. He was earning $15,000 a year, which was ridiculous when you consider that in addition to being an All-Pro safety, he was the team's punter and punt returner, and he held for placekicks. He wanted to be paid $60,000, or $15,000 for each of his jobs. He thought the request was a bargain, considering that he was also the emergency quarterback. "Hell," he said, "I'm giving 'em that for free."

Retzlaff, the general manager, called his demands outrageous.

When training camp opened, Bradley was there, but not in uniform. Instead, he parked his VW van next to the practice field and set up a table where three attractive young ladies in T-shirts and short shorts sold bologna sandwiches and cold drinks to the spectators. The sign on the van read: "Bill Bradley Relief Fund." Bradley sat there in a straw hat, smiling and signing autographs while Retzlaff fumed.

When the '72 season ended, Tose fired Khayat and his entire coaching staff. Retzlaff stepped down as general manager. The highlight of the press conference was Jack Zilly, the special teams' coach, walking behind the podium where Tose was speaking, surveying the luncheon buffet, and carrying away an entire cheesecake. It was like a raised middle finger to Tose, the media, and Philadelphia in general.

A few weeks later, we were back in the same room to see Tose introduce Mike McCormack as his new head coach. McCormack's resume was stellar: He had been an All-Pro tackle with Cleveland in the 1950s and an offensive line coach with Washington for eight seasons. That meant he played for Paul Brown and coached under Vince Lombardi and George Allen. All three coaches are in the Hall of Fame.

McCormack spoke optimistically about turning around the franchise. He was familiar with the personnel because the Redskins played them twice a year in the NFC East. He knew the offense needed help, but he said the defense was "as good as any team we faced." He called Bradley "the best safety in football."

Naturally, McCormack was asked whether he had rules regarding long hair and mustaches. He did not.

"I believe in discipline," he said, "but with common sense."

McCormack had all the right answers. He was also smart enough to know what he was taking on. Tose had fired two head coaches in three seasons. The new coach knew that he had to win in a hurry.

McCormack came from Washington, where Allen coined the phrase "The Future Is Now." Allen took over a losing Redskins team and turned it around by trading draft picks for veteran players. In his first year, he improved the team's record to 9–4–1. The next year, he led them to the Super Bowl.

McCormack used the same playbook to rebuild the Eagles. He traded away three picks in the 1974 draft (including the first and second picks), seven picks in the 1975 draft (including the top six), six picks in the 1976 draft (including the first four), four picks in the 1977 draft (the first four), and seven picks in the 1978 draft (including the first two).

In return, he acquired quarterbacks Roman Gabriel and Mike Boryla; running backs Norm Bulaich, John Tarver, and James McAlister; defensive linemen Jerry Patton and Dennis Wirgowski; offensive linemen Stan Walters, John Niland, and Bill Lueck; linebackers Bill Bergey and Dick Absher; and placekicker Horst Muhlmann. Only Gabriel, Bergey, and Walters had a real impact.

Because McCormack traded away so many high picks, he wound up sifting through the leftovers on draft day. In 1974, the draft was winding down—more than three hundred players had been selected already—and I pulled McCormack aside. For the first and only time in my life, I tried to play general manager.

"Mike, you should take Billy Johnson," I said, referring to the 5'9", 170-pound halfback who broke all the records at Widener College.

"Too small," McCormack said.

"It's the fourteenth round," I said. "What do you have to lose?"

The Eagles had just used their thirteenth-round pick to select Lars Ditlev, a defensive tackle from the South Dakota School of Mines. I had never heard of the school, much less the player. Ditlev never even reported to camp. He might still be in the mines, for all I know. But Billy Johnson scored 62 touchdowns at Widener, plus he was a local kid. Why not give him a shot?

I saw Johnson play at Chichester High School, and I saw him run wild at Widener. I really believed that with his speed and elusiveness, he could make it in the NFL—maybe not as a running back, but certainly as a kick returner, and maybe a wide receiver.

"Are you his agent?" McCormack said with a laugh.

"I'm telling you, he's *really* good," I said.

"He's just too small," McCormack said, noting the Eagles had just moved their training camp to Widener, and if they drafted Johnson and later had to cut him, it might cause hard feelings at the school.

Johnson finally was drafted by the Houston Oilers in the fifteenth round, the 365th player selected overall, and he became one of the best kick returners in NFL history. Famous for his white shoes and "Funky Chicken" end-zone dance, Johnson played thirteen NFL seasons and retired as the game's all-time leader in punt return yardage (3,317).

I never let McCormack forget it.

Gabriel's arrival did energize the Eagles offense. The thirty-three-year-old former MVP with the Los Angeles Rams was the NFL's comeback player of the year with the Eagles in 1973.

Harold Carmichael led the league with 67 catches and 1,117 yards. Teaming with 6'5" tight end Charles Young and 6'4" wide receiver Don Zimmerman, they became known as the "Fire High Gang."

The high point of the season was a 30–16 win over Dallas, a victory that ended with hundreds of fans pouring onto the field to mob McCormack and the players. It was the Eagles' first win over the Cowboys since 1967, snapping an eleven-game losing streak to their division rival. They were unable to build on that, however, and after a 4–10 finish in 1975, McCormack was fired.

I was sorry to see how things ended for McCormack. He was a nice man. Everyone in the organization liked him. In announcing McCormack's dismissal, general manager Jim Murray said, "I feel lousy, I feel terrible, but this is pro football. You gotta win."

4

The Broad Street Bullies

IN THE EARLY 1970S, the sports landscape in Philadelphia was as bleak and arid as the Sahara. The 76ers, having dealt away Wilt Chamberlain, made history by winning just nine games in the 1972–1973 season. The Phillies, despite the Cy Young efforts of Steve Carlton, won only fifty-nine games in 1972. We've already discussed how bad the Eagles were that year. They led the league in only one department: most sacks allowed.

The Flyers still had not produced a winning season and seemed to be going backward. They won thirty-one games in their first season (1967–1968) but slipped to seventeen wins two years later. The team had yet to win a playoff series and twice had missed the postseason altogether. For many Philadelphians, hockey still was a foreign sport.

All that changed in 1973.

The Flyers assembled a feisty young team that became known as "the Broad Street Bullies." Led by a gap-toothed captain named Bobby Clarke—Montreal coach Scotty Bowman called him "the dirtiest player in hockey"—and a superb goaltender in Bernie Parent, the Flyers stunned the hockey world by winning the Stanley Cup in only their seventh season.

But it wasn't just the winning—it was *how* they won that captured the heart of Philadelphia. They didn't just outscore the opposition; they outhit them and outfought them. They won back-to-back Cups, leaving a trail of blackened eyes and bloody noses in their wake.

The fans didn't know the finer points of hockey, but when one of the Flyers splattered an opposing player against the glass, the crowd stood up and cheered. This was our kind of team.

No one understood that better than Ed Snider. He was the vice president of the Eagles under owner Jerry Wolman, but at heart, he was a hockey guy. He had seen a game at Boston Garden years earlier and had fallen in love with the sport. When the NHL talked about expanding in 1967, he jumped to the front of the line.

Snider and Wolman convinced the NHL to put one of the six expansion franchises in Philadelphia. They built a new arena in South Philly—they called it the Spectrum—and then they built the team.

The Flyers were the best of the six new teams during the regular season, but in the playoffs, they were ousted in the first round by the St. Louis Blues. Snider watched as the Plager brothers—Bill, Barclay, and Bob—and other St. Louis tough guys pushed the Flyers all over the ice. The scene was repeated numerous times over the next few years as the Flyers were outmuscled by the NHL's bigger teams.

Snider knew this would never sell in Philadelphia, a town that worshipped Chuck Bednarik and Smokin' Joe Frazier. These fans were not going to get behind a team that got slapped around. Snider told his scouts to search the Canadian provinces and bring back the meanest, toughest guys they could find. If they could skate, well, that was a bonus.

That's how the Broad Street Bullies came to be. The revamped roster included Bob "the Hound" Kelly, Don "Big Bird" Saleski, Andre "Moose" Dupont, Bill "Cowboy" Flett, and Dave "the Hammer" Schultz. They had size and were willing to drop the gloves every night. The best player and leader was Clarke, whose blond curls made him look like an innocent schoolboy but who was the fiercest competitor on the team. He didn't fight as much as the others, but he was brutally efficient with his stick.

Playing in the 1972 Summit Series for Team Canada, Clarke took out the Soviets' best player, winger Valery Kharlamov, with a slash across the ankles. With Kharlamov sidelined, Team Canada rallied to win the final two games in Moscow and win the series. Clarke did not deny that his stick work was deliberate.

"Kharlamov was killing us," Clarke said. "Somebody had to do something about him. It's not something I'm really proud of, but I honestly can't say I was ashamed to do it."

Clarke brought that fire to the ice every night for fifteen seasons. He won three NHL Most Valuable Player Awards and two Stanley Cups, and in the process, he pinned the city's heart to his suspenders. He went from a shy rookie to an All-Star to a legend right before our eyes. His growth paralleled the growth of the franchise, from strangers to champions. The kid from Flin Flon, Manitoba, brought the game to our neighborhoods and taprooms.

His was the first NHL name I heard on the Broad Street Subway. Guys talked about Clarke the way they talked about Bill Bergey and Greg Luzinski. That was significant, because it meant that the game was now part of the city's sports dialogue. When general manager Keith Allen surrounded Clarke with better talent and the wins started piling up, the Flyers owned the town.

I was delighted for several reasons. One, I was a hockey fan. I talked earlier about my affection for the Ramblers, the minor league team that played here in the 1950s. When I heard the NHL was coming to town, I was thrilled at the prospect of seeing Gordie Howe, Bobby Hull, and Stan Mikita in person. But more than that, after covering the Eagles for several years, it was refreshing to have the opportunity to write about a winning team.

In the '70s, the football beat was not the year-round job that it is today. There was no free agency and no off-season minicamps. The NFL basically went into hibernation after the Super Bowl. For six months, from February until the start of training camp in July, I was free to write about other things. I covered some golf, and with the success of the Flyers, I was assigned to help out on the hockey beat.

It was funny to see the excitement, because I remembered what it was like that first year. On the day before the home opener, the team scheduled an open practice. It was billed as "Meet the Flyers" day.

I cut my afternoon classes at Temple so I could be there when the doors opened. Frank Bertucci, a fellow journalism major and hockey fan, came with me. We talked hockey all the time. In Philadelphia circa 1967, it was like speaking a foreign language. We would be talking about power plays and penalty kills, and people would stare at us like we were from another planet.

We were excited about getting a sneak preview of our new team. We planned to arrive early, because we thought it would be crowded. Even if the city wasn't all that into hockey, we figured that people would come to check out the new arena. Plus, it was free.

On the ride to South Philadelphia, we tried to guess how many people would be there. I said three to four thousand. Frank said it would be twice that. Boy, were we wrong.

I counted twenty-four people in the lower deck, including the ushers. A car towing would have drawn a bigger crowd. Stu Nahan, the team's play-by-play voice, introduced the players to a smattering of applause. Frank and I left, shaking our heads.

The next night, the Flyers played their first home game. Only 7,812 fans turned out to see them defeat the Pittsburgh Penguins, 1–0. Frank and I paid $2 for general admission tickets and sat in the upper deck, first row behind the goal. We had the entire row to ourselves.

Just a few people sat behind us, and they clearly knew nothing about hockey. When Lou Angotti came on the ice, one guy asked, "Why does he have a 'C' on his jersey?" The guy sitting next to him said, "I think it means he's Canadian."

Frank turned around and said, "They're *all* Canadians."

"So what does the 'C' mean?" the guy asked.

"It means he's the captain," Frank said.

Under his breath, Frank muttered, "Nitwit."

In those days, gazing around at the empty seats, I thought back to my conversation with Bill Putnam. I thought about how confident he was that hockey would catch on in Philadelphia. He had said that a great game in a great sports town couldn't miss. I hoped that he was right, but I had this awful fear that the Flyers might be playing in another city before long.

But for two college kids with no money—that was Frank and me—it was a cheap night out. Two bucks got you in the door, and you could sit anywhere. Concessions were a bargain. A roast beef sandwich cost 75 cents, and a Coke was a quarter. If you wanted to splurge, you could get an order of French fries for 50 cents.

I made it a point to get to the arena early so I could watch the warmups. I stood in the visitors end so I could see the superstars up close. Certain images stick in my mind. A crew-cut Bobby Orr. A graying Gordie Howe. An aged and scarred Johnny Bower, the Toronto goalie.

Back then, players would sign autographs during warmups. Kids would hold their programs over the glass, and players would go down the line, signing each one. I remember Bobby Hull, the Golden Jet, signing one program after another while the Zamboni inched along behind him.

The team was fairly successful that year—the Flyers were 31–32–11, the best among the expansion teams—so attendance picked up as the season went along. However, a portion of the Spectrum roof blew off in a windstorm, and the team was forced to play March "home" games in New York (one), Toronto (one), and Quebec (five).

It wasn't until the seventh year, when the Flyers emerged as a legitimate Stanley Cup contender, that they filled the house every night. By then, I was working for the *Bulletin* and was the second hockey writer, assisting beat man Jack Chevalier.

Chevalier was the one who came up with the name "the Broad Street Bullies." His initial suggestion was "the Bullies of Broad Street," but night editor Pete Cafone thought "Broad Street Bullies" worked better in a headline.

Each beat man tried to put his own stamp on the team. Chuck Newman of the *Inquirer* called them "Freddie's Philistines" after coach Fred Shero. Bill Fleischman of the *Daily News* called them "the Mad Squad," a play on the TV show *The Mod Squad.* But "Broad Street Bullies" was the name that stuck.

They were a fun team to cover. For one thing, they were winning, and that was a nice change. But more than that, they were fun to be around. Most were in their early twenties, kids from small towns buried deep in the Canadian timber, places with funny names like Flin Flon and Moose Jaw. They weren't spoiled by success, because it was all too new to them. They hung out at a South Jersey bar called Rexy's, ate pizza, and drank beer with the blue-collar crowd.

It was amusing to see how they were treated in other cities. Newspapers, especially those in Canada, vilified them. There were cartoon drawings of the Flyers as cavemen carrying clubs. They were called thugs and savages, but that was far from the truth. Off the ice, they were regular guys. They didn't go looking for trouble. On the rare occasion when a drunk tried to start a fight at Rexy's, the players just walked away.

On the ice, it was a different story. They shattered the league record for penalty minutes. There were fights and bench-clearing brawls almost every night. Sometimes the fights spilled over into the stands. Seven Flyers were hauled off to jail one night in Vancouver after a fan reached over the glass to grab Saleski's hair. His teammates rushed in, and pretty soon they were duking it out with the fans and the security guards.

Schultz was their most feared player. He wasn't that big—6'1", 185 pounds—but he would fight anyone anywhere. He played left wing on the third line and scored 20 goals in the first Stanley Cup season, but he wasn't there to score goals: He was there to handle the rough stuff.

Critics accused the Flyers of tarnishing the sport. They said the team was winning through violence and intimidation rather than skill. It wasn't true. The Flyers had skill—Bobby Clarke, Bernie Parent, and winger Bill Barber are all in the Hockey Hall of Fame—and Shero was ahead of the other coaches in terms of strategy. But the intimidation factor was real. Teams didn't want to play the Flyers, especially in the Spectrum, where they were virtually unbeatable.

"I remember talking to Jim Gregory [Toronto general manager] during the '73–'74 season," Keith Allen said. "He said, 'Keith, your team is going to win the Stanley Cup this year.' I was surprised. No one else thought we could play with the New Yorks and Bostons.

"I said, 'We're getting better, Jim, but we've got a lot of young players. I don't know.' He said, 'Your team works so damn hard, you'll just wear down these other teams. Your kids are too hungry to lose.' He turned out to be right."[1]

That season, the Flyers won fifty games. In the first round of the playoffs, they swept the Atlanta Flames. In the second round, they defeated the New York Rangers in a seven-game series but lost three players to injury: Bob Kelly hurt his knee, Gary Dornhoefer separated his shoulder, and Barry Ashbee suffered a career-ending eye injury when he was struck by a Dale Rolfe slap shot.

The final game of the New York series was played at the Spectrum. In the first period, Schultz squared off with Rolfe, a big man but not much of a fighter. Schultz literally punched Rolfe from one side of the ice to the other. Rolfe's teammates stood and watched. They let Rolfe take a bloody beating.

"That would never happen with our team," Clarke said. "This is a sport where you have to stick up for each other. I know we do. It's one of the reasons we made it this far."

After the game, Rangers' defenseman Brad Park tried to rationalize it. He said the Rangers didn't want to stoop to the Flyers' level.

"I was so fed up with the shit they were pulling, I wanted to give it right back," Park said. "But when I thought about it more carefully, I almost got sick. If I had to maim someone to win another game and win the Stanley Cup, then it wasn't worth it.

"We have a lot of class guys on our team. I look around our locker room and I'm prouder to lose with these guys than I would be winning with another club."[2]

A New York writer repeated Park's words to Clarke. The Flyers' captain sneered, "He's proud to lose? Good for him. I'd rather win."

Park predicted that the Bruins would rout the Flyers in the Stanley Cup finals. He was not alone. Few hockey people gave the Flyers a chance against the Bruins. They had no history of success against Boston, winning just four of thirty-eight games against them. They were 1–17–2 all-time in Boston Garden, and the Bruins had home-ice advantage in the best-of-seven series.

The atmosphere in the Garden for Game 1 was decidedly hostile. I was in the auxiliary press section. We were not in a box; we were in the cheap seats, surrounded by Boston fans. When the Flyers took the ice, the fans were all over them, cursing and pelting them with garbage.

Tom Brookshier was seated next to me. Brookshier was the sports director at Channel 10, but he was also a former Eagles cornerback and still plenty tough at age forty-two. He kept looking over his shoulder at the fans. I could see the anger building. Finally, he turned and shouted, "Why don't you shut the hell up?"

A big guy in a Bobby Orr jersey shot back, "What are you gonna do about it?"

Brookshier stood up and said, "I'll come up there and *make* you shut up."

The big guy spread his arms across the row of fans, all young and flexing their beer muscles.

"You gonna take us all on, Dad?" he said.

Brookshier pointed at me and the other reporters from Philadelphia.

"These guys are with me," he said. "We'll kick your ass, big mouth. You and all your friends."

Inquirer columnist Frank Dolson spun in his chair.

"What's this 'we' stuff?" he said.

Fortunately, the security guards arrived to calm things down. Then the game started, and we got back to business. Later, I polled the other reporters: Who would have gone to battle with Brookie?

Charlie Swift of WIP said he had been ready to go, but Charlie stood 5'5" in his Cuban heels—I don't know how much help he would have been. Everyone else was a conscientious objector. My feeling was the Flyers didn't need me to fight their battles. They were more than capable of standing up for themselves.

They demonstrated it, too, by splitting the first two games in Boston. Clarke won Game 2 with a goal in overtime. The Flyers won the next two games at the Spectrum to take a 3–1 lead. The Bruins won Game 5 in the Garden, so the Flyers pulled out all the stops for Game

6 in Philadelphia, including bringing Kate Smith in to sing their good-luck anthem, "God Bless America," before the opening faceoff.

The Flyers scored when Rick MacLeish deflected a Dupont shot past Boston goalie Gilles Gilbert and Parent withstood the desperate Bruins' attack in the final period to preserve a 1–0 victory. The Flyers were the first expansion team to win the Stanley Cup and Parent—simply magnificent throughout the season—won the Conn Smythe Trophy as the Most Valuable Player in the playoffs.

When the game ended, hundreds of fans poured onto the ice to celebrate with the players. After the presentation of the Cup, it seemed like most of the fans followed the players into the locker room. It was jammed wall to wall with people—some players, some family, some total strangers—all sipping champagne from the Stanley Cup.

The only one missing was Shero, who fled to the solitude of his office. On the locker room blackboard was the message he had written for the team before the game: Win today and walk together forever.

No doubt, there is a special bond among players who win a championship, and that was particularly true of those Flyers. They won with hard work and sacrifice, the very essence of teamwork. They didn't have the most talent, but in the end, they were the best team.

"They had the greatest courage and discipline," Shero said. "Sure, you'd get more on the open market for Bobby Orr than Terry Crisp or Orest Kindrachuk. You'd get more for Phil Esposito than Bill Clement. But it takes 21 men to make a team."[3]

In the locker room, Schultz and his father, Edgar, shared a tearful embrace. The elder Schultz was an auto mechanic. It was inspection time back in Saskatchewan, he said, and the work was piling up. "I told 'em there's no damn way I'm coming back now," he said. "My son is going to win the Stanley Cup, and I want to be there."

As they held the Cup, Schultz told his father, "I'm still just a small-town kid from Saskatchewan. I'm no big deal." His father smiled and said, "As far as I'm concerned, you are."

Ashbee was celebrating with a patch over his injured eye. Dornhoefer was there with his arm in a sling. Frank Rizzo, the mayor who knew nothing about hockey but felt as though he needed to be there, was looking around for Parent. "Where's the goal guy?" he asked. "I want to meet the goal guy."

I went back to the *Bulletin* office to write my game story, but Jack Wilson gave me another assignment. He had heard something about a victory parade. He wanted me to contact someone from city government to find out whether it was really happening.

It took several calls, but I got a confirmation: There would be a parade the next morning. It would start at the Spectrum and wind through Center City, ending with a rally on Independence Mall. The city projected a crowd of one hundred thousand.

I told Wilson, "I think it will be bigger than that."

"There aren't that many hockey fans in Philadelphia," he said.

"Today there are," I said.

Monday dawned, and it became clear that the parade would far exceed the city's estimate. The streets of Center City were jammed. The cops were overwhelmed.

The players were riding in open convertibles, and the fans mobbed them. Clarke and Parent were pulled from the parade for their own safety. Shero shook so many hands that he ended the day with a dislocated thumb.

I was riding in the press bus with a dozen other reporters as well as the families of the players. These were humble folks from small Canadian towns, and they could not believe their eyes. People of all ages were lining the streets and rooftops, showering their sons with ticker tape and confetti.

Joe Watson Sr., the father of defensemen Joe and Jimmy Watson, was next to me. The elder Watson was a butcher in Smithers, British Columbia, population 750. He was gazing at all the people—some in Flyers jerseys, others in three-piece suits—leaning out windows and hanging from streetlights. Watson was a burly man with a thick gray beard, and his eyes were wide with wonder.

"I didn't know there were this many people in the world," he said.

Andrea Mitchell, now an NBC news anchor, was a reporter for KYW news radio. She was phoning in live reports. She said the police estimated that two million people were at the parade.

"All of this for a hockey team," she said.

Well, not just a hockey team, but a Stanley Cup champion. And the outpouring wasn't about hockey—it was about winning. Philadelphia had been down for so long that it was labeled "the City of Losers." The Flyers had broken the spell, and people wanted to celebrate.

Daily News columnist Tom Fox summed up the city's mood when he wrote, "It had to be the single greatest and most joyous day in this town's history. I never saw anything like the crowds that lined the streets and jammed Independence Mall. I always thought the Mardi Gras mobs in New Orleans were the greatest, but this was bigger and a lot more spirited.

"There's been so much bad news to distress the soul, but here were these hockey players from Canada, kids who all wore their hair like the Three Musketeers, and they brought this town together again and even cynics like me were caught up in the happiness."[4]

After the parade, Clarke and his father, Clifford, tried to put it in perspective. The elder Clarke, who spent his life in the zinc mines, talked about coming to Philadelphia for the first time after his son was drafted by the Flyers.

"They flew us to town, Bobby and me," Clifford said. "They put us up in a fancy hotel. They told us we could go to the Phillies game that night. Bobby wouldn't go. He stayed in the room. Bud Poile [the general manager] told us our room was paid through the next day. He said, 'Relax. Look around town. Enjoy yourselves.' Bobby said, 'C'mon, Dad, let's go home. So we left.'

"It wasn't that Bobby didn't like Philadelphia, it was just so big. We had never seen anything like it."

"I was scared as hell," Clarke said. "I remember the first time I walked through the Spectrum and saw all those seats. The building held more people than lived in Flin Flon [population 12,000]. I thought, 'What am I doing here?'

"I signed my contract in the parking lot outside the Hershey Arena. That's where we had our training camp. I didn't have an agent. Keith [Allen] handed me the paper and I signed. I got a $5,000 bonus and $14,000 for my first year. It seemed like all the money in the world. My father was making $6,000 a year working in the mines. All I wanted to do was play hockey. Look how it turned out."

The next year, the Flyers increased their regular-season win total to fifty-one and stormed back to the playoffs, where they swept Toronto, defeated the New York Islanders in seven games, and overcame a dangerous Buffalo Sabres team to repeat as Stanley Cup champions.

They beat the Sabres in six games, winning the clincher in a steamy Buffalo Memorial Auditorium, 2–0. It was the second year in a row that Parent won the final game by shutout. He became the first player to win back-to-back Conn Smythe trophies.

The Flyers returned home to another parade. This time, the city planners knew what to expect. They knew there would be a huge crowd, so they started the parade uptown and went south on Broad Street, finishing in JFK Stadium. This time, the team rode on a flatbed truck preceded by several string bands.

In other cities, the media bemoaned the Bullies' success. It was clear the NHL did not love the team's pugnacious style. The sour look on league president Clarence Campbell's face as he handed the Cup over to Clarke and Parent spoke volumes. The Flyers didn't care.

"The people who have a problem with how we won can go to hell as far as I'm concerned," Clement said. "We won playing hard. We sacrificed. It took an incredible amount of work, but all the things we should have gotten acclaim for kind of took a back seat. But we earned everything we got, that's for darn sure."[5]

It was sweetly ironic the next season when the Flyers found themselves in the position of defending the league's honor when the Soviet Red Army team came to North America for a series of games against the NHL. The Soviets easily defeated the Rangers and Bruins and played Montreal to a tie in the Forum. They had one game left on their tour, and it was against the Flyers at the Spectrum.

Campbell and others from the league office, as well as owners and coaches from the other clubs, all of whom had accused the Flyers of hurting the sport with their brawling style of play, now saw the Broad Street Bullies as their last hope. It was up to the Flyers, the NHL establishment said, to take down the Soviets and restore the league's pride. The same people who had spent two years wagging their fingers at the Flyers and calling them names now were their biggest boosters—for one day at least.

Parent was out with a neck injury, but his backup, Wayne Stephenson, was playing well. Shero had studied the Soviets and came up with a defensive system that kept them bottled up in the neutral zone. That combined with the Flyers' physical play put the visitors on their heels.

Defenseman Ed Van Impe knocked Kharlamov to the ice with a solid but legal body check. Kharlamov stayed down, and while the trainers attended to him, the Soviet coach took his team to the locker room. The head of the Soviet delegation complained to the officials about the Flyers' rough play and said their team would not return to the ice. Snider informed them that if they did not finish the game, they would not get their $200,000.

The Soviets went back on the ice, including Kharlamov, but the Flyers dominated them, winning 4–1. The NHL brass celebrated their success, as did the rest of Canada. Of course, by the next day, everyone hated them again.

The Flyers finished that season with their highest-ever point total (118), and they defeated Toronto and Boston in the playoffs, but in the finals they were swept by Montreal. Injuries to Parent and MacLeish ruined their chances of winning a third consecutive Stanley Cup. The league also was putting in more rules designed to get the rough stuff out of hockey. The Flyers found it harder to play their game.

Over the next two seasons, their win totals slipped to forty-eight and then to forty-five. Shero stepped down after seven years as coach. The most crushing blow came in February 1979, when Parent suffered an eye injury that ended his brilliant career.

It was a Saturday matinee at the Spectrum. The Flyers were playing the Rangers, and Jimmy Watson and New York's Don Maloney were fighting for position in front of the net. Watson wrestled Maloney down, but as he fell, his stick struck Parent in the eye. It was a freakish thing. He was wearing a mask, but the tip of Maloney's stick went in the eye hole. Parent skated off the ice in obvious pain.

Stephenson came on, and the game continued, but we received word that Parent was being taken to Wills Eye Hospital. Chevalier said to me, "You go. I'll stay here and cover the game."

I was the only reporter there when the thirty-four-year-old goalie was wheeled down the hall with white gauze taped over both eyes. The doctors determined that he had suffered two conjunctival tears of the eye. I had two thoughts: First, the injury was even more serious than we had initially thought, and second, I probably shouldn't be there.

Parent and his wife were visibly upset. They didn't need a visitor, especially a reporter, but Parent recognized my voice and said it was OK. The nurse glared at me and tapped her watch.

"You have five minutes," she said.

I asked Parent what he remembered. He still was unclear.

"There was a scramble in front of the net," he said. "Two guys were fighting next to me, then I got hit with a stick. I don't know how the stick got through my mask. All I know is everything went black and there was so much pain.

"This is a terrible feeling. I've had injuries before, but this is different. An eye injury isn't like a bruised arm. An eye injury, you never know how it will turn out. The way the doctor downstairs was talking, it [the eye] is badly damaged."

Parent reached up and felt the gauze over his eye. His wife was sitting next to him, holding his other hand. He talked about the trend among younger goalies to wear a helmet with bars instead of the flat mask. He tried wearing the newer model in practice but discarded it. He found the bars in front of his eyes distracting.

"I said I wanted to play another four or five years," he said, "but now I don't know. This scares the hell out of me. The doctor tells me there is bleeding in the front and back of my eye. It makes you appreciate your health, eh? This is what happens to old goalies, I guess. You forget to duck."

The initial prognosis was that Parent would be sidelined for at least one month, but I had a bad feeling after talking to Edward Viner, the team physician. He said there was hemorrhaging into the chamber of the eye, and it was very serious. The tone of his voice was even more troubling than his words. I left the hospital convinced that we had seen Parent's final game.

On June 1, 1979, he made it official when he announced his retirement.

It was an enormous blow to the franchise to lose a Hall of Fame goalie, but the team rebounded the next season under coach Pat Quinn. They alternated Pete Peeters and Phil Myre in goal, and with six holdovers from the Stanley Cup team, including Clarke, Barber, and MacLeish, they were the best team in the league for most of the season.

They lost just once in their first thirty-seven games and compiled a thirty-five-game unbeaten streak, an NHL record. They finished the regular season with a 48–12–20 record. In the playoffs, they swept Edmonton and then defeated the Rangers and Minnesota, each in five games. That put them in the finals against the Islanders.

The Flyers lost the opener in overtime and split the next four games, setting up Game 6 at the Nassau Coliseum. The Islanders could claim their first Stanley Cup with a win, but the Flyers could even the series and bring it back to the Spectrum for Game 7.

The Islanders scored an early goal when Denis Potvin appeared to tip the puck past Peeters with a high stick. Referee Bob Myers didn't call it, so the goal counted.

Later, linesman Leon Stickle missed an offsides call that led to another goal, this one scored by Duane Sutter. It was hard to believe, because it was so obvious. Clark Gillies left a drop pass for Butch Goring that crossed the blue line. When Goring carried the puck into the zone, the Flyers froze, expecting the linesman to whistle the offsides. However, Stickle did not blow his whistle, and Goring fed Sutter, who wristed the puck past Peeters for a 2–1 lead.

The Flyers rallied to tie the game and force overtime, but the Islanders won it on a Bob Nystrom goal, setting off a wild celebration. Everyone in the press box was scrambling to get to the locker rooms. I was not that familiar with the Coliseum. When I got caught in the mob scene on the concourse, I didn't know where to go. I saw an unmarked door, pushed it open, and hustled down the stairs.

I did not know where I was, but I figured I'd get to the lower level and find my way from there. I didn't realize that I was in a restricted area where no press was allowed. I turned a corner, and there was Snider, pacing back and forth and fuming about the officiating. When he saw me, he exploded.

"The officials killed us, the bastards," he said. "It was an absolute, total f—king disgrace."

I hadn't asked a question. I hadn't said a word. I didn't have to. The Flyers' owner was writing my story for me. I pulled out my notebook and started writing as fast as I could.

"Anybody who is impartial knows we took a screwing today," he said. "This was a travesty. Their first two goals should have been disallowed. The one Potvin knocked in with the high stick. The other one came on an offside pass. It was obvious to everyone except the linesman.

"Well, I'm damn sick of it. I walk in that locker room and see those guys, knowing how hard they worked only to have this game taken away from them. It's a f—king disgrace. Why do we have to beat the other team and the officials too? Every f—king night.

"I believe the [officials] who come out of Montreal and Toronto don't want the Flyers to win. I believe that down to the pit of my stomach. They don't want us to win so they take every opportunity they can to screw us. I'll be damned if I'm going to be quiet about this. I don't care how much [NHL president] John Ziegler fines me. Let him suspend me as an owner, I don't care. I'd just like to watch the film of this game with him. I'll go over it inch by inch with him anytime at his convenience. I'd like to have him look me in the eye when it's over and say this was a well-officiated game. I'd like to see if he has the nerve to do that."

Snider paused but his eyes were still blazing.

"The problem with this league is Scotty Morrison, he should be shot," Snider said, referring to the NHL's referee-in-chief.

Excuse me? The head of officiating should be shot? It was an outrageous thing to say. I expected Snider to catch himself and say something like, "I shouldn't have said that." Or "Don't quote me on that." But he didn't. He just kept going.

"Every time I complain, Ziegler sticks it to me one more time and the rest of the league laughs at me," Snider said. "I want Ziegler to read this. I hope he does fine me. I'll make plenty of noise then. What's he going to say? He knows I'm right."

It was a familiar complaint by the Flyers. They were always griping about the league having a vendetta against them dating back to the Broad Street Bullies days. They had cleaned up their act—well, sort of—but they believed that they still were paying the price for all that brawling. They were like the neighborhood thug who tries to go straight, except nobody on the block believes him.

After the game, Stickle admitted his mistake. He saw the tape, so he realized that the Islanders' second goal was offsides. "I guess I blew it," he said.

"That does us a lot of good, doesn't it?" Snider said bitterly.

I called the *Bulletin* office to let the editors know I had an exclusive. No one else was there when the Flyers' owner went off on the officials. When I read back some of the quotes—including the one about Morrison—the editors immediately decided that my story would lead the paper. They commended me for a great job of reporting.

Great job of reporting? The only reason I got the story was because I got lost and went down the wrong staircase. If I had followed the other reporters and gone where I was supposed to go, I never would have run into Snider. It was dumb luck. I was in the wrong place at the right time. But OK, I'll take it.

My story was picked up by newspapers across the United States and Canada, which wasn't surprising. Snider's outburst made for great reading. He was fined $5,000 by the league, which seems pretty lenient, given what he had said. I think it was the league's way of acknowledging that Snider had a point—not about shooting Morrison but about the fact that it was a poorly officiated game.

I thought Snider would claim that he was misquoted or use the old "I was taken out of context" routine. He didn't do that. He did not deny anything in the story. He said that he had made his comments after a painful loss and his emotions had gotten the better of him, but other than offering an apology to Morrison, the owner stood behind his words.

The next season, everyone waited to see what would happen when Stickle returned to Philadelphia to work a Flyers game. He did not appear at the Spectrum until November, four weeks into the season. That night, as Stickle sat nervously in the dressing room, there was a knock on the door. He opened it a crack and peeked into the hallway.

He saw the Reverend John Casey, the Flyers' team chaplain, standing there in his clerical collar, his hands folded solemnly in front of him. Stickle's knees almost buckled.

"Oh my God," he thought. "They sent a priest to walk me to the ice."

Stickle thought it was like prison, where a priest walks the condemned man to the electric chair. As it turned out, Casey was just stopping by to say hello and wish Stickle well. The priest told Stickle that he didn't have anything to worry about. There would be some boos, maybe a heckler or two, but it would pass soon enough.

"The Philadelphia fans are good people," Casey said, "contrary to what you might have heard."

Stickle was greeted with a chorus of boos when he skated onto the ice to work the Flyers game against the Los Angeles Kings. A fan leaned over the glass and waved a pair of eyeglasses at Stickle as he skated past. Another fan carried a sign with a tin can mounted on top. "Help the Handicapped," it read. "The Leon Stickle Foundation for the Blind."

There were derisive cheers when Stickle made his first offsides call of the game. One fan held up a sign that read: "Six Months Too Late." There was extra security in the building, but it wasn't necessary. There were no incidents—just a few catcalls, and even those dissipated after one period. It helped that the Flyers routed the Kings, 8–2.

Stickle met with reporters after the game.

"I'm glad I got this over with," he said. "I know the Philadelphia fans can be rowdy at times. They really support their club, and they get upset. But this [reception] wasn't bad at all. I thought it would be much worse. Really, it's a credit to these fans. They just solidified what I always thought of them. They have a lot of class.

"It's tough, but I have to face the fact, I blew the call. It couldn't even qualify as a controversial call. I was definitely wrong. The puck was well over the line when Goring picked it up. I committed the cardinal sin. I followed Gillies [with my eyes]. When I looked back, Goring was already in the zone. It was my mistake, and I'll have to live with it."

Clarke was on that Flyers team, the kid from Flin Flon now an aging veteran. That was his last best shot at a Stanley Cup. He played four more seasons and never advanced beyond the quarterfinals. He retired as a player in 1984, and the team honored him by retiring his jersey number 16. Shero came back for the ceremony.

"I counted on that number so often," Shero said. "Probably too much. He's the only man I ever coached who made me cry. He worked so hard night after night. I thought, 'No one should have to work that hard.'

"I saw a game on TV last year. He had thirty stitches in his eye, and he still checked his man and stole the puck to set up the winning goal. Most players would say, 'Let it go. Better to play another day.' Not Clarke. He's the greatest ever."

"Better than Gordie Howe?" I asked.

"Detroit could have won the Stanley Cup without Howe," Shero said. "We could not have won without Clarke, yet we won it twice. You can talk about players who were bigger and faster with harder shots, but show me a player who accomplished more. You can't. There will never be another player like him."

Typically, Clarke made the night—*his* night—about everyone else. He talked about the Stanley Cup teams, what they had accomplished, and what they meant to Philadelphia. He talked about the work ethic that carried them farther than anyone thought possible.

"It is something when you think about a bunch of guys who have loved each other as long as we have," Clarke said. "Not a day goes by that I don't think about them. What Freddy wrote on the board that day: We walk together forever, it's true. All these years later, it's still true.

"People never get tired of talking about our team. Even kids who weren't born then know us. It's a great feeling, you know? Who wouldn't want to be remembered for the best thing they ever did?"

5

High School Harry

JIM MURRAY, the West Philadelphia leprechaun who grew up to become the general manager of the Eagles, has a million great stories, but this one may be his favorite. It was New Year's Day, 1976. He was watching the college bowl games with his boss, Leonard Tose.

Tose had just fired his third head coach in five years, and he was looking for a new man. He had interviewed Norm Van Brocklin, Hank Stram, Allie Sherman, Joe Paterno, Arizona State coach Frank Kush, and Harvard coach Joe Restic, but he wasn't sold on any of them. He wanted to make sure that his next hire was the right one.

They were flipping around the TV dial and saw UCLA upsetting top-ranked Ohio State in the Rose Bowl. The camera zoomed in for a close-up of the UCLA coach, a fiery young guy named Dick Vermeil.

"He lit up the screen," Murray said. "He looked like Robert Redford and coached like General Patton."

Tose had never heard of him, but he was intrigued.

"Let's go talk to him," Tose said.

Just like that, Tose and Murray were off to Los Angeles. Tose was impulsive that way. Sometimes it got him into trouble, often in casinos, but this time it led him to a man who would change his life and the arc of pro football in Philadelphia.

It was a long shot, but Tose wasn't averse to those. Vermeil was born in California, went to school in California, coached exclusively in California, and wasn't in any great hurry to leave. He had just won the Rose Bowl, and he had blue-chip recruits lining up at his door, wanting to enroll at UCLA.

As far as Vermeil was concerned, he had the perfect situation. Pro football was the farthest thing from his mind. When Murray asked for a meeting, Vermeil said he wasn't interested.

"You mean he doesn't even want to talk about it?" Tose said. "What kind of idiot . . . ?"

Then the phone rang. It was Vermeil calling back. He said, "OK, I'll meet with you." Tose and Murray had flown all the way to Los Angeles just to talk to him, and so it would be pretty rude to say no. But Vermeil told Murray up front that he had no desire to leave UCLA. It would be more of a courtesy visit than an interview.

"Just hear us out," Murray said.

So Vermeil drove to the Beverly Hills Hotel in his baby blue Mustang. He met Tose and Murray in their suite.

When Vermeil asked, "Why would I want to come to Philadelphia?" the general manager took over. Murray is a formidable salesman, especially when he is selling Philadelphia. It would be hard to find anyone who loves the city more, and Murray articulates that love in a way that can win over even the most skeptical audience.

When Vermeil mentioned seeing the Philadelphia fans throwing golf balls from the upper deck during a 42–3 Monday night loss to the Rams, Murray was prepared. He told Vermeil it was the reaction of a passionate but frustrated fan base. He pointed out that the Vet was full that night, even though the Eagles were 1–6. In most other cities, he said, the stadium would have been empty.

Murray told Vermeil, "Our fans are so desperate, you'll get a standing ovation if you win the coin toss."

He followed up with a prediction.

"If you come to Philadelphia," Murray said, "you'll never leave."

It was one of the greatest sales jobs in history. Not only did it work—Vermeil left UCLA to take over the moribund Eagles—but everything Murray said came true. Vermeil came to Philadelphia and never left. He took other jobs—coaching St. Louis to a Super Bowl victory and finishing his career in Kansas City—but he stayed rooted in Philadelphia. He fell in love with the people, and they loved him back.

It did not feel that way when Vermeil was introduced as the Eagles' coach. At his press conference, all the right things were said while Tose and Vermeil posed for photographers, but we had been down this road before. This was Tose's fourth head coach. Each new hire talked about bringing a winner to Philadelphia, and yet none delivered. Why, the city asked, would this guy be any different?

I was more willing than most to give Vermeil a chance. That's because I covered the Rose Bowl and had seen Vermeil up close. I saw him share a dais with Woody Hayes. The thirty-nine-year-old Vermeil looked like a schoolboy sitting next to the curmudgeonly Hayes. Vermeil deferred to him, addressing him as "Coach." He said it was an honor to share the stage with a legend, which Hayes surely was.

But when the teams played, Vermeil kicked the legend's butt. The 23–10 UCLA victory was one of the biggest upsets in Rose Bowl history. In the final minutes, with the game still going on, Hayes walked across the field to shake Vermeil's hand.

"Fine job of coaching, young man," Hayes said.

Hayes was not the most gracious of losers, but even he could appreciate what Vermeil had accomplished.

The UCLA players mutinied in the days leading up to the game. Vermeil had them practicing twice a day, long and hard, right through the Christmas holidays. Meanwhile, the Ohio State players were riding floats at Disneyland and frolicking in the pool with the Rose Bowl queen.

Why are they having fun, the Bruins wondered, and we're out here killing ourselves?

So, the UCLA players rebelled. Team captain John Sciarra walked into Vermeil's office and said the players were going on strike. He told Vermeil the players would only return to practice if he agreed to lighten up. They believed that going to a bowl game should be a reward for a successful season. Two-a-days in full pads didn't seem like much of a reward.

Vermeil went into the locker room and told the players they had fifteen minutes to suit up and get on the field. If they refused, he said, he would put out a call to the student body for volunteers.

"I won't have any trouble finding fifty kids who want to play in the Rose Bowl," he said.

With most coaches, it would have been a bluff, but the players knew Dick Vermeil. He didn't bluff.

The players dressed and reported to the field, where Vermeil put them through the usual three-hour practice. He never addressed the protest. His focus remained, as always, on the game.

Ohio State was a two-touchdown favorite. The Buckeyes were 11–0 and fresh off a big win over Michigan. Their star halfback, Archie Griffith, had just won his second Heisman Trophy. Earlier in the season, Ohio State had played UCLA and won convincingly, 41–20. Most believed that the rematch would be more of the same.

Yet the Bruins went out and played their best game of the year, dominating the Buckeyes for sixty minutes. When it was over, the players thanked Vermeil for what he had done, which was to drive them to play better than they had ever played in their lives.

So, a few weeks later, when Vermeil stepped to the podium at the Vet, I thought Tose might have finally found the right guy. Jack McKinney, the veteran football writer for the *Daily News*, took one look at the handsome Vermeil and dubbed him "California Slick." McKinney said Vermeil would last two years, three at the most, in Philadelphia.

I knew this much: With Vermeil in charge, the Eagles' summer camp would be hell. And it was.

Vermeil was a workaholic. He didn't like the term, but he did nothing to discourage it. Indeed, the first sign he hung in the Vet Stadium locker room read: "The Best Way to Kill Time Is to Work It to Death."

He invited one hundred players to his first training camp at Widener. He ordered them to report on July 3, a full week ahead of every other NFL team. On the second night, Vermeil was watching film when he was jolted out of his chair by what sounded like gunfire. He looked out the window and saw fireworks.

"What's going on?" he barked at Carl Peterson, an assistant coach he brought from UCLA.

"Dick, it's the Bicentennial," Peterson said. "It's the two-hundredth birthday of the country."

"I don't care whose birthday it is," Vermeil said. "Make 'em stop."

Vermeil was surprised that anyone would think his reaction was unusual. This was football camp. There was serious work to be done, especially when he was trying to rebuild a team as run down as the Eagles.

"There is no such thing as a holiday when you lose," Vermeil said. "Only winners have luxuries like holidays. When I made out our schedule, I never even thought about the Fourth of July; it was just another block on the calendar."

Vermeil brought in Tom Tellez, the UCLA track coach, and put him in charge of conditioning. He put the team through a series of 110-yard sprints. A player would run a sprint and have his pulse rate checked. When it dropped to 120 beats per minute, the player would run again. The process was repeated ten times. On a scorching 95-degree day, it was enough to bring grown men to their knees. And it did.

"It's more of an evaluation," Vermeil said. "It measures each individual's cardiovascular recovery rate. That's the surest way of determining what kind of condition a man is in. If a man's pulse rate recovers quickly, it means he worked hard in the off-season. If he recovers slowly, it means he loafed.

"I'll put a lot of stock in the results. When it comes to cut down time, I'll keep the man who has worked hard over the man who has shown a tendency to cop out. He'll do the same thing in a game."

The camp was all about work, because the head coach was all about work. Vermeil had grown up in a blue-collar family in Calistoga. His father, Louie, operated a garage in the back yard. He called it the Owl Garage, because he worked all night.

Behind his desk, Vermeil had a picture of his father. It wasn't a shot of Louie smiling or putting his arm around his son, because he rarely did either. It was a photo of Louie's back as he walked toward the garage. That was how Vermeil remembered him—always going to work.

As a kid, Vermeil worked in the garage with his father, taking apart car engines and rebuilding them. Louie thought his son would take over the business one day, but the son had a passion for football that was greater than his desire to please his father.

After completing his studies at San Jose State, Vermeil took a coaching position at Hillsdale High School. He worked his way up from there, including a stint as the NFL's first special teams coach, working under George Allen with the Rams.

Vermeil learned from every coach he worked for, including Allen, John Ralston at Stanford, and Tommy Prothro at UCLA, but when he became a head coach himself, he brought something unique to the job. It was what he had inherited from his father: a willingness—almost a compulsion—to work around the clock. He demanded it of himself, and he demanded it of the people around him.

The camp schedule was particularly hard on the assistant coaches. Not only were they on the practice field for seven hours a day; they also were in meetings that went into the wee hours of the morning. One day, I was interviewing backfield coach Johnny Roland after lunch. We found a bench outside the dining hall, and five minutes into the interview, Roland was sound asleep.

I didn't know what to do. I didn't want to wake him, because it was obvious the poor guy was exhausted, but at the same time, I couldn't very well leave one of the team's coaches sleeping on a bench like a homeless person.

I cleared my throat, hoping that might wake him up. It didn't. I coughed. Still nothing. At this point, Roland was starting to snore. Finally, I nudged him. His eyes popped open. He looked around and realized what had happened. He was embarrassed.

"How long was I asleep?" he asked.

"Just a minute or two," I said.

"I'm sorry about that," he said. "Can we do this later? I gotta go lie down."

Roland picked up his playbook and headed for the dorms.

"I love Dick," he said, "but, man, he's killing us."

Vermeil kept up the relentless pace right through the summer. The only one who never appeared tired was Vermeil.

"People need to be pushed," he said. "They need to be driven. They thrive on it. They need to be disciplined, even if they bitch."

They bitched all right. Not only did Vermeil have the players on the practice field for three hours in the morning and three hours in the afternoon; he insisted that they keep their helmets on with their chin straps buckled. They were in full pads for every practice, because there was live hitting every day.

Bill Bergey, the Pro Bowl linebacker, took an immediate dislike to Vermeil. He called him "High School Harry." He didn't understand all the rules, he didn't understand all the hitting, and he didn't understand why they had to keep running the same plays over and over again.

Bergey had broken into the NFL with Cincinnati, playing for Paul Brown, a Hall of Fame coach. Brown was aloof and stern, but he treated the players like professionals. Vermeil, by comparison, was a nit-picking martinet.

After one week of camp, Bergey ached all over. One day, he went through the motions in the morning practice. All he wanted to do was go back to his dorm room, crank up the air conditioner, and lie down. That evening, Vermeil called him to his office. He put on a film of the morning practice, which showed Bergey being pushed around by a rookie guard, a bottom-of-the-roster free agent.

"You see this kid?" Vermeil said. "I'm gonna have to cut him in another week, because he's not an NFL player, but look at this. He's giving me a helluva lot more than you're giving me. You're gonna make this team because you're Bill Bergey, but how do you think I'll feel when I have to look that kid in the eye and tell him he's going home?"

Vermeil ran the film of a goal-line series, stopping, rewinding, and running it again. Bergey watched in silence. The rookie was pushing him all over the field.

"You should be embarrassed," Vermeil said.

He handed Bergey the film.

"I want you to take this and watch it," he said, "then I want you to burn the damned thing."

Bergey knew that Vermeil was right. He had gone through the motions that morning. He thought he had gotten away with it, but he hadn't. Vermeil saw it; he saw everything on the practice field. But rather than embarrass Bergey by chewing him out in front of the team, he had done it in his office.

The way Vermeil handled it made a lasting impression on Bergey. It was a turning point in their relationship.

"It was a great lesson in what it means to be a professional," Bergey said. "You give your best effort all the time. I understood where Dick was coming from. He was all about accountability. I realized this guy will bring out the best in all of us if we just buy into his program. I did. Eventually, we all did."

Vermeil had a prickly relationship with the beat writers, especially me. He believed that I was undermining his program. He spent all day trying to build up the players and convince them they could compete with the rest of the NFL. My columns told a different story.

"Everything you say is negative," he said.

Vermeil said the writers who covered his UCLA teams wrote positive stories. He thought that I should do the same. I said there was a big difference. At UCLA, he had good players and good teams. With the Eagles, he had neither. It was my job to write what I saw, and what I saw was a team that would be lucky to win four games.

"You're hurting morale," Vermeil said.

"I'm just being honest," I said.

I really did want to see the team improve. It was my seventh year on the beat, and I still had not covered a winner. The best season was 7–7 in 1974 under McCormack. As high-water marks go, that wasn't very high.

It was depressing to be one week into a training camp and know the team was going nowhere. You had five more months of watching practices and cranking out stories every day, and you already knew where the season was headed. It would be one dispiriting loss after another until finally the team wound up in a snowy ditch in December.

I hoped that Vermeil could change that storyline, but looking at what he had to work with, I knew it was not going to happen that season. I had no doubt that he was working harder than any other coach in the NFL, but it didn't change the fact that when he opened the regular season against the Cowboys, he would be armed with a peashooter while Dallas coach Tom Landry would be driving a tank.

Three weeks into camp, Vermeil did his first big cut down. He released more than a dozen players, including a veteran who was one of the better players on the roster. I wrote a piece questioning his decision. The *Bulletin* ran my story with a cartoon of Vermeil as a medieval executioner. The headline read: "The Axe-Man Cometh."

That afternoon, I walked into the dining hall, and Vermeil was waiting for me. He waved the paper in my face, yelling, "You think this is funny? This is bullshit."

The players looked on, thankful he was chewing out someone else for a change.

Vermeil threw the paper on the floor and stormed off.

The next day, he pulled me aside. He said the reason he cut the veteran was because of drugs. Not only was the player using drugs, Vermeil said, he was selling drugs in the locker room.

"I couldn't come out and say that," Vermeil said. "I didn't want it in the paper, but that was the reason."

I wished I had known that when I wrote the story. I would not have put the drug stuff in the paper, but I would have been less critical of Vermeil's decision. If he had told me the full story and stipulated it was off the record, I would have honored that, but he didn't know me well enough to trust me. He didn't trust any of us that first year.

Vermeil's first camp was the most grueling camp I've seen in fifty years of covering football. The hitting was nonstop. The practices were endless. He insisted on running plays over and over again until the players got them right. With the '76 Eagles, that took a long time.

I lost count of how many players quit. We would see them every night in the parking lot, tossing their bags in the trunk and waving goodbye. Vermeil said, "I'd rather have them quit now than in the fourth quarter of a game."

One guy who didn't quit was Vince Papale. He had everything going against him. He was thirty years old and had never played college football—he went to St. Joseph's University on a track scholarship—but he caught Vermeil's eye at an open tryout. Papale was so determined to fulfill his dream of playing for the Eagles that he simply outlasted the competition.

Most NFL coaches would have rejected someone with Papale's resume, but Vermeil was building his team around players with heart and desire. Papale, a schoolteacher and bartender from Glenolden, just a five-minute drive from Widener, fit that description. His father was in the stands every afternoon, usually with his buddies from Westinghouse, cheering as Vince, a 6'2", 195-pound receiver, caught passes from Roman Gabriel and Mike Boryla.

Papale's quest to make the team was a great human-interest story, especially since he was a local guy. I wrote something about him almost every day.

When Papale officially made the team, it was a big story. I went to the office to write it. The editor said he would run the story across the top of the sports section.

"You have a suggestion for the headline?" he asked.

"How about 'Invincible Papale'?" I said.

That was the headline in the next day's paper. I never imagined that it would one day appear on a movie marquee, although I did half-jokingly raise the possibility of Papale's story finding its way to Hollywood.

I was standing with the other writers at practice one day when Papale jogged by. I said to no one in particular, "Someday they're going to make a movie about this." Everyone laughed, but I didn't think it was that far-fetched.

Rocky had just won the Oscar for Best Picture by telling the story of a scrappy Philly guy who came out of nowhere to fight for the heavyweight title. Why couldn't Papale be another studio's Italian Stallion?

It took thirty years, but Hollywood finally got around to making the Vince Papale story. It was produced by the Walt Disney Studios in 2006 and—what do you know?—they called it *Invincible*. Mark Wahlberg played Papale, and Greg Kinnear played Vermeil. The movie was a hit, finishing number one at the box office the week it was released. I was an extra in a few scenes.

Other than Papale's underdog tale, there wasn't much to feel good about during that Eagles season. The team finished its first year under

Vermeil with a 4–10 record. They weren't much better the next year, winning five games.

Vermeil was handicapped by a lack of draft picks—they had been traded away by the previous regime—so he collected what he could in the late rounds. Several bottom-of-the-barrel picks played significant roles, including defensive linemen Carl Hairston and Charlie Johnson (seventh-round choices) and running back Billy Campfield (an eleventh-round pick).

The real coup was finding Wilbert Montgomery in the sixth round of the 1977 draft. He was a 5'10", 190-pound running back from Abilene Christian who scored 76 touchdowns in three seasons despite missing eleven games due to injury.

Several teams wrote Montgomery off as a medical risk. Vermeil, with no high picks to work with, could not afford to be choosy. He took Montgomery with the 154th selection. It proved to be one of the best picks in franchise history.

Montgomery was quiet and painfully shy. He expected to get cut every day at training camp. Vermeil saw the natural talent, but he didn't think Montgomery was ready to play a big role. He spent most of that first season on special teams, but he led the NFL with a 26.9-yard average on kickoff returns.

He did not start a game until the final week, when the Eagles hosted the New York Jets. Only 19,241 fans turned out on a cold, rainy day at the Vet, the smallest crowd for an Eagles home game since their final game at Connie Mack Stadium in 1957.

Montgomery rushed for 103 yards and scored two touchdowns in a 24–0 Eagles victory. Jim Brown, the Hall of Fame running back, was doing the TV broadcast. After the game, Brown and I were on the same press box elevator. He asked, "That number 31, where have they been hiding him?"

"He's a rookie," I said. "The coaches didn't think he was ready."

Brown chuckled.

"He looked ready to me," he said. "You watch that young man. He's gonna do big things."

I told Montgomery what Brown said.

"Jim Brown said that?" he asked.

"Yes, he did," I said.

"I'm honored," Montgomery said.

Brown's prediction came true. The next season, Montgomery rushed for 1,220 yards and scored 9 touchdowns as the Eagles posted their first winning record in thirteen years. Ron Jaworski was maturing at quarter-back, and Harold Carmichael was on his way to becoming the team's all-time leading receiver, but the coach built his offense around Mont-gomery and the running game.

The fans wanted to know more about Montgomery, but he did not like doing interviews. The only way to tell his story was to fly to his hometown of Greenville, Mississippi, and talk to his family and friends. I called his mother, Gladys, and asked whether it would be OK for me to visit. She worked late most nights but said that I was welcome to wait for her at the house.

Greenville is a quiet town tucked away on the western edge of Mis-sissippi next to Lake Ferguson and the Arkansas border. It is in the heart of the delta country, with lush cotton and soybean fields sprawl-ing for miles. The family lived in a small, one-story brick house at the north end of town near the airport.

In the '70s, Greenville enjoyed a growth in industry. A large gypsum plant was built less than a mile from the family's front door. Gladys worked as a machine operator at the Greenville Mill, a local rug factory. Prior to that, she worked in a laundry. She separated from her husband ten years earlier. Of the nine children, six still lived with Gladys. It was not easy, but few things in Greenville were.

When I arrived at the house, Wilbert's teenage brothers, Jerry and Leonard, answered the door. They looked puzzled; they weren't expect-ing visitors. I introduced myself and explained the reason for my visit. They let me in without saying a word.

I told them I was there to write a story about their brother. I asked whether they had seen him play for the Eagles.

"We've seen highlights," Jerry said.

"So, what do you think?" I asked.

"He's doing good," Leonard said.

We sat there in the living room, just staring at each other. Jerry and Leonard weren't used to being interviewed. Finally, I said something like, "I'm sure you guys have things to do" and excused myself. I waited outside in the car until Gladys pulled in the driveway. She laughed when I explained what had happened.

"They're just shy," she said, "like Wilbert."

We went to the kitchen, where Gladys made a pot of tea. She said she never wanted her sons to play football. A boy in the neighborhood had broken his neck playing football, and so she told her sons they were not allowed to play the game.

But Wilbert was determined. He had a classmate forge his mother's signature on the permission slip. Gladys worked long hours, so she didn't know that he was staying late for football practice. On game nights, he told his mother he was at a friend's house. He couldn't get away with it for long, though—he was too good.

College recruiters started calling, so Wilbert had to fess up. Gladys was not happy, but she saw an opportunity for her son to go to college on a football scholarship, so she relented.

"What could I do?" she said. "I already said no, and that didn't stop him. I told him, 'All right, go play. But don't come running to me if you get hurt.'"

She worried about him all through college when he was sidelined with an assortment of injuries. She was not unhappy when she heard they might keep him from playing in the NFL. Bigger men, harder hits—she didn't want that for her son. But the Eagles drafted him anyway, and now he was a star for a team on the rise.

In the '78 season, Montgomery was the third-leading rusher in the NFC, trailing only Walter Payton and Tony Dorsett. His 1,220 yards set a club record for rushing yards in a season, breaking the mark set by Steve Van Buren in 1949. The Eagles brought Van Buren to the Vet to pass the torch to the new rushing leader. The Hall of Famer went to Montgomery's locker after the game and stuck out his hand.

"I'm Steve Van Buren," he said. "I'd like to say congratulations and tell you that you're a great, great player."

"Uh . . . thank you," Montgomery said. "You were a great player, too."

The photographers asked the two men to pose together. As they smiled for the cameras, Van Buren told Montgomery he considered him one of the two best backs in football. Payton was the other.

"Well, there's Tony Dorsett," Montgomery said, almost embarrassed to put himself in that company.

"You're better than Dorsett," Van Buren said. "Dallas would be a lot happier if they had you."

"I don't know about that, sir," Montgomery said, "but thank you."

One month later, Montgomery was in Hawaii, participating in his first Pro Bowl. The NFC running backs were Payton, Dorsett, and Montgomery. During the week of practice, Montgomery felt out of place. Every time he made a mistake, he was sure the other players were asking, "What's he doing here?"

But on game day, Montgomery was the NFC's best player. He had 9 carries for 53 yards and scored a touchdown. Payton and Dorsett managed just 51 yards between them.

After the game, Montgomery flew back to Abilene, where he spent the winter in a small apartment with no telephone. He wanted to rest up and not even think about football. Back in Philadelphia, the Eagles' publicity department fielded dozens of calls from corporate groups that wanted Montgomery to speak and sign autographs. The team's management had to say, "Sorry, but we have no way to reach him." He liked it that way.

It was fascinating how similar Montgomery and Van Buren were. The two great runners—the best in franchise history to that point—played thirty years apart, but they were almost the same guy. Both had their roots in the South. Van Buren was born in Honduras but grew up as an orphan in New Orleans. Both did physical labor in their teens: Van Buren worked in a steel mill, and Montgomery mixed cement for a construction company. Both saw football not as a glory trip but as a way to escape poverty.

Like Montgomery, Van Buren was a man of few words. Although he was pro football's biggest star in the 1940s, he ducked the press whenever possible. He didn't like being singled out. He saw football as a team game—a quaint notion, even in those days—so he believed that the praise should be shared by everyone. He led the league in rushing four times, but he never took the credit. He said he played on a great team. Montgomery was the same way.

Their humility was reflected in how they lived off the field. When Montgomery hit it big with the Eagles, he lived in a one-bedroom apartment in the shadow of an oil refinery in South Philadelphia. He drove a leased Dodge Aspen. He rarely went out at night. Mostly, he watched TV, read the Bible, and talked to his mother on the phone.

When I met Van Buren, he was in his sixties, a widower living in a tiny apartment in Northeast Philadelphia. He had a cat named Spike, and he spent most of his time at Philadelphia Park racetrack. Even at that age, he still had the broad shoulders and thick chest of an athlete. He always wore an Eagles baseball cap. When he walked through the stands, people recognized him and called his name. He would smile and wave, but he usually kept on walking.

I first visited Van Buren in 1978, right before Montgomery broke his rushing record. I wanted to get his thoughts about seeing his record fall. Most athletes are protective of their places in history, even if they don't like to admit it. They roll out the old cliché—"Records are meant to be broken"—but usually there is a hint of regret. There was none of that with Van Buren.

"Regrets?" he said. "What for?"

I told him about a conversation I had with Bosh Pritchard, his former teammate, when Montgomery broke his record for the longest run from scrimmage. Pritchard had a 77-yard touchdown run against Washington in 1949. That stood as the team record for thirty years.

When the record fell, Pritchard was watching on TV.

"I thought, 'There goes the last bit of me,'" he said. "You feel a loss. It's only natural."

"That's Bosh," Van Buren said. "He feels that way, and that's OK. I don't. I'm happy for Wilbert. He's a great kid and a great player. I hope he breaks all my records. I'm an Eagles fan. I want 'em to do good."

I asked Van Buren whether he knew which records he still held.

"I have no idea," he said. "I never paid any attention to that stuff. It wasn't important to me. All I cared about was winning. I figured if we won, I did my job.

"The way I see it, if a player is good enough to break your record, let him. Wilbert is a great player. He's better than I was. Why shouldn't he have the record?"

I had the utmost respect for Montgomery and still do, but he wasn't better than Van Buren. I still believe that Van Buren was the greatest running back in Eagles history. Others have rushed for more yards—LeSean McCoy is now first, Wilbert Montgomery is second, and Brian Westbrook is third, all ahead of Van Buren—but they were not as dominant as the 6'1", 210-pound force they called "the Moving Van."

Van Buren led the league in rushing and touchdowns four times in a five-year span (1945–1949). He carried the Eagles to back-to-back world championships. He was the first Eagle inducted into the Pro Football Hall of Fame, and when he retired in 1951, he was the leading rusher in NFL history, with 5,860 yards.

"Montgomery is faster than I was and shiftier," Van Buren said. "I look at the old films and think, 'Look how slow I am.' I couldn't play with these players today. Well, maybe I could play, but I wouldn't be as good as Montgomery."

I told Van Buren he was being modest.

"No, I'm being honest," he said.

Van Buren had no football memorabilia in his apartment. The only

photographs on display were family pictures, mostly of his ten grandchildren. There were no trophies or game balls. If you didn't know who
he was, you would have no idea he had even played pro football, much
less that he had been one of the league's biggest stars.

I asked what he did with his awards. In Chuck Bednarik's house,
every inch of wall space was taken up with plaques and photos of "Concrete Charlie."

"I gave it all away," Van Buren said. "Someone would come to visit
and see a trophy. I'd say, 'You like it? Take it.' I didn't need it. I never
cared about trophies and scrapbooks, things like that."

He tapped his head.

"I have it all right here," he said.

Van Buren and Montgomery were similar in another respect: They
excelled in big games. Van Buren scored the lone touchdown in the
1948 championship game when the Eagles defeated the Chicago Car-
dinals, 7–0, in a blizzard at Connie Mack Stadium. The following year,
he set a championship-game record by rushing for 196 yards in a 14–0
win over the Los Angeles Rams. The game was played in torrential rain
at the Coliseum.

"I felt like I was running in glue," Van Buren said. "When they told
me how many yards I gained, I couldn't believe it."

After the game, Clark Gable visited the Eagles' locker room. He
sought out Van Buren, shook his hand, and said, "You're the greatest
athlete I've ever seen." The other Eagles looked on in awe. They could
not believe that Hollywood's biggest star was in their locker room.

Later, Van Buren asked teammate George Savitsky, "Who was that
guy?"

"You didn't recognize Clark Gable?" Savitsky said.

"I don't go to the movies much," Van Buren said.

The players laughed about that for years.

Montgomery rushed for a career-high 194 yards in the NFC Championship game against Dallas. No one was sure he would even play that
day. He was so physically battered that teammate John Bunting said, "It
hurt just to look at him."

Montgomery had a strained knee, bruised hip, and bruised thigh.
It was an accumulation of the pounding he had absorbed over three
seasons. He had 275 rushing attempts and 35 pass receptions in 1978,
377 rushing attempts and 47 pass receptions in 1979, and 261 rushing
attempts and 59 pass receptions in 1980. That was a lot of wear and tear
on a small body.

He sat out four games in the 1980 season with various injuries, but Louie Giammona filled in, and the team kept winning. To get past the Cowboys in the NFC title game, however, the Eagles needed Montgomery. The Dallas defense had not allowed an opposing ball carrier to rush for 100 yards in their previous twenty-nine postseason games.

It was a brutally cold day in Philadelphia (–20 degrees windchill), which would limit the passing game. To win, the Eagles had to run the ball, and to run the ball, they needed Montgomery.

The team spent the week practicing in Tampa away from the harsh weather, and Montgomery limped through the workouts. On Thursday, his knee buckled, and he fell to the ground. Otho Davis, the Eagles' trainer, worked on him all night before the team flew back to Philadelphia.

On Sunday morning, Montgomery was in the trainer's room four hours before kickoff. Davis massaged his bruised thigh for ninety minutes and then taped it. He sent Montgomery onto the frozen turf, and everyone held their breath. Would the leg hold up for a quarter? A half? No one knew.

On the second play from scrimmage, Montgomery took a handoff from Jaworski, started left, cut back to the right, and sprinted 42 yards to the end zone. The roar of the 70,696 fans literally shook the press box. For a moment, I thought the whole thing might collapse.

The play was executed to perfection. Left tackle Stan Walters blocked Harvey Martin. Left guard Petey Perot blocked Randy White. Center Guy Morriss fired out on Bob Bruenig. Right guard Woody Peoples trapped John Dutton, while right tackle Jerry Sisemore cut off Ed "Too Tall" Jones, giving Montgomery a cutback lane. Once he broke through the line of scrimmage, he was gone.

It was a masterful piece of coaching by Vermeil. He had coached against Tom Landry often enough that he knew his methods. Landry coached by computer. He spent hours logging tendencies to determine what plays teams ran in every down and distance situation. He played his defense accordingly, so if a coach was willing to gamble and try something different, he might make a big play. Vermeil did exactly that in the championship game.

The Eagles used the shotgun formation extensively but always as a passing formation. When Vermeil sent in Billy Campfield and Rodney Parker, it was a tip-off that the shotgun was coming. When Landry saw that, he countered by sending in extra defensive backs and taking out his linebackers. He also played man to man in the secondary.

Vermeil sent in his shotgun personnel, but for the first time, he had them line up in the I-formation, with Campfield as the fullback and Montgomery as the tailback. Vermeil was counting on Dallas to stay with man-to-man coverage, because that would mean the defensive backs would be running with their backs to the line of scrimmage. If Montgomery could get into the secondary, he would literally run up their backs.

The play worked beautifully. As Vermeil said later, "We could run that play a hundred more times and never hit it as perfectly as we did there."

Montgomery also had a 55-yard run in the second half that set up a Tony Franklin field goal. Eagles radio play-by-play announcer Merrill Reese described it well when he said, "Wilbert Montgomery is having his day of days." The Eagles won the game, 20–7.

Tom Cushman of the *Daily News* wrote a column likening Montgomery to a knight from Camelot: "Sore of body, small in stature, but of great spirit, Wilbert darted here and there over the frozen pasture, inflicting grievous wounds until the men of Dallas gradually scattered, were then routed and finally fled for the plains of Texas."[1]

As usual, Montgomery credited his teammates. "The guys up front won the battle," he said. "They made it easy for me."

The next day, I received a phone call from Van Buren. He had watched the game on TV while babysitting two of his grandchildren. He was excited about the prospect of the Eagles going to their first Super Bowl, but he was most excited by Montgomery's performance.

"Remember when I said Wilbert was better than Dorsett?" he asked.

"Yes, I remember," I said.

"How many yards did Dorsett have yesterday?" Van Buren asked.

"Forty-one."

"Wilbert had what?"

"A hundred ninety-four."

"So tell me who's better now?" Van Buren said.

6

The Big Doolies of the World

"**D**O YOU BELIEVE in miracles?"

When Al Michaels made that now-famous call at the 1980 Winter Olympics, I was watching on TV and thinking, "I should be there." I was supposed to cover those Olympic Games for the *Bulletin*, but one week before the opening ceremony, I came down with the flu.

Already, there were reports of logistical problems in Lake Placid. The buses chartered to shuttle the media to and from the various events were running late, and sometimes not at all. Reporters were standing in the freezing cold for hours, waiting for transportation that never came.

I was in bed with a fever two days before I was scheduled to leave. I was still planning to go. I had my credentials and research material. I knew everything there was to know about speed skater Eric Heiden. I knew the difference between a toe loop and a triple axel. I even knew how to keep score in the biathlon—well, sort of.

I spent five months writing profiles on the Olympic athletes. I found them fascinating. How does a 9-to-5 office worker wind up piloting a bobsled? Or whizzing down a luge track? It is a world far removed from professional sports, where players are treated like royalty. These were working-class people, many of whom trained in their own garages, but for a few weeks in Lake Placid, they would be prime-time TV stars.

I had grown up watching the Olympics on TV—the U.S. hockey team winning the gold medal in 1960, Peggy Fleming winning the women's figure-skating gold in 1968, Franz Klammer flying down the mountain in Innsbruck in 1976—and this would be my first chance to experience it. I couldn't wait. Then the flu grounded me.

The *Bulletin* had one credential, which meant whoever went to Lake Placid would have to cover everything. It would mean working around the clock, rushing from one event to another, all in frigid conditions. I wanted to give it a try, but my doctor said no.

"If you go, you'll wind up in the hospital," he said.

So, I called Jack Wilson with the bad news.

Wilson went around the sports department, looking for a volunteer. No one wanted to go.

Crazy, right? I mean, who doesn't want to cover the Olympics? But the other writers had heard the horror stories coming out of Lake Placid, so they weren't eager to sign on, especially on such short notice. They took a pass.

Still, the paper had to send *someone* to the Games, so Wilson posted a notice in the newsroom: Want to cover the Olympics? Here's your chance. No sports-writing experience necessary.

Drew Strunk, a features writer and skiing enthusiast, accepted the assignment. He came to the house to collect my credentials and media guides. He asked what he should be looking for. Obviously, Heiden was the headliner. He was favored to win five gold medals, which would be a first for the Winter Games.

I gave Strunk a scouting report on the hockey tournament. The Soviets were prohibitive favorites. They had won the gold medal in each of the previous four Olympics. The Czechs were very strong. Sweden would challenge for a medal. I thought the U.S. team might surprise. They were young, but they had talent and the home-ice advantage, which helped the United States win the gold medal in Squaw Valley, California, in 1960.

"Could they win it?" Strunk asked.

I said with a few breaks, the Americans could win the bronze. But gold? No chance. What followed, of course, was "the Miracle."

The U.S. team tied Sweden in its first game, trounced the Czechs, and then shocked the world by upsetting the Soviets, 4–3. Mike Eruzione, a blue-collar journeyman who had played a handful of games for the minor league Philadelphia Firebirds, scored the winning goal and sent millions of Americans into the streets, chanting, "U-S-A, U-S-A."

It was a victory that set off flag-waving celebrations across the country, even in the Deep South, where folks wouldn't know a power play from a power mower. It came at a time when America's morale was sagging. Our hostages were being held in Iran, our flag was burning in the streets of Tehran, and we were waiting in line for hours to buy gasoline.

The underdog U.S. team was like an Alka-Seltzer for America. When they beat the Soviets, the whole country turned a Fourth of July cartwheel. We love a big upset, and they don't come any bigger than this one. The image of goalie Jim Craig wrapped in the Stars and Stripes, gazing into the crowd and asking, "Where's my father?" brought a lump to millions of throats, including mine.

I so wished I was there. Instead, I was on my couch, far removed from the best sports story of the year.

The U.S. team won the gold medal by defeating Finland on Sunday just before the closing ceremonies. I heard they would be visiting the White House the next day. I contacted the *Bulletin*'s Washington bureau to find out whether I could get a pass to cover the event. It took some doing, but I got a call an hour later saying there would be a credential in my name at the White House gate.

I was still feverish the next morning, but I was determined to get a piece of this story. I took the train to D.C. and waited with the other reporters at the White House. As the buses rolled through the gate, a military band played "Stars and Stripes Forever." The athletes, who had lived a cocoonlike existence in Lake Placid, were wide-eyed. They knew there would be a reception, but they didn't expect *this.*

All the U.S. Olympians were there: The figure skaters, the skiers, the bobsledders, they were all there to meet President Carter. Heiden, who made history by winning his five gold medals and setting four Olympic records, was there as well, but no one seemed to care. The day belonged to the "big doolies of the world." That's what coach Herb Brooks called the U.S. hockey team.

Asked what's a doolie, Brooks said, "A big wheel, a big gun, a big shot."[1]

Yes, they were all of that.

Craig walked along the driveway, shaking hands with senators and congressmen. Crusty old politicians turned into shrieking teenyboppers reaching out to touch the twenty-two-year-old goalie who was unknown outside his native New England a month earlier.

"I feel like I walked on the moon or something," Craig said.

He lifted the gold medal from his chest and kissed it softly, the way a nun might kiss her rosary beads.

"I don't know if I'll ever take this medal off," he said. "I might even wear it on the beach this summer."

Eruzione was shaking hands with Massachusetts governor Ed King. The U.S. hockey captain was still wearing the blue sweat suit he wore on the medal platform the previous day. He was wearing a white cowboy hat with a tiny American flag in the band. King said, "You made us proud, Mike. You made the whole country proud."

Eruzione made his way over to where the reporters were standing. He looked like he hadn't slept much. It was just beginning to dawn on him, the enormity of what he accomplished. His goal was being talked about as one of those "I'll-always-remember-where-I-was" moments that people carry with them for the rest of their lives. A humble, lunch-pail kind of guy, Eruzione was the new American Dream.

"My father works in a sewage disposal plant during the day and tends bar at night," Eruzione said. "He says this is the greatest thing that ever happened to him. I heard that from a lot of people. It's like we gave them hope."

The reception was about to begin in the East Room, and the Olympians were expected inside. A Secret Service agent wanted to pull Eruzione and Craig away from the media scrum, but he wanted to do it as gently as possible.

"Anytime you want to go," the agent said.

"Go?" Craig said. "I'm having the time of my life."

The only trouble was that time was running out. After a year spent together, traveling around the globe, playing hockey, and finally winning Olympic gold, they had come to the end of the journey. It was ending in a memorable way and in a memorable place, but it was ending just the same.

The players won the gold medal on Sunday, got on a plane and flew to Washington on Monday, met the president and the first lady, and just like that—it was over. After lunch, they were escorted to a waiting area where the gold medal team would be dismantled, one piece at a time.

The players had plane tickets for other destinations. Most of them were going off to join NHL teams. White House staffers were tapping guys on the shoulder and saying, "Mr. Craig, your ride is here." Or "Mr. Ramsey, your ride is here." Or "Mr. Morrow, your ride is here."

The players who just one day earlier stood shoulder to shoulder on the medal stand now were breaking up, knowing they would never have that opportunity again.

This wasn't like a team that wins a Stanley Cup and comes back the next season to defend its title. An Olympic team is one and done. The players scatter; all that remains is a memory. You could see in their faces that realization was just now setting in. A day that had started so joyously was ending with tearful hugs and goodbyes.

"It was like we were going one hundred miles an hour then, bam, we hit a wall," Eruzione said. "It was like a family breaking up. Heck, it *was* a family breaking up."

Ten years later, I visited Eruzione to do a story about his life since Lake Placid. He was back at Boston University (BU), working as a fundraiser. He was still flying all over the country, giving motivational talks. He had offers to sign with several NHL teams after the Olympics, but he chose to go out on top. He knew that nothing—not even a Stanley Cup—could match the thrill of Lake Placid.

If there was to be an enduring image of Mike Eruzione, he wanted it to be standing on the medal platform, his hand over his heart, singing the national anthem as they raised the Stars and Stripes. What could be better than that?

He still laced up the skates now and then—alumni games at BU and beer league games with his buddies—but he admitted, "The shifts are getting shorter every year."

"The amazing thing," Eruzione said, "is that moment never fades. It never gets old. If I'm on the golf course, someone will yell, 'Do you believe in miracles?' The other day I was walking through an airport, and somebody called out, 'Do you believe in miracles?'

"It gives me goosebumps to think I was part of something like that, something that special. I mean, how many sporting events touch a nation? I got to experience that. I feel blessed."

In 2004, the Walt Disney Studios turned the '80 Olympic team into a feature film, *Miracle*. It starred Kurt Russell as Brooks, with Patrick Dempsey as Eruzione and Eddie Cahill as Craig. The studio made a wise decision by casting former collegiate players rather than actors to fill out the team. The part of Buzz Schneider was played by his son Billy, a college star. Having real players on the ice made the game action more convincing.

I was blown away by Russell's performance. He totally became Brooks, right down to the ugly plaid slacks and Minnesota accent. Russell made the abrasive taskmaster understandable and even sympathetic. As Eruzione said, "Herbie loved us, but as the coach, he couldn't let it show." Russell brought that sense of emotional conflict to the character.

The film was much better than I thought it would be. How could Disney build drama into such a well-known story? The U.S. team was going to beat the Soviets. Where was the suspense? But director Gavin O'Connor and screenwriter Eric Guggenheim told the story so well that you sat back and enjoyed the ride.

Ed Swift, who covered the 1980 Olympics for *Sports Illustrated*, gave the film high marks. He wrote: "Who could have known that two superlative weeks of play by that group of fresh-faced kids would keep its hold on the American imagination for so long?

"Herb Brooks brought out in them qualities they didn't know they had. Together, as a team, they did the same for us. For Americans, I've always believed that was the miracle, that a hockey team could do such a thing."[2]

———

I MET UP WITH TEAM USA again four years later. There were only two returning players from the gold medal team: wingers Phil Verchota and John Harrington. The rest were playing professionally, most of them in the NHL.

Ken Morrow had won three Stanley Cups with the New York Islanders. Mike Ramsey was an all-star in Buffalo. Mark Johnson was playing in Hartford. Herb Brooks was coaching the New York Rangers; Mark Pavelich and Dave Silk were playing for him there.

But the Winter Olympics were coming around again, and this time a very different team was preparing to carry America's hopes into Sarajevo. It was a younger team: The average age was twenty-one. They were just kids watching on TV when the U.S. team won the gold at Lake Placid.

When I caught up with the team, it was on its pre-Olympic tour playing exhibition games, mostly against college teams. I met them at a hotel in Worcester, Massachusetts. They had trounced BU the previous night, 10–2, and they were busing to Rhode Island for a game against Providence that night. It would be their fifth game in six days.

The woman behind the counter, a gray-haired lady with a smile as warm as a pot-bellied stove, was looking at Pat LaFontaine, the team's eighteen-year-old star. He was dressed like the others in a USA windbreaker and ski cap, but with his slight 5'9" frame and baby face, he looked like a choir boy.

"Is this the team that's going to play the Russians?" she asked.

"This is the Olympic team, yes," I said.

"But they are so . . . ," she paused, searching for the right word.

"Young?" I said.

"Yes, young," she replied.

They didn't just look young—they *were* young. Five of the players were in their teens. Two were still in high school, keeping up with their classes through correspondence courses. They had talent—notably LaFontaine, but also defensemen Chris Chelios and Al Iafrate and winger Ed Olczyk—but they were under enormous pressure. The 1980 team was a tough act to follow.

That team was seeded fifth in the twelve-team field. They had flown under the radar, which helped. They did not have to live in a fishbowl for an entire year. It was different for the '84 team. These players were the focus of media attention from Day 1. LaFontaine, Olczyk, and the others were on magazine covers. They were asked to do meet and greets in every town.

The day I met them, five players were scheduled to film a TV commercial for Snickers. The next day in Providence, there would be a photo shoot for *Vogue* magazine.

"At first it was glamorous," said defenseman Mark Fusco, "but it got old in a hurry. Last week, we went to a reception in Manchester [New Hampshire]. We were told it would be a little pregame deal. We got there, and there were six hundred people, a band, TV cameras, reporters. All of that on top of the travel is exhausting."

Mark Johnson, the leading scorer on the '80 team, was playing for the Whalers. They played the U.S. team, and the Olympians smoked them, 8–4. Johnson was impressed with their play, but he worried about the pressure they faced, as fans and media now expected a sequel to "the Miracle."

"They've already been to the White House, they've been on TV," Johnson said. "That's a load for kids in their teens to carry around. In '80, there were no expectations for our team. By the time we started making news, we were already in the [Olympic] village, and Herb was able to keep things under control."

Coach Lou Vairo could have built his team with older players, but he had chosen to go with the talent and speed of youth. Vairo believed that the players would grow up during the exhibition tour. He also had two holdovers from the '80 team to provide leadership as well as a link to the past.

Verchota, the twenty-six-year-old captain, was the most sought-after interview on the team. In 1980, he had been a quietly efficient left wing on a line with Pavelich and Rob McClanahan. He was comfortable in that role. Now as the captain, he was in front of the media every day, answering the same question: "How does this team compare to the team of 1980?"

His stock answer: "They're two different teams."

Follow-up question: "Does this team have a chance to win the gold medal?"

"You just go out and play," he said. "See what happens."

Verchota was not as quotable as Eruzione. The '80 captain was a chatty wise guy from Winthrop, Massachusetts. His college coach, Jack Parker, called him "Pete Rose on skates," and it was a good comparison. Eruzione had Rose's competitive nature and outgoing personality.

Verchota was low-key in a typically Midwestern way. Win or lose in Sarajevo, he was not going to make a living as a motivational speaker. He already had a job lined up at a bank in Minnesota.

"Mike loved being the captain, it came naturally to him," Verchota said. "I'll do what they ask me to do, but I'm not much of a talker."

That afternoon, the team bus pulled into a McDonald's for a combination lunch and photo op. The store owner had agreed to make a donation to the Olympic Committee if the hockey team made an appearance. He had a banner draped across the golden arches—Welcome U.S. Olympic Hockey team—and five hundred people were waiting with cameras and autograph books.

Vairo and Verchota said a few words, and then the players posed for pictures. Verchota and I found a quiet booth where we could talk. I asked what he remembered about the epic game against the Soviets.

"We played very well, and the Russians didn't play their best," he said. "They struggled the whole week. They weren't as dominant as they had been in the past. We knew we had a shot. Herbie said that over and over, and we believed it.

"Both teams had good chances in the third period. Jim made some big saves. We got the bounce of the puck a few times. Then Mike scored, and for the last ten minutes, we checked and checked. We were diving in front of pucks and blocking shots. Herbie kept the shifts short, and we just battled our butts off. Those ten minutes felt like an eternity.

"People say, 'If it was a seven-game series, you would've lost four games to one.' That may be true, but so what? It was one game, and we won it. It was an upset, but it wasn't a fluke. We worked too hard for anyone to call it a fluke."

At the final buzzer, the American team had a wild celebration, tossing their sticks in the air and rolling around on the ice. The Soviets stood stone-faced, leaning on their sticks, waiting for the Americans to finish so they could have the customary handshake. I asked Verchota what he recalled about that.

"Most of them had no expression on their faces, but a few had a hint of a smile," he said. "Maybe it was a mocking smile, maybe they had never seen a team react the way we reacted to that win. Who knows what they were thinking?"

Harrington, Verchota's 1980 teammate, came over to join us. They had gone their separate ways after the Olympics. Verchota had no desire to play professionally in the United States. Instead, he went off to play for the Jokerit team in Finland. Harrington signed with the Buffalo Sabres, which sent him to their farm team in Rochester. He played just a few games before an opponent leveled him with a vicious cross-check. He woke up in the hospital with a concussion and a broken jaw.

"The guy was quoted as saying, 'These aren't the Olympics. This is professional hockey. If he can't take it, let him get out,'" Harrington said. "There was a lot of jealousy towards us in the pros, particularly the minor leagues. I didn't enjoy the life. It seemed silly to continue."

Harrington signed with a team in Switzerland. He played there for one year and enjoyed it, but he came home for another tour with the U.S. national team. He was wearing the "A" on his jersey as the team's alternate captain. Like Verchota, he spent much of his time answering questions about 1980.

"Everyone said we won that [Soviet] game for America," Harrington said. "We didn't think of it that way. We were just trying to win a hockey game. It wasn't until later after we left Lake Placid and toured the country that we realized the impact we had. We didn't solve all the world's problems, but we made a lot of Americans feel good about themselves, and that's a good thing."

"I didn't get to bed for three days," Verchota said. "It was one party after another. We visited the White House and met President [Jimmy] Carter. We were national heroes, which was pretty funny if you knew the guys on the team."

"Yeah, we were a rowdy bunch," Harrington said.

A few weeks later, I rejoined the team in Cincinnati to begin covering a six-game exhibition series against the Soviet Wings, their national "B" team. The Red Army team, the one the Americans had vanquished in Lake Placid, was at home, honing its game for Sarajevo. So, while this was not a true Olympic preview, it was the first meeting between U.S. and Soviet teams since the 1980 Winter Games.

Tensions were high between the two nations. The very day the exhibition series began, U.S. and Soviet diplomats broke off strategic arms talks in Geneva. The Soviets were in Afghanistan, and it was becoming apparent that the Eastern Bloc countries would not be taking part in the Summer Olympics in Los Angeles—this after the United States had boycotted the Summer Games in Moscow four years earlier.

Given that backdrop, it was surprising to find the U.S. and Soviet teams traveling on the same plane during their exhibition tour. On the same day that the diplomats broke off talks in Geneva, the two hockey coaches, Lou Vairo and Anatoli Bogdanov, shared a booth in the airport coffee shop. Two hockey coaches—one born in Brooklyn, the other in Moscow—talked and laughed like any two businessmen waiting for a flight.

Meanwhile, the U.S. and Soviet players browsed through the newsstand and video arcade. There is nothing like watching two young Soviets inspect a *Playboy* centerfold to make you realize we aren't so different after all.

As near as I could tell, the Soviets liked Christie Brinkley, Donkey Kong, blue jeans, and cheeseburgers. In other words, they could fit in comfortably at any American shopping mall. They didn't trudge around in fur hats and trench coats. Several Soviet players were wearing T-shirts from a Cincinnati radio station. They had picked them up in exchange for a few autographed hockey sticks.

They smiled a lot and nodded when we passed in the hall. They were, on the whole, more pleasant than most major league baseball teams.

"The Russians?" Verchota said. "They're like anybody else. They like to drink beer and have a good time."

"Great athletes," Fusco said. "Great discipline. Better than ours, frankly."

At a time when U.S. and Soviet tensions were high, the two hockey teams traveled on the same plane. They passed magazines and pillows to each other across the aisle. They used gestures and a few words to re-create plays from the previous night's game. The teams coexisted happily, despite the competitive nature of the series.

The Americans won the series, three games to two with one tie, thrilling the large crowds who seemed intent on turning the games into a political statement, with their flag waving and patriotic songs. It was a series where there were more right-wingers in the seats than on the ice.

There were anti-Soviet demonstrations. In Cincinnati, a crowd rallied outside the arena, calling for an end to the persecution of Soviet

Jews. In St. Louis, a spectator threw a cardboard missile onto the ice. The Soviet players looked puzzled. The American players looked embarrassed. After the game, Bogdanov had nothing but praise for his hosts.

"Everywhere we have seen very warm receptions and enjoyed good conditions," the Soviet coach said through an interpreter.

Asked whether there were political overtones to the tour, he said no.

"We are sportsmen," he said. "We came here to strengthen our ties with American sportsmen. The political issues, let them be decided by the diplomats."

That's the problem: Diplomats can't meet on the same terms as athletes. They can't hang out in a video arcade or snack bar. They are locked into the rigid framework of politics.

"I've been to the Soviet Union," Verchota said. "The World Tournament was there in 1979. I got to travel around, and the people I met seemed very nice. They're just trying to get by. The average Russian leads a hard life. I wouldn't want to live there, I know that.

"The housing is inferior to what we have. The food isn't as good or plentiful. There is a lot of standing in line for consumer goods. Every aspect of our life is better. I was glad to come home. But they don't hate Americans. They listen to what their government tells them about the United States, but if they believe it, they don't show it. At least, I don't feel it among the Soviet players."

I found it ironic that our athletes, not our scholars or statesmen, were the ones who were the closest to finding the path to world peace. "It's simple, really," said Olczyk, putting diplomacy in terms any seventeen-year-old could understand. "I treat [the Russians] OK, they treat me OK."

I enjoyed traveling with the U.S. team and getting to know the players. Their youth was a constant source of amusement. I still remember the sight of Iafrate eating an ice-cream sundae for breakfast. They were so guileless, I felt sorry for them as they headed off to Sarajevo, because I feared it would be a painful journey.

They had plenty of talent. LaFontaine, Iafrate, Olczyk, and Chelios would become stars in the NHL. But their youth combined with the pressure of living up to the expectations of the American audience proved to be too much.

They lost the first two games—4–2 to Canada and 4–1 to the Czechs—and the people who tuned in to see "the Miracle, Part II" tuned out. The team did not lose another game—it routed Austria, 7–4, and tied Finland and Norway—but no one noticed. The Soviets recaptured the gold. The United States finished seventh. There would not be a return trip to the White House.

One year later, I met Verchota for breakfast in the Twin Cities. He was wearing a suit and dark-rimmed glasses. He blended in with the business crowd, and that was fine with him. He was vice president at his bank and doing well. He shrugged when I asked about the disappointing finish in Sarajevo.

"We did our best," he said, "but nobody wants to hear that if you don't win."

I FINALLY GOT A CHANCE to cover the Olympics in the summer of 1984. The games were held in Los Angeles, and I was part of a twelve-person team dispatched by the *Philadelphia Daily News* to blanket the event. We divided up the crowded Olympic calendar, with each writer assigned to different sports, but we doubled up for the big events.

The biggest story at the '84 games was Carl Lewis. He was the greatest track athlete in the world, and he was from Willingboro, New Jersey. The plan was to have something about Lewis in the paper every day. It should have been easy, but Lewis and his management team made it hard.

I warned our sports editor, Mike Rathet, that it would be difficult, if not impossible, to get near Lewis at the Games. I had done my usual pre-Olympic tour, visiting with the top American athletes. If you went through their agents, you could set up interviews with even high-profile athletes like hurdler Edwin Moses, diver Greg Louganis, and distance runner Mary Decker.

Lewis was another story. His coach, Joe Douglas, insisted on controlling everything. He may have been a good coach, but he was a lousy public relations man. If you wanted time with Lewis, you had to get in line, and it was usually behind the TV networks and national magazines.

I left phone messages for Douglas, and they were rarely returned. When he did call back, he sounded annoyed. I asked if I could schedule a one-on-one interview with Lewis. Douglas said it was out of the question. I knew he was doing one on ones with *Sports Illustrated*, *Time*, and *Gentleman's Quarterly*, but that was Douglas's marketing strategy: Cater to the big dogs and leave the scraps for everyone else.

Douglas suggested I come to an indoor meet in New York. He said Lewis would be there, and maybe I could grab him for a few minutes. I went to the meet, where I was one of a dozen reporters chasing after Lewis. He walked past us, with Douglas at his side saying, "Not now, guys." When Lewis finished his event, he headed for the door. There were a few shouted questions, a few hurried replies, and just like that, he was gone.

So, we knew what to expect when Lewis came to Los Angeles. He would be available only on his terms. The U.S. Olympic Committee scheduled a press conference for Lewis that drew a huge contingent of international media. Lewis arrived thirty minutes late, which rankled everyone waiting in the press tent outside the Coliseum.

His entourage included his parents; his sister Carol, who was competing in the women's long jump; and assorted handlers, including Douglas, who sat next to Lewis on stage. Douglas must have sensed the chill in the air, because he opened by saying, "We'd like to keep all questions in a positive tone. Be nice."

Here was a track coach telling a tent full of reporters to mind their manners after he kept them waiting for a half hour. There was grumbling, but no one walked out. Lewis was the story of the Games. He was trying to equal Jesse Owens's feat of winning four gold medals in one Olympic Games. If he was running late, that wasn't the story. The story was Lewis running for a place in Olympic history.

If he won four gold medals, he would stand shoulder to shoulder with Owens, who was revered for his magnificent performance in the 1936 Berlin Games. That was why Lewis's face appeared on no fewer than eight magazine covers. Douglas compared Lewis to Michael Jackson in terms of his marketability. The world press had a field day with that.

A British journalist asked Lewis whether he felt at all hypocritical discussing such matters at the Olympics. In 1984, the Olympics were still considered the high altar of amateur sport. Athletes were getting paid in all sorts of ways, much of it under the table, but some purists still believed in the Olympic ideal.

Lewis wasn't the only one selling himself in the marketplace, but he was the most visible and the least apologetic.

"Hypocritical? Not at all," he said. "ABC is paying $225 million to televise the Games. Corporations have paid millions to be Olympic sponsors, and they will make millions in return. What we're talking about here is miniscule compared to that."

The reporter asked Lewis to define what's amateur and what's professional.

"Professionals can do whatever they want financially," Lewis said. "Amateurs must abide by their particular governing body. I live on a trust fund. That's the rules my governing body [the Athletics Congress] set up. That's who should be judging. You shouldn't be judging. I shouldn't be judging, and the public shouldn't be judging who's an amateur."

It was a reply worthy of an Olympic gold medal—in fencing.

We had seen pictures of Lewis's lavish home in Houston. We had seen his crystal collection and his shiny BMW. His annual income was a reported $1 million, and that was probably conservative. Yes, he was an Olympian, but he wasn't bunking at the Olympic Training Center and eating meat loaf in the cafeteria. He was living like a 1980s sports superstar, which he was.

He chose not to live in the Olympic Village during the games. He was quoted as saying the Village was OK "for other people," which made him sound arrogant. The other Olympians already viewed Lewis that way. They saw him as a selfish prima donna who was competing for himself and his shoe company.

"I'm a very visible athlete," Lewis said, "and it is difficult for me to move around there without being interrupted. It's distracting, and it would make it difficult for me to prepare for competition. The most important thing is to be ready to compete well. I need some privacy to get ready. That's the bottom line."

Like him or loathe him, Lewis was taking on an enormous challenge. He would compete in the 100-meter dash on Friday, the long jump on Monday, the 200 meters on Wednesday, and the 400-meter relay on Saturday. That was four events in eight days, competing against the best athletes in the world as well as the ghost of Jesse Owens.

He was expected to win gold in every event. If he fell short in even one event, some people would say he had failed, or worse, that he choked. Asked about that, Lewis smiled confidently and said, "There are going to be some absolutely unheard of things coming from me."

Lewis delivered on his boast. He won the 100-meter dash in 9.99 seconds. He won the long jump with a leap of 28 feet. He won the 200 meters in 19.8 seconds, an Olympic record. He anchored the 400-meter relay team to victory with a time of 37.83. But even in victory, there was controversy.

Lewis said he hoped to break Bob Beamon's record for the long jump. Beamon had set the mark of 29'2.25" in the thin air of Mexico City at the 1968 Summer Games. Track experts said it was the one record that may never be broken. Lewis talked openly about doing that. The crowd who filled the L.A. Coliseum that night almost expected it. Just winning wouldn't be enough.

When Lewis jumped 28 feet on his second attempt, he had the gold medal locked up. No one was going to beat him. But Lewis still had four more jumps, and the crowd wanted to see him go for the record. He talked it over with his coaches, pulled on his sweat pants, and called it a night.

When the fans saw what was happening, they began to boo. The boos got louder when it was announced that Lewis was passing on his remaining jumps.

What? He's *not* going for the record? But that's what we came to see.

The people who understood track and field had no problem with Lewis's decision. It was a cool night, and Lewis had a mild twinge in his thigh. He had the 200 meters coming up in two days and the 400-meter relay after that. If he tried another jump and injured himself even slightly, what sense would that make?

The idea was to win the four events. Breaking Beamon's record would be a nice bonus, but it wasn't the real mission. However, because Lewis had turned off so many people, the storyline became the selfish superstar once again putting himself first, and although Lewis finished the L.A. Games with four gold medals draped around his neck, he wasn't warmly embraced.

He captured everything, it seemed, except America's heart.

A gymnast, Mary Lou Retton, emerged as the darling of the Games. She was the one the press and the public loved. She was the one the big-money boys—Wheaties, Vidal Sassoon, and McDonald's—came after for endorsements. The Olympics are funny that way. They aren't like other sports. They are more like a TV show, and it becomes more about personality than performance.

Retton was cute and bubbly, with a telegenic smile. Lewis beat her, four gold medals to one, but it didn't matter. America loved Mary Lou; it didn't love King Carl.

Former U.S. decathlon champion Bob Mathias, the first athlete to appear on a Wheaties box, summed up the general feeling when he called Lewis's attitude toward the Game "cold and calculating."

One year after the L.A. Games, I went to see Lewis. It was a lot easier to get an interview. He missed part of the 1985 track season with a sore hamstring and was dividing his time between Houston and New York, where he was enrolled in the Warren Robertson Theatre Workshop. He was taking acting lessons in the same prestigious school that produced James Earl Jones, Jessica Lange, and Diane Keaton.

Lewis was in a curious position. He was a four-time Olympic gold medalist who needed to rebuild his image. I mean, how crazy is that? He had done everything he said he would do in L.A., yet he left town less popular than when he arrived. The quickie paperback on his life published one week after the Games was greeted with scorn.

"When you talk about image, you talk about public perception," said Bob Mazza, business adviser to gold medal sprinter Evelyn Ashford, "and most people see Carl as a pompous figure. I'm not saying he is or isn't. I'm just saying that's how he comes across to the guy in the forty-fifth row."

Douglas, who orchestrated the Lewis victory tour, rejected the criticism.

"All this talk about [the public] turning on Carl is so much bullshit," Douglas said. "People say he missed out on [endorsements]. A lot of them Carl turned down. He was selective. He was looking for long-term deals, not quickie stuff. He has done well. It's the press that would have you believe otherwise.

"We can't go anywhere without people coming over to shake his hand and congratulate him. He still gets fan mail every day. He set attendance records everywhere he competed last year."

That was the party line: It was the press, not the public, that was hostile. It was the press that referenced his negative image, thereby creating the negative image. Most people, Lewis insisted, were behind him.

"You ask if I've been treated fairly," he said. "It all depends. Are we talking about the press or the public? I haven't had one fan say, 'Gee, I haven't seen you on a Wheaties box. What's wrong?' They say, 'It was great watching you in the Olympics. How's the acting going?' It's the media that wants to know about the endorsements.

"You ask about my negative image; I don't see it. We're dealing in personal opinion. I'm sure there are people out there who don't like me, maybe they resent me for whatever reason, but I don't meet them very often."

Douglas claimed it was the press that made money an issue. And why would the press want to tarnish Lewis's golden image? Douglas claimed it was because he had limited the media's access to Lewis in 1984.

"I found the definition of aloof and arrogant," Douglas said. "Both mean denying an interview to a reporter."

"It's a two-way street. The athlete has to respect the media too," said swimmer John Naber, who won four medals at the 1976 Olympics. "Carl didn't do that. He showed up thirty minutes late for his press conference. You can't do that. I don't care who you are. Carl is his own man, he has his own priorities, and that's fine, but he has to understand the consequences of his actions. To be late like that is asking to be called a prima donna."

Lewis said he had no regrets. He said if he had the chance to do 1984 over again, he would do it the same way.

"My goal was to win four gold medals in Los Angeles, and I did that," he said. "I did the things I had to do to put forth my best effort. I was put in a lot of impossible situations, but I made the best of them. I've matured a lot. I have a better understanding of myself.

"I'm not a phony, and I'm not plastic," Lewis said. "I'm a winner."

No one could deny that. Lewis returned to compete in the next three Olympics, an amazing feat. He won the gold medal in the long jump in four consecutive Summer Games. He finished his career with nine Olympic gold medals and one silver. He won eight world championships and set three world records. He will go down in history as one of the great Olympic athletes of all time.

He just wasn't Michael Jackson.

7

"It's All Gene Mauch's Fault"

I GREW UP A PHILLIES FAN. The conversation in my grandfather's bar was dominated by baseball talk. In the 1950s, baseball truly was the national pastime. The guys in Ray's Tavern talked about the Phillies 365 days a year.

Behind the bar, my grandfather had a dozen autographed baseballs. They were so yellowed by the nicotine in the smoky air that you couldn't read the names. My grandfather would say, "I think this ball is signed by Elmer Valo." I took him at his word.

When the Phillies blew the pennant in 1964, losing a six-and-one-half game lead with twelve to play, I was just starting my freshman year at Temple. No sooner had I started classes than Chico Ruiz stole home against Art Mahaffey, and the misery began.

The Phillies dropped ten games in a row. Jim Bunning and Chris Short each started three games, twice on two days' rest. The once insurmountable lead melted away.

By October 1, the Phillies had fallen out of first place. I was numb. I allowed myself to believe that 1964 was, in the immortal words of catcher Gus Triandos, "the year of the blue snow." In other words, this was the year when the unexplained phenomenon would be commonplace. It was a year for dreams coming true.

I fully believed that the '64 Phillies were a team of destiny. In June, Bunning pitched the first perfect game in franchise history. In July, outfielder Johnny Callison won the All-Star game with a ninth-inning home run. Third baseman Richie Allen was the National League Rookie of the Year.

The Phillies reeled off three triple plays—that's right, *three* triple plays—that season. How much more proof did you need? Surely, this was their year.

Until it wasn't.

It was the cruelest twist of fate, sucking in Philadelphia's long-suffering fans and, just when their World Series tickets were arriving in the mail, snatching them away and shredding them into so much confetti.

Walking into Ray's Tavern that September was like walking into a funeral parlor. All the regulars were hunched over their Ballantine drafts, but instead of the usual happy buzz, there was an awful silence.

One afternoon, a guy walked in and got a pack of Chesterfields from the cigarette machine. He went to the jukebox, dropped a quarter in the slot, pushed a button, and suddenly Dean Martin was singing, "Everybody Loves Somebody."

It was like a scene from an old Western where everyone in the saloon turns to stare at the stranger in their midst. Big Dom, the burly mechanic at the end of the bar, shouted, "Turn that shit off!" The man looked bewildered.

"Don't you like Dean Martin?" he asked.

He had no idea what was wrong. Clearly, he was not a baseball fan. He didn't know Ed Roebuck had just blown another ninth-inning lead. No one was in the mood for music.

Joe Donnelly, one of the bartenders, walked over and pulled the plug on the jukebox. It remained unplugged for the remainder of the baseball season.

It was a particularly brutal time for me. It was my first month on a college campus, a time of adjustment, especially for a kid who had spent the previous four years at an all-boy's Catholic high school. Suddenly, I was surrounded by pretty girls in short skirts, which was distracting enough, but when you combined that with the Phillies' meltdown, it was more than I could handle.

I sat in class all day thinking about the game that night. I didn't hear a word the professors said. I didn't take a single note. If I wrote down anything, it was a new lineup. Why not let Cookie Rojas bat lead-off? Maybe they should try Callison in the two hole. Let Triandos bat against the right hander. Why wasn't manager Gene Mauch using Jack Baldschun more out of the bullpen?

These were all the things I was thinking when I should have been paying attention to—what was it?—oh yeah, sociology.

Each night, I expected the Phillies to break the spell. Richie Allen will hit a tape-measure home run, Bobby Wine will turn a clutch double play, Baldschun will pitch a perfect ninth inning, and the Phillies will win. They had done it all year. Of course, they would do it again.

One win, just one lousy win, and they could end this nightmare.

Then I would sit by the transistor radio and listen to them lose.

My plan was always the same: I'll study after the game. But when the game was over and they had lost again, I would be too depressed to study. I would stretch out on the bed and stare at the ceiling. I had an English test the next day, but so what? The lead was down to two games, and Dennis Bennett had a sore arm. Who cares about Emily Brontë?

The Phillies choked away the pennant, finishing one game behind St. Louis. It was the worst collapse in baseball history. We had climbed aboard the bandwagon—all of us, the skeptics as well as the true believers—and the Phillies drove us off a cliff.

I was catatonic for a month. Midterms were approaching, but I had fallen so far behind in my studies that there was no way to catch up. I totally bombed that first semester. I don't remember my grade-point average, but I know I wound up on academic probation. I was one step away from being booted out the door and into the draft.

When my parents saw my grades, they were stunned. I had been an honor student all through high school. What the hell happened?

"It's all Gene Mauch's fault," I said.

OK, it was a bad joke, but there was some truth to it.

The Phillies wrecked my life, and the manager's mishandling of the pitching staff was a big part of it. I'd be willing to bet there were many otherwise sane people in the Philadelphia area whose lives fell apart in much the same way. All the stricken faces I saw on the Broad Street subway each morning—I did not imagine them. They were real, and so was their anguish.

I pulled myself together over the winter and got back on track academically, but the scars of 1964 never fully healed. I still have my Phillies Yearbook from that season. Every so often, I page through it and ask myself why Gene Mauch didn't give Ray Culp a chance down the stretch or maybe go back to Art Mahaffey. Why didn't he give Wes Covington more at bats? We'll never know.

My grandfather could have turned in his unused World Series tickets for a refund, but he chose to keep them. He believed that was as close as the Phillies would ever come to playing in the Fall Classic, so he was determined to hang on to those tickets. I found them in his desk after he died. I had them framed and hung in our kitchen. I looked at them every morning when I poured my Cheerios.

So, with that as a backdrop, you can imagine how enthused I was in 1977 when I had a chance to write about baseball, especially knowing that the Phillies had a legitimate shot at the World Series. I was the new sports columnist at the *Bulletin,* succeeding Sandy Grady and Jim Barniak. Grady had moved to Washington to write politics—this was post-Watergate America, and he wanted to have his say—and Barniak was going into broadcasting, so the paper needed to find a new columnist.

I had covered the Eagles for seven seasons that ranged from mediocre to pitiful. I was finally seeing signs of promise under Dick Vermeil, and I was looking forward to covering a team with a chance to win something. I assumed Jack Wilson would bring in an experienced columnist from another paper to take over for Barniak and Grady. Those were big shoes to fill.

I certainly didn't expect Wilson to offer the job to me, but he did. I was surprised when he said Grady himself had recommended me.

"He thinks you're ready," Wilson said. "So do I."

At thirty-one, I was the youngest sports columnist in the country. I had been down this road before, of course, as the youngest NFL beat writer in 1970. I had some trepidation, but it was a fabulous opportunity. Philadelphia was in the midst of a sports renaissance. The Flyers and Sixers were winning, and after a decade of wandering in the desert, the Phillies were emerging as real contenders.

In 1976, they won the National League East and went to the postseason for the first time since 1950. They were swept in the playoffs by Cincinnati's Big Red Machine, but there was no disgrace in that. The Phillies had a talented young nucleus and a bright future, and they were fun to watch. The problem, at least from a journalist's standpoint, was that they were no fun to cover.

The players were at war with the media, and as the *Bulletin* columnist, I was on the front line. When I came aboard, the bad feeling was already there. It had started with Steve Carlton's vow of silence in 1974. The great left-hander was upset with some things written by Bill Conlin in the *Daily News* and slammed the door on the media. From there, the divide between the players and the press grew wider and more hostile.

Shortstop Larry Bowa was a volatile personality who could go off at any time. Pitcher Ron Reed was a 24/7 grump. Greg Luzinski was moody. Mike Schmidt was aloof. Second baseman Ted Sizemore sneered at anyone carrying a notepad. Outfielder Bake McBride shoved a sock into his mouth to let everyone know he wasn't talking. Even some of the younger players caved to the peer pressure and went silent.

"A Phillies versus Scribes bout has simmered all summer," wrote Thomas Boswell in the *Washington Post*. "Philadelphia probably leads the majors in boo birds, flip writers who walk the line between wit and sarcasm and surly players who hide in the trainer's room and tell their sorrows to their hair dryers."[1]

Over the years, I found baseball players to be the hardest athletes to deal with. Hockey players were by far the easiest. I think it is because so many of them grew up in Canada. They were not as spoiled as the Americans who populated the other sports. In those days, hockey players were not making the huge salaries that athletes in other sports were making.

Hockey players were, by and large, regular guys. It was a different story with the other sports, but it was particularly true in baseball. I felt an uncomfortable vibe in most baseball clubhouses. I think there is too much media access, which seems like an odd thing to say, considering that access to the people we cover is an important part of doing our jobs, but I believe that there is too much of it in baseball.

It changed in 2020 during the COVID-19 pandemic, when baseball—along with every other major sport—barred reporters from the team locker rooms. Most interviews were done via teleconference. But prior to that, the press was allowed in the locker room and in baseball, the clubhouse was open before the game and after the game. When you have a 162-game regular season plus spring training, that's a lot of time spent staring at each other. The players see the writers as intruding on their space—which, when you get right down to it, we are. It is their clubhouse, after all.

There is a big difference between being allowed in a room, which we were, and being welcome in that room, which we certainly were not. That was particularly true with the Phillies of the '70s. After years of losing, they finally had a team with a chance to win it all, but they lost in the '76 playoffs to the Reds, and when they lost again in the '77 and '78 playoffs to the Dodgers, we didn't hold back in our criticism.

I wrote a column for the *Bulletin* with the headline "The Phillies: Legends in Their Own Minds." I wrote they were a bunch of under-achieving prima donnas. When I walked into the clubhouse the next day, I was greeted with icy glares. The only player who was unaffected was reliever Tug McGraw, who approached me at the batting cage. He had been through the media wars in New York when he played for the Mets, so this stuff just rolled off his back.

"I read your column," he said.

"What did you think?" I asked.

"We deserved it," he replied.

As he walked away, McGraw gave me a wink.

"But we will win," he said. "Mark it down."

We thought 1977 would be the year. The Phillies won 101 games. Carlton (23–10), Larry Christenson (19–6), and Jim Lonborg (11–4) were a formidable rotation. The bullpen was four deep, with McGraw (7–3, 2.62 earned run average [ERA]), Reed (7–5, 2.76), Warren Brusstar (7–2, 2.66), and Gene Garber (8–6, 2.36).

Luzinski and Schmidt combined to hit 77 homers. McBride batted .339 after joining the team in midseason. They were a superb defensive team, with Gold Glove winners Schmidt, Bowa, and centerfielder Garry Maddox. That was the summer I wrote the line, "Two thirds of the earth's surface is covered by water, the other one third is covered by Garry Maddox." The line has since been widely attributed to Mets broadcaster Ralph Kiner, but he was merely repeating my line on the air.

The Phillies were favored to beat the Dodgers in the National League Championship Series and, indeed, they were in control of the best-of-five series. They split the first two games in Los Angeles and were leading 5–3 with two outs in the ninth inning of Game 3 at the Vet, but they let it slip away on what became known as "Black Friday."

Garber retired the first two hitters in the ninth. Just one more out was all they needed. I was packing for the dash to the clubhouse when the Dodgers' manager, Tommy Lasorda, sent Vic Davalillo up to pinch hit. The 5'7" Davalillo was a thirty-nine-year-old journeyman who looked more like a jockey than a ball player. He laid down a perfect bunt to reach first base, but it hardly seemed to matter. All Garber had to do was get the next hitter, and the game was over.

Lasorda sent up another pinch hitter. This time, it was forty-year-old Manny Mota. I felt like I was watching an Old-Timers' game. Who was Lasorda going to send to the plate next, Pee Wee Reese? Duke Snider?

Mota fell into a 0–2 hole, and the 63,719 fans were on their feet, anticipating strike 3. Instead, Mota lofted a fly ball to left field. Luzinski went back to the wall and got his glove on the ball but couldn't hold it. Davalillo scored, and when Sizemore bobbled the relay throw, Mota took third.

A better left fielder would have made the catch. The Phillies had a better left fielder, Jerry Martin, but he was on the bench. To this day, no one knows why manager Danny Ozark left Luzinski in to play the ninth inning. All season, Ozark had gone to Martin when the Phillies had the lead late in the game. Martin could get to balls that the lumbering Luzinski could not.

So why in Game 3 of the NLCS was Luzinski in left field and Martin on the bench? Ozark said he wanted to keep Luzinski's bat in the lineup in case the Dodgers tied the score, but it made no sense. The Phillies were up by two runs. I think Ozark got caught up in the moment and simply forgot to make the switch. Whatever, the result was devastating.

Davey Lopes followed with a hot shot that bounced off Schmidt. Bowa speared it barehanded and threw a strike to first base. Replays show that the ball beat Lopes by half a step, but umpire Bruce Froemming called him safe. It was a great defensive play by Bowa that should have ended the game, but instead it was just one more gut punch that left the Phillies gasping.

Lopes went to second when Garber threw wide on a pickoff attempt, and he scored the winning run on Bill Russell's single up the middle. The Phillies lost the game, 6–5, and the clubhouse was deathly silent afterward. The next night, Tommy John outpitched Carlton, 4–1, in a cold steady rain to win the series.

It happened again the following year, as the Phillies lost to the Dodgers in the NLCS, three games to one. Three straight playoff losses began a conversation about what this Phillies team lacked. It wasn't talent; they had plenty of that. So why did they keep coming up short in October?

The consensus view was that the Phillies needed leadership, preferably from someone with a history of excelling in big moments. Someone like Pete Rose.

Rose was a free agent after playing out his contract in Cincinnati. He was thirty-seven years old, but he was coming off a season in which he had made headlines by hitting safely in forty-four straight games. He was a fierce competitor, a proven winner, and exactly what the Phillies needed.

Other teams were pursuing him, but Rose favored the Phillies because he was buddies with Bowa and Luzinski. All signs indicated that he was coming to Philadelphia. It was just a matter of time, we were told.

Then, on November 30, the Phillies announced they were dropping out of the Rose sweepstakes. Team president Ruly Carpenter said the bidding had reached a point where they could no longer compete. The price was too high, even for a three-time batting champion.

Most of the press corps gave Carpenter a pass. They believed that it was too much money to spend for a singles hitter. There was a lot of hand-wringing about the skyrocketing salaries and what they meant for the future of baseball. Even Conlin and Stan Hochman, who often were critical of Phillies management, supported them this time.

I disagreed. I wrote a piece that ran under the headline "Phillies Are Rose-Less and Red-Faced."

In a week when the Consumer Price Index broke 200, a week when we learned the dollar is now worth half of what it was worth in 1967, Phillies president Ruly Carpenter declared war on baseball inflation. Carpenter put Pete Rose, the caviar of free agents, back on the shelf and wheeled his empty shopping basket to next week's winter meetings.

After a month of talking about what Pete Rose would mean to his team, Carpenter decided [Rose] is too expensive for his tastes. For a while Ruly was browsing in Tiffany's but now he is back shopping at Korvette's.

The point is if the Phillies had to pay Pete Rose a million dollars a year, you know he would have given a million dollars' worth of effort. He would have made the team take off. Ruly Carpenter had his shot to bring a hunk of Cooperstown to Philadelphia and maybe win a National League pennant at the same time. He booted it.[2]

We know now that Rose isn't likely to wind up in Cooperstown, but that's a separate issue. This is about what he represented in 1978, and that was a bold step forward for the franchise. The Phillies had gone to the postseason three years in a row and lost. How many more chances would they get? If they really cared about winning, they couldn't afford *not* to sign Rose. At least, that was how I saw it.

One week later, the Phillies did a stunning about-face. They signed Rose for $3.2 million over four years. Vice president Bill Giles convinced Taft Broadcasting, the Phillies' TV partner, to kick in some money to sweeten the bid. With Rose in the lineup, Giles said, the TV ratings would soar, allowing the network to charge more for advertising. In other words, everyone wins.

Philadelphia Magazine credited me with making the deal happen. The magazine said my column made the Phillies change their minds and sign Rose. For that, the magazine put me in its annual power issue with the city's top politicians and labor leaders.

It was a nice compliment, but that's not how these things work. Teams don't spend millions of dollars based on a columnist's opinion. We like to think we have that kind of clout, but the truth is we don't. Teams spend money to make more money. Ultimately, signing Rose was a business decision, but it was the right one.

When I ran into Carpenter at the winter meetings, he didn't say hello. He said, "You got your wish."

It wasn't the warmest of greetings, but I'm sure he was pleased when Rose helped the Phillies win their first World Series in 1980. I don't think the club would have won it without him. He made that much of a difference.

"Pete concentrated better than any human being I've ever seen on every pitch," Bowa said in his book, *I Still Hate to Lose,* "and he literally loved the game. He put us over the hump. We kept coming close before he got there but he put us over the hump."[3]

I first met Rose in January on the press caravan, a weeklong bus tour through the distant precincts of Phillies fandom. It was bitter cold with snow in the air as the traveling party made its way from Reading to Lancaster. Schmidt and Bowa were on board along with Ozark, Harry Kalas, and the Philly Phanatic, but the star of the show was Rose. It was his introduction to the Phillies Nation, and every luncheon was a wall to wall lovefest.

I introduced myself to Rose in the coffee shop of the Reading Motor Inn. He was sitting in a booth with Schmidt, who was reading the morning paper. I said I needed to interview him at some point during the trip.

"Let's do it right now," he said. "Pull up a chair."

Schmidt never looked up from his newspaper, but I wasn't surprised. I was not very popular with the Phillies veterans. I had a blowup with Bowa the previous season. It started with Bowa confronting Ray Kelly Jr. of the *Courier Post* in the clubhouse. He was upset with something Kelly wrote. Bowa shoved Kelly, setting off a wild scene that ended with a table getting knocked over and Kelly nursing a bruised eye.

When I tried to intercede, Bowa came at me cursing and swearing. I said something back, and the next thing I knew, Ruly Carpenter and clubhouse manager Kenny Bush were shoving me out the door. Carpenter issued a statement saying, "Bowa and Didinger got into a shouting match."

Yes, we were definitely shouting. Even Ozark, who rarely left his office, came out to see what was going on.

Within an hour, it was a national story. It was probably inevitable that something like this would happen, given the simmering tension that existed with the players and the media. We all felt it coming. I just didn't think I would wind up in the middle of it.

Predictably, the players circled the wagons around their teammate. They insisted that nothing had happened. Bowa said, "I did not touch anyone. I'll swear to that on a million Bibles." Carpenter said the incident was "blown out of proportion." I was the only other media member in the room, so I was the only one who could support Kelly's version of the incident.

I wrote a column for the next day's *Bulletin* in which I described exactly what took place. I wrote, "The Phillies aren't a baseball team anymore; they are a home for delinquent boys. . . . They have become a distasteful collection of raging antisocial misfits, bullies who believe intimidation is as much a part of their daily routine as batting practice."[4]

Here is the irony: I liked Bowa. I admired the way he had made himself into a big league player. He was a skinny kid who was written off as "a Little Leaguer" by Associated Press sports editor Ralph Bernstein, and he worked his butt off to become a three-time National League All-Star. He was a brilliant defensive shortstop and an underrated hitter who finished his career with 2,191 hits.

His competitive fire got him to the big leagues, but the flip side was that the same fire made him hard to live with. Perhaps bringing Rose aboard would help. Rose and Bowa were similar: both overachievers, not blessed with the natural gifts of a Mike Schmidt, but driven by a fierce desire. That hunger formed the basis of their friendship. The difference was that Rose combined that competitive drive with an engaging personality. Bowa was short-tempered and thin-skinned.

Boswell painted an accurate picture of Bowa when he wrote, "Larry Bowa has the metabolism of a hummingbird, the piercing cry of a sassy jay and the frenetic look of a sparrow among cats."[5]

Bowa was always on edge. Even though he was established as a major league player, he still carried the memory of being cut from his high school team, so he lived with the fear that tomorrow he would walk into the clubhouse and find someone else—younger, stronger, better—dressing at his locker. That was why even the mildest criticism—and Kelly's reference to Bowa's "immature tantrums" was pretty mild—set him off.

Rose, on the other hand, had bulletproof confidence. He did not care what anyone said or wrote about him—he knew that he was Pete Rose, and that was enough. He enjoyed coming to the ballpark, putting on the uniform, and being Pete Rose. He was the most media-friendly player in baseball. He talked before games. He talked after games. He talked between swings in the batting cage. He talked to the bat boys in the on-deck circle. He just enjoyed talking, so I wasn't surprised when he asked me to join him for breakfast.

"People are funny," he said. "They've never been within three hundred feet of you, but they think they know you. Last night in the bar, this guy came over a dozen times to ask me questions. He said, 'I can't believe it. You're Pete Rose. You're a superstar. You can't be this nice.' I said, 'What do you want me to do? You want me to stop talking to you? If that's what you want, I'll stop.'"

I brought up the forty-four-game hitting streak of the previous season. It tied the National League record for the longest hitting streak, set by Wee Willie Keeler in 1897. It was the first time anyone really threatened the all-time record of fifty-six consecutive games set by Joe DiMaggio in 1941. It was such a big story that TV networks interrupted their programming to show Rose's at bats. You could argue that the biggest stories of 1978 were the touring King Tut exhibit and Rose's hitting streak.

"Pete was a bigger story than King Tut," Schmidt said. "He's older."

"Sparky [Anderson, the Reds' manager] said he didn't think any other player could've done it," Rose said. "He didn't think any other player could have put up with all the hoopla. If anything, the excitement kept me going. Every day, the crowd of reporters got bigger. It was like being the only player in the World Series. I could hardly swing the bat in batting practice because there were so many photographers around. But it didn't bother me. I loved it."

It was that attitude the Phillies were looking for when they signed Rose. Yes, they wanted his bat in the lineup. They knew he would be the team's best leadoff hitter since Richie Ashburn. They knew he could handle the move to first base. He had played second, third, and the

outfield in nineteen seasons with the Reds, so switching positions was
nothing new to him.

"Just a different mitt, that's all," he said.

But they also wanted his bravado and the air of confidence he projected. I interviewed Anderson, who predicted that Rose would be the
final piece to the Phillies' championship puzzle.

"Pete will spark them, especially in the playoffs," Anderson said.
"He has always responded in those situations. I remember the sixth
game of the '75 World Series. That was the game where [Carlton] Fisk
hit the home run off the foul pole. We were walking to the bus. Pete
said, 'Sparky, that was the best damned game I've ever played in.' I was
surprised. I figured he'd be as upset as I was. He said, 'Relax, we'll win
it tomorrow.'

"Sure enough, the next day we came from 3 runs down and beat
Boston to win the series. Pete drove in the tying run in the seventh, and
he was on base when we won it in the ninth. A man with confidence like
that, he makes everybody on your team play better."

I mentioned Anderson's comments to Rose. He agreed that's what
the Phillies were looking for when they signed him.

"These guys want to win, and that's something I know how to do,"
he said. "I'm not talking about winning with rah-rah. That's bullshit.
I'm talking about winning with production. If I'm a leader, it's not
because I have a big mouth. It's because I produce. Show me a leader
who hits .210. There ain't one. Leadership isn't slapping guys on the ass.
It's getting on base, scoring runs, doing the things that win games.

"I hear people say, 'Rose will be the leader the Phillies need.' What
do they expect? Do they think I'm gonna walk through the clubhouse
every day and tell Schmitty he's gotta start hitting home runs or tell
Bowa he's gotta start stealing more bases? Can you see me walking up to
Carlton and telling him he'd better go nine? He'd tell me to drop dead.

"What I will do is break my ass every day. I'll be out there doing my
job when it's 35 degrees in April and when it's 110 degrees in August.
I'm not gonna be up one day and down the next. I'll get my 200 hits,
my 100 runs, my 40 doubles. When I talk like this, people say I'm cocky.
They can say whatever they want because I got the stats to back it up."

Rose played more games (3,562) than any other player in major
league history and finished his career with the most hits (4,256). He
was a lock for the Hall of Fame, and it was something he talked about,
how much it would mean to him to be in the cathedral of baseball with
Babe Ruth, Ty Cobb, and Lou Gehrig. That's why it was sad to see him

lose that immortality with his involvement in gambling, a sickness that earned him a lifetime ban from baseball.

Over the years, people have accused us—the media—of covering for Rose. They think we turned a blind eye to what he was doing because we did not want to knock him off his pedestal. Besides, he filled our notebooks every day. It was a mutually beneficial relationship: He was good for us, so we looked out for him. I can see how some people may think that, but it never occurred to me. Call me naïve, but that's the truth.

I knew Rose went to the dog track pretty much every night during spring training, but so did many other players and even some team executives. I didn't see any red flags there. He went to jai alai, but OK, it was something to do. He talked about betting on the NCAA basketball tournament, but who doesn't have a bracket sheet or two in their desk drawer? Again, no big deal.

I often saw Rose in the Eagles' locker room—the two teams shared the same shower at the Vet—and he would be talking to players, but I didn't think anything of it. He was a big football fan. It never occurred to me that he might be looking for inside information—who has a bad knee, who has a sore hamstring?—that would help him bet on the next game.

Knowing what we know about Rose now, it all fits the profile of a compulsive gambler. But at the time, I did not even consider the possibility of his betting on baseball. He knew the consequences of betting on the game. I could not imagine him risking his career—and his legacy—to do something so foolish. I could see him betting on just about anything, but not baseball.

I was wrong. He broke the rules and wound up ruining his life.

I know he brought it on himself and lied about it for years. I can't defend him, and I'm not about to try, but I still find it sad, because I have the memory of the guy I covered in Philadelphia and the excitement he brought to the city. That first season, Rose hit .331 and drew 2.7 million fans to the Vet even though the team failed to make the playoffs. Ozark was fired and replaced by Dallas Green, with his throaty, no-bullshit brand of leadership.

Ozark indulged the players and protected them from criticism. Green had a different style. Instead of coddling the players, he told them to "look in the f—king mirror." He challenged them. He ripped them in the press, which Ozark never did. The players resented Green's methods, but he didn't care.

"I'm in this for one f—king thing, and that's to win it," he said. "I'm beyond the point of caring about people's feelings."

With Green calling the shots, loudly and often, the Phillies were back in the pennant race in 1980. They went to Pittsburgh for a big series in August. I had just changed jobs, leaving the *Bulletin* after eleven years to become a columnist at the *Daily News*. My first assignment was covering a Phillies doubleheader in Pittsburgh. The Pirates won the first game, 7–1, and Green was seething.

When we went downstairs, we found the clubhouse door locked. Green told the guard not to admit the press, but it didn't matter. He was so angry, his words cut through the steel door like a blow torch. We were in the hallway, but we could hear the whole thing. Hal Bodley of the *Wilmington News-Journal* got every word, clear as a bell, on his pocket tape recorder.

"You've gotta stop being so f—king cool," he roared. "Get that through your f—king heads. If you don't, you'll be so f—king buried, it ain't gonna be funny. Get the f—k off your asses. You're a good f—king baseball team, but you're not now, and you can't look in the f—king mirror and tell me you are.

"You tell me you can do it, but you f—king give up. If you don't want to f—king play, get the f—k in my office and f—king tell me, because I don't want to f—king play you."

When the shouting stopped and the door finally opened, Rose was the only one at his locker. The other players had fled to the showers or the trainer's room, which was off limits to the media. Rose never hid out. Win or lose, he was always available.

"Dallas is pissed," Rose said, "but he has a right to be. We were horseshit."

"We were out in the hall, and we heard the whole thing," I said.

"They probably heard him back in Philadelphia," Rose said, "but maybe a good kick in the ass is what we need."

The Phillies lost the second game of the doubleheader, 4–1, to complete a four-game sweep by the Pirates. The Phillies dropped to third place, a full six games off the pace, and the road trip was just beginning. They had three games coming up in Chicago against the Cubs and four in New York against the Mets.

The temptation was to write the Phillies off, and some people did, but they won two out of three against the Cubs and swept the Mets to climb back into the race. Still, there were problems. Boone, Luzinski, and Maddox were slumping, so Green benched them. He put Keith

Moreland behind the plate, Lonnie Smith in left field, and Del Unser in center.

It was a gutsy move, especially going with the youngsters Moreland and Smith. The veterans who came up through the ranks under Ozark were furious with Green for benching core players like Boone, Luzinski, and Maddox in the heat of a pennant race. Bowa went on a pregame radio show and accused Green of "talking out of both sides of his mouth" by saying he believed in his veterans while telling them to take a seat.

That night, the Phillies pulled out a 6–5 win over Chicago in fifteen innings. The length of the game put most writers on a tight deadline. They did not have time to follow up on Bowa's comments. They barely had time to file their game stories. I was lucky because the *Daily News* was an afternoon paper, which meant that our deadline was four hours later.

I waited for the other writers to leave the manager's office. When I had Green alone, I asked him whether he knew about the Bowa interview. "What interview?" he said. I read him the transcript. With each line, his face became a deeper shade of red. When I finished, he sat silent for a moment, letting the words sink in. He walked to the door and stared into the empty clubhouse.

"I get the feeling we're not all together in this thing," he said. "I wouldn't be surprised if there aren't a few guys out there rooting against us."

It was a jaw-dropping statement. The Phillies were in a pennant race, and the manager was wondering aloud whether some players actually wanted the team to lose. I know things got a little crazy with the Yankees under George Steinbrenner—Billy Martin and Reggie Jackson certainly had their differences—but no one thought that the players didn't want to win.

"I stayed with my veterans," Green said. "Hell, I stayed with them the whole month of September. It gets to the point where I felt I had to change. I'll play the guys who I think can do the job. We've got six games left, and I'm gonna battle like hell to win those six games. What will straighten all this out is if we win the whole damn thing, [and] then we [the front office] are allowed to do what we want to do."

He was talking about trading players even if the team won the World Series. It was a huge story. I called the office to let them know what I had. Mike Rathet, the sports editor, redesigned the back page, putting my story on top. The headline: "A Bitter Taste to Phils Win." My final line: "It would be fascinating to see the Phillies win the World Series now just to see that many players ordering champagne to go."

Once again, the Phillies responded to the sting of the manager's words. They completed a four-game sweep of the Cubs and flew to Montreal for the final weekend of the regular season. They met the Expos in a head-to-head showdown for the division title and won it by taking the first two games. Boone, back in the starting lineup, had a clutch hit to win one game, and Schmidt crushed a two-run homer to put the team in the playoffs.

In the NLCS, Luzinski had two game-winning hits and Maddox another as the Phillies outlasted Houston in a classic five-game series. Maddox caught a fly ball to secure the final out. In the World Series, Boone batted .412 and Bowa excelled offensively and defensively as the Phillies defeated Kansas City to win their first world championship.

The players Green rode the hardest were the ones who came through for him in the end. They may have done it just to shove it in his face, who knows? The "why?" didn't matter. What mattered is the Phillies won their first World Series, and in the end, they all celebrated together.

Rose's influence was felt every day. He was particularly good in helping Schmidt through his emotional highs and lows. For a great player, Schmidt was hard on himself. He was a worrier who never seemed to trust his enormous talent. In many ways, he was the opposite of Rose. Schmidt had a fear of failure. Rose never even considered the possibility. Fail? Me? Never.

With Rose chirping in his ear, Schmidt had a career year, raising his batting average to .286 and hitting 48 home runs, the most ever by a National League third baseman. He had 17 game-winning runs batted in, including 4 in the last five Phillies victories as they stormed to the pennant. Schmidt was a landslide winner for Most Valuable Player, and when he accepted the award, he credited Rose for keeping him going.

As Sparky Anderson had predicted, Rose was huge in the postseason. In the NLCS, he batted .400 and scored the go-ahead run in Game 4, bowling over catcher Bruce Bochy at the plate. In the World Series, he made the most Rose-like of plays, catching a pop foul that bounced out of Boone's mitt in the ninth inning of the final game.

"How many guys would've even been over there to make that play?" Green said as he bathed in the winners' champagne. "Only Pete Rose. That's why we got him. He's a f—king winner."

Rose's heads-up play retired Frank White for the second out of the inning. The final out was recorded by Tug McGraw pumping a third strike past Willie Wilson to end the game and begin the celebration. Fireworks filled the sky, and the cops rushed onto the field, but I was looking down from the press box to where my grandfather was sitting behind home plate.

The press box was virtually deserted. The other writers had gone to the interview room to watch the final inning on TV. I did the same thing at most big events. You don't want to get caught in the crowd when the game ends. You don't want to be trapped on an elevator. You want to be downstairs safely away from the madness.

But not this time. This was different. I had waited my whole life to see the Phillies win a World Series, and I wanted to see it live with my own eyes. I did not want to be in a windowless room watching it on TV. I wanted to take in the whole scene. I wanted to hear it and feel it the way the other fans did. I wanted to wrap myself in the moment,

Most of all, I wanted to share that feeling with my grandfather. On the final out, he turned and looked up to the press box. I looked down. Our eyes met. He smiled up at me and flashed the thumbs-up sign.

I asked later what he was thinking.

"I was thinking it was a long wait," he said, "but it was worth it."

My grandfather passed away two years later. He often said he was glad he lived long enough to see the Phillies win a World Series. He was like thousands of older fans who really needed that moment, that opportunity to celebrate. He had seen the Eagles, Sixers, and Flyers win it all. He needed the Phillies to take him there too.

He wasn't around to see Joe Carter's Game 6 home run end the Phillies' magical run of 1993. I'm sure he would have blamed it on manager Jim Fregosi. Sadly, he wasn't here to see the powerhouse team of the 2000s that won five straight Eastern Division titles and a World Series in 2008. He would have loved that team, especially Chase Utley, who was the kind of hard-nosed throwback player my grandfather remembered from his days on the Southwest Philly sandlots.

I had a different perspective on that team because, unlike in 1980, I wasn't around it as much. By 2008, I was working at NFL Films and doing TV and radio, so I was fully immersed in football. I watched those Phillies as a fan, taking in the games from Ashburn Alley. When Brad Lidge threw that last unhittable slider past Tampa Bay's Eric Hinske to close out Game 5 of the World Series, I was actually able to cheer, something I could never do in the press box.

And it felt *so* good.

8

March Madness, Indeed

IN MY FIFTY YEARS OF JOURNALISM, I've walked out on only one assignment. It was on March 30, 1981.

It should have been a great day. The NCAA basketball championship game was scheduled for that night in Philadelphia. The Spectrum was dressed for the occasion, with red, white, and blue banners rimming the court.

North Carolina fans and Indiana fans were having impromptu pep rallies on street corners in Center City. It was fun, it was colorful, it was joyous.

Then, at 2:27 P.M., President Ronald Reagan was shot.

On the streets, people overheard other people talking. What did you say? The president was shot? Are you sure?

It wasn't like today, when everyone has a cell phone and Internet connection. People ran to their cars to turn on the radio. In offices, people gathered around the TV.

"Please no," we thought, "not again."

The basketball game that once seemed so important now felt insignificant. I was on my way to the Spectrum when I heard the news. I knew there would be a press conference with the NCAA brass and representatives of the two schools.

I never considered the possibility that they would play the game that night. It was unthinkable. President Reagan was in emergency surgery, fighting for his life. This was a time for prayer and reflection, not basketball. In my mind, there were only two choices: Postpone the game or cancel it altogether.

Playing the game tonight as scheduled? They wouldn't do that. They *couldn't* do that.

But they did.

I was at the Spectrum most of the afternoon, waiting for the NCAA to decide what to do. Again, I assumed it was a choice between postponing the game or canceling it. My guess was they would postpone it, but I would not have objected if they had canceled.

The nation was reeling. Was it really that important to find out which college had the best basketball team?

Mike Lupica, a sports columnist for the *New York Daily News*, said he had heard the game might still go on. He said the NCAA officials were waiting for updates on the president's condition. If he survived the surgery, Lupica said, we would have tip-off shortly after 8 P.M.

Lupica believed, as I did, that it was a wrong-headed decision. I didn't think it could happen. He said, "That's not what I'm hearing."

We walked the Spectrum halls, talking to everyone with an NCAA badge. It was 7 P.M., and they still were holding off on making a decision. They were monitoring the news from Washington. If Reagan died, they likely would have postponed the game, but if he was still alive in an hour, they were going to play.

"Mike, they can't do this," I insisted.

"They're doing it," he said.

It had been announced that the Academy Awards ceremony in Los Angeles was being postponed. Even the people in the movie industry—people we mock for being shallow and narcissistic—had enough sense to put their red-carpet gala on hold out of respect for the president.

How could these university leaders—educators, presumably—go ahead and play a basketball game?

"Is it just about the money?" I asked.

"What do you think?" Lupica replied.

Shortly before 8 P.M., Wayne Duke, the chairman of the NCAA basketball committee, announced the game would go on. There was a murmur of disapproval in the press room. Duke picked up on it immediately.

He said all the reports on the president were positive, and he was out of danger. He explained it would be very difficult—and costly—to push the game back even one day. Changing all those hotel and flight reservations would be a hardship for the fans.

Yes, but the president had been shot. Wasn't that more important?

Apparently not, because right after Duke finished his press conference, the Indiana and North Carolina players were on the court, going through layup drills. The bands were playing, the cheerleaders were cheering, and the TV networks were smiling because they had their big game. March Madness, indeed.

What would have happened if thirty minutes later, with the game underway, the president had taken a turn for the worse? What if he died? Given what we now know about his injuries, it easily could have happened. What then? Would they have stopped the game? If so, when would they have resumed? Would they have continued playing? Would anyone care? Going ahead with the game made no sense to me.

I took my seat in the press box, but I had no interest in the game. The teams were running up and down the floor; Indiana's Isiah Thomas was putting on a show; Bobby Knight, the bullying tyrant who coached the Hoosiers, was screaming at the officials; and I wasn't jotting down a single note.

Several other writers must have felt the same, because we left our seats and went into the stands to find the people in charge and ask why this game was even happening.

We found Dr. John Ryan, the Indiana University president, at halftime. He was in the Hoosiers' cheering section behind the band. We shouted our questions over the ear-splitting music. He shouted back. He said he was fine with the decision to play. He said this was not like when President Kennedy was shot in 1963.

"Mr. Kennedy was killed," Ryan said.

I went back to the press box and called my sports editor, Mike Rathet.

"Mike, I can't do this," I said.

"What do you mean?"

"I can't cover this game," I said. "I can't even bear to watch it. I want to leave."

"It's the national championship game," he said, "and it's being played here."

"I don't care," I said. "I think it's a disgrace they're playing after what happened today."

"You feel that strongly about it?" he asked.

"Yes, I do," I replied.

"OK, come back to the office and write a column about it," he said. "Tell people how you feel. We have plenty of other guys there to write about the game."

"You're OK with that?" I asked.

"You're a columnist, you're supposed to have opinions," he said. "I'm fine with it."

So, I went back to the *Daily News*, found a quiet desk in the corner, and wrote my column. I could see the game on a TV across the newsroom, but I didn't bother to check the score. I didn't care.

I thought about what was happening in the country. I thought about the child murders in Atlanta that had claimed twenty-eight victims over the past year. It became a national story, and a Philadelphia grandmother came up with idea of people wearing green ribbons to show their support for the heartbroken families. It was a nice gesture, but ultimately, we had to do more.

All those thoughts were swirling around in my head when I wrote this:

> We sat numbly in front of our color TVs watching the Apocalypse of American politics. We saw a sidewalk littered with bodies; we saw men waving submachine guns and we shuddered at the awful memories of Dallas, 1963, and Los Angeles, 1968. Surely, it was a night to bow our heads, hold hands and try to pull this sick society together before it is too late.
>
> Ah, but they cranked up the Great Fun-and-Games Machine anyway. Just moments after they showed us James S. Brady bleeding on the street, they brought the Indiana and North Carolina basketball teams dribbling onto our TV screens. The show, after all, must go on. This was the NCAA championship game and that, you understand, is big stuff. A bullet had just missed the President's heart. The nation's capital was spinning on its edge. But so what? We had to find out how Bobby Knight would defend against Carolina's Al Wood.[1]

I had never felt so conflicted about covering a sports event. I didn't like feeling that way, but I couldn't help it. I was pleased the NCAA men's final was being played in Philadelphia. I had covered a few Final Fours in other cities, but this was the first time I would see it play out in my hometown. It was great for the city, with all the visitors, all the parties, and all the excitement.

But the shooting of President Reagan and the NCAA's shameless behavior afterward pushed me over the edge. To stay and write about it would have made me complicit in something I believed was a huge mistake. I was glad Rathet allowed me to leave and return to the office. As I left the Spectrum, I could hear the cheers behind me. I could still hear them when I sat down to write:

> The NCAA acknowledged the events of the day. It moved the starting time back fifteen minutes and added a special pre-game prayer. The NBC-TV folks made sure they had a close up of a tearful Carolina cheerleader. They made every attempt to tell you how sorry they were. Then the national anthem ended and the 18,276 fans cheered and the game began. Within a minute, the bands were blaring, the fans were hurling profanities at the officials and ten kids in sneakers went about settling an issue that should have mattered to no one.
>
> They say sports are a reflection of our society and, sadly, that is true. What we learned about ourselves last night is that Isiah Thomas is a more compelling prime time story than a President with a tube in his lungs. I guess that's what our country has come to. You have to kill the President before they lock up the basketballs and turn off the gymnasium lights. Put a bullet in his chest and we can get by with a moment of silence.[2]

For the most part, the basketball writers focused on the game and let columnists like me deal with the bigger picture. Opinions were split. Some believed that the game should go on. "Why cheat the kids?" they said. Others shared my feeling that the NCAA showed very poor judgment in playing the game.

And this wasn't about the kids, by the way. It was about the money. It is *always* about the money.

When I think back on that night, the thing I'll remember is walking down the Spectrum hallway, hearing the cheers behind me and thinking, "This is so wrong."

9

The Peddler's Son

 I MET MICHAEL NOURI on the set of *Invincible*. Nouri, an actor best known as the romantic lead in *Flashdance*, was cast as Leonard Tose in the 2006 film about Vince Papale.

"They tell me you knew Leonard Tose," Nouri said.

"I wrote about him for thirty years," I replied.

"So, you knew him pretty well," the actor said.

"I'm not sure anyone really knew Leonard Tose," I said.

Nouri said if he was going to play Tose, he wanted to get it right. Actors like to research their roles, especially when they are portraying a real person.

Mark Wahlberg, who played Papale in the film, practically moved in with Vince's family. Greg Kinnear, who played Dick Vermeil, spent time in Kansas City, following Vermeil around while he coached the Chiefs. It obviously helped, because both Wahlberg and Kinnear did superb work in the film.

Tose died in 2003, one year before *Invincible* went into production, so Nouri had to piece together his character by talking to people who were around the team in those years. I was one of those people.

We found a shady spot in the Franklin Field bleachers and talked for an hour. We talked about Tose's sixteen years as owner of the Eagles. We talked about his lifestyle, his marriages, his drinking, his gambling, his chain smoking, his temper, and also his generosity. Nouri was taking notes and shaking his head.

"We should be making a movie about *this* guy," Nouri said.

"No one would believe it," I said.

Over the years, I wrote about his good deeds (which were numerous) and his misdeeds (which were legendary), but I couldn't say I knew him. If you talked to his ex-wives—there were four of them—they didn't really know him either. Even Jim Murray, who was his closest friend as well as the Eagles' general manager, called him an enigma.

At the time, Doctor Pepper had a jingle: "Doctor Pepper . . . so misunderstood." That was Murray's nickname for Tose—Doctor Pepper. Murray felt that people saw the public Tose—flashy clothes, flashy women, flashy everything—but they didn't see his many acts of kindness.

For years, they were inseparable—Murray was Sancho Panza to Tose's Don Quixote—yet when Tose abruptly fired him in 1983, Murray never saw it coming. He said, "It was like being dropped from the top of the Empire State building without a bungee cord." Yet Murray loved Tose to the very end.

"He hurt me deep, but he loved me deep," Murray said. "I never doubted that."

Tose was mercurial, which was reflected in our relationship. We got along fine at times, but at other times, he would call me at home to curse me out for something I had written. Those calls always started the same way: "How the hell can you write that?" It was never, "Hello," and there was never a "Goodbye." He would slam the phone down, sometimes in mid-sentence.

We didn't speak for five years after I ripped him for almost moving the Eagles to Arizona, but after we patched things up, he called me almost every day. At the time, he was living alone in a Center City hotel room. He needed someone to talk to, someone who could reminisce about the good old days when he owned the Eagles. Back then, he was a Gatsby-like figure riding in a chauffeur-driven Rolls Royce, peeling off $100 bills for maître d's and bellboys. At the end, those memories were all he had left.

He talked about hanging out with Frank Sinatra and Don Rickles. He talked about the parties in Beverly Hills and the vacations in Acapulco, where he chartered a yacht and paid for a private fireworks show. He talked about inviting Dick and Carol Vermeil to join him in Mexico and hiring a mariachi band to greet them at the airport. He loved those stories.

But most of all, he enjoyed talking about the big wins over Dallas and how much fun he had walking into Old Original Bookbinder's the next day with everyone patting him on the back.

"Remember that?" he would say wistfully.

But Tose lost everything to gambling. He lost his Villanova mansion in a sheriff's sale—on his eighty-first birthday, no less. He squandered his entire fortune—an estimated $50 million—and he was forced to sell the thing he loved most, the Eagles. In the end, he was flat broke.

Vermeil, the coach he brought to Philadelphia, found him a place to live and gave him enough money to keep going. Vermeil never wanted anyone to know, but it is hard to keep a secret like that. The word got out, which Vermeil regretted. Tose had lost everything at that point except his dignity, and Vermeil did all he could to preserve that. He insisted this wasn't charity. It was an old friend repaying a debt.

"Leonard gave me more than I ever gave him," Vermeil said. "He gave me a chance to coach in the National Football League. Everything I have, I owe to him."

It is rare to find that kind of loyalty, especially in professional sports, but Vermeil is a rare individual. The relationship he had with Tose went far deeper than owner and coach. I always believed that Tose saw Vermeil as the son he never had.

Vermeil believed that too. That's why when he came off the field after beating the Giants to clinch a playoff spot in 1978, he wept when he saw Tose in the locker room. He hugged the owner and said, "That was for you."

Tose joked about Vermeil getting tearstains on his Oleg Cassini tie, but he cherished that moment. You could see it in his eyes. They were an odd couple—the laser-focused young coach and the roguish playboy—but their partnership brought winning football back to Philadelphia.

I'll always remember the sight of Tose at the victory party following the NFC Championship win over the Cowboys. He had taken over the entire second floor at Bookbinder's. Patti LaBelle was singing, the Dom Perignon was flowing, and Tose was sitting with his arm around Caroline, the stunning brunette he had married one month earlier. He was on top of the world.

"You think this is good?" he said. "Wait 'til you see the party we have in New Orleans."

Two weeks later, Tose was slumped on a chair in the losing locker room at Super Bowl XV. He was so sure the Eagles would win that game and bring home the championship, but they were hammered by Oakland, 27–10. They turned the ball over on their first possession, fell behind immediately, and never recovered. It was the worst game they played all season, and they played it at the worst possible time.

After the game, Tose sat with his head down, a Marlboro Light cupped in his manicured fingers. A small group of writers surrounded him, but no one knew what to say. Tose looked up when I joined the circle. His eyes were bloodshot and lifeless.

"What the hell happened?" he asked. "We looked unbeatable against Dallas. What the hell happened?"

Needless to say, there was no party in New Orleans.

The loss took a lot out of everyone, including Vermeil, who stepped down as coach two years later, but it devastated Tose. He had flown eight hundred friends and associates to New Orleans for the game. He gave them tickets, paid for their hotels, and hired a fleet of limousines to shuttle them from party to party. He had everyone from Don Rickles to Caroline's hairdresser to Philadelphia's Cardinal John Krol there, all on his tab.

On Super Bowl Sunday, the cardinal told Tose he prayed for an Eagles victory. Tose was elated.

"How can we lose?" he said. "We have Cardinal Krol."

Late in the game, with the Eagles losing, Tose turned to the cardinal, who was seated behind him in the owner's box.

"I thought God answers our prayers," Tose said.

"God does answer our prayers," the cardinal replied, "but sometimes the answer is no."

Tose dropped a bundle in New Orleans that week, so it was a crushing blow to lose to the Raiders. Some people blamed Vermeil for working the team too hard while the Raiders partied in the French Quarter. I never believed that. Hard work is what got the Eagles there. It would have been foolish to change.

I think the team put everything it had, physically and emotionally, into beating the Cowboys and didn't have anything left for the Super Bowl. I know it sounds crazy—the Super Bowl, a letdown?—but I think that's what happened to the Eagles. Vermeil's team played a lot on emotion, and there just wasn't enough left in the tank after the Dallas game.

On the flight home, Tose drank his Scotch and stared out the window. It wasn't long before rumors started coming out of Atlantic City about Tose and his gambling. We all knew Tose was a player—and not a very good one—so tales of him losing money in the casinos was nothing new, but these reports were different. He was losing crazy amounts of money, millions of dollars in a single night.

The casinos were setting him up at his own blackjack table with his own dealer. He would play seven hands at a time, $10,000 on each hand, which meant he could lose $70,000 on the turn of a single card. Two waitresses were assigned to the table with orders to keep his glass full. Some nights, Tose was so drunk that he needed help to get to the men's room. Yet all the while, he kept signing markers for more and more credit.

"This wasn't gambling, it was robbery," said Sam Procopio, who worked in the Eagles' front office and often accompanied Tose to Atlantic City. "They might as well have put a gun to his head. We tried to stop him—me, Jimmy Murray, Caroline—but it was no use. He shoved us all away."[1]

Tose was an alcoholic and a gambling addict, a deadly combination. Years later, he sued the casinos, claiming they had taken advantage of him by overserving him and extending obscene lines of credit.

"It was like watching a man skydive without a parachute," Procopio said.[2]

During the trial, Tose presented a marker trail of ten IOUs written only minutes apart for a total of $400,000. His signature was a drunken scrawl. He lost more than $14.5 million at the Sands. He lost another $20 million at Resorts International. The worst part, Tose said, was that he did not remember any of it.

"The only reason I stopped," he said, "was because I ran out of money."

In 1982, the NFL players went on strike, and the league shut down for eight weeks. Other club owners were able to weather it, but Tose needed that revenue to cover his losses. The strike was settled, and the players came back to finish the season, but Tose was in a hole he could not escape. The strain was felt throughout the organization, and it contributed to Vermeil's emotional collapse at the end of the year.

"Leonard was so depressed, he wasn't himself," Vermeil said. "He always had a great relationship with our players, but that changed [during the strike]. The first game back, we lost to Cincinnati. He came in the locker room and ripped into the team. He told them to go back on strike. We were never the same after that."

"I could feel the fabric of the team coming apart," said tight end John Spagnola. "I felt so sorry for Dick because he was caught in the middle. We could all see the emotional toll it was taking on him."[3]

Vermeil was exhausted after seven years of working around the clock. Assistant coaches Marion Campbell and Sid Gillman urged him to ease up and not push so hard, but Vermeil couldn't do it. He still was the kid in the Owl Garage, his sleeves rolled up, working under the hood of a sputtering football team and trying to fix what was wrong.

There also was the matter of his players, who had become like sons to him, especially the dozen or so who were with him from the beginning. He worked them so hard day after day, and surely he got the very best out of them, but the grind had taken a toll on them as well. They were aging and breaking down. He knew he should cut them loose and move on, but the thought of calling a Wilbert Montgomery or a Harold Carmichael into his office and saying goodbye tore him to pieces.

"Dick always believed work was the answer," Jim Murray said. "He thought if you worked hard enough, you could solve everything. He often said there is no limit to human energy, and he really believed that. He wanted to save everybody—the players, Leonard, the fans, the organization, the city—and he put it all on his shoulders. In the end, it was too much, even for him."[4]

He lived on coffee and energy bars. The muscles in his neck grew so tense that he could barely turn his head. His emotions, always close to the surface, became cause for concern. He would tear up in the middle of a team meeting. He would be drawing up a play on the blackboard, and, suddenly, his voice would crack, and tears would roll down his cheeks.

"Guys would be looking at each other, like, 'What's going on?'" tackle Stan Walters recalled. "We had all seen Dick get emotional, but usually it was after a big game, something like that. Now it was like coming out of nowhere and all the time."

Monsignor John Sharkey, the team's chaplain, saw what was going on, and, like everyone else, he grew concerned. He gave Vermeil a book about burnout, a condition first identified by psychologist Herbert Freudenberger as placing "the sufferer in a hellish place where he or she always feels like they are chasing the next task or they haven't done enough."[5]

Vermeil read it and realized that everything in the book, especially the hellish part, applied to him. At the urging of his wife, Carol, and their three children, he stepped down as coach after the final game of the '82 season. To the fans, the announcement was sudden and shocking. To those closer to the situation, it was not. We had all seen it coming.

"I'm just burned out," he said, introducing the term to the sports world. "I'm my own worst enemy. I'm far too intense and far too emotional. I hope my coaches and players understand where I'm coming from."

Tose sat nearby, wiping away tears as Vermeil spoke. His own depression was now deeper than ever. The young coach he had discovered, the one he sweet-talked into coming to Philadelphia, the one who rebuilt his team and led it to a Super Bowl, the one he loved like a son was leaving. The downward spiral of Tose's life only accelerated. The trips to Atlantic City became more frequent and more destructive.

Jack Edelstein was a fixture around the team, a jokester who served as statistician on the radio broadcasts. During the good years, he and Tose would party for weeks at a time, but Edelstein saw the path Tose was on and, like many others, tried to pull him back.

"No one could keep Lenny from going out," Edelstein said. "What I tried to do was steer him away from the casinos. One night I said, 'Why don't we go to a movie?' He said, 'There are no chips at the movies.' I hated the whole casino scene. People were fawning all over him, treating him like a movie star when all they wanted was his money. He kept throwing in more chips. I'm like, 'Lenny, what are you doing?'

"Jimmy [Murray] brought in this doctor who specialized in helping people with a gambling addiction. He shows up, and Lenny is sitting here, smoking a cigarette and drinking a Scotch. Lenny says, 'Who are you?' The doctor says, 'I'm here to talk about your gambling.' Lenny says, 'I beat smoking and drinking, what makes you think I can't beat gambling?' He's saying this while he is smoking a cigarette and drinking a Scotch. The doctor left, and we never saw him again.

"Lenny and I had great times together," Edelstein said, "but by the end, I was begging off. I made up excuses why I couldn't go out with him. I couldn't stand watching him do this to himself. Night after night, losing so much money, losing everything, it broke my heart. Lenny is a great guy, so generous, always reaching in his pocket to help people, but he was his own worst enemy."[6]

Campbell succeeded Vermeil as head coach, and the team fell apart. The final week of the 1984 season, the Eagles were playing out the string. They had one more game left, a "who cares?" trip to Atlanta, and that would be the end of the season.

At 2 A.M. on Tuesday, my phone rang. I was half asleep, but I recognized the voice of Caesar Alsop, the night sports editor.

"Did you hear anything about the Eagles moving to Arizona?" he asked.

"What?" I said, now fully awake.

"The story just moved on the wire," he said. "A reporter in Phoenix broke it."

He read the story over the phone. A wealthy real-estate developer named James Monaghan was in negotiations to become a partner with Tose in owning the Eagles. The agreement called for the team, founded in Philadelphia in 1933, to move to Arizona. The story said the deal was almost complete, which meant that Sunday's game would likely be their last as the Philadelphia Eagles.

I didn't have a clue any of this was going on. I had never heard of James Monaghan. We knew Tose was in trouble, but moving the team to Arizona? I would have said it couldn't happen, but a few years earlier, we saw another beloved franchise, the Colts, move from Baltimore to Indianapolis. All it takes is a desperate owner and a U-Haul.

We went into scramble mode, waking people up and asking them about the report. Within a few hours, we pieced together a story that said a move was in the works. Arizona senator Dennis DeConcini said, "I have a very reliable source who says that this is going to happen."

This was no rumor—this was real.

For the next two days, we chased after Tose and his daughter, Susan Fletcher, who took control of the front office with the firing of Murray. They hustled past the reporters and TV cameras, with security guards clearing a path. Fans protested outside the gates. Death threats were phoned into the team's offices.

Meanwhile, Mayor Wilson Goode and NFL commissioner Pete Rozelle did everything but pile sandbags around the Vet to keep the Eagles from leaving town. Negotiations went on between Tose, Fletcher, and Goode to work out a deal to keep the Eagles in Philadelphia.

On Saturday night, Tose and Goode held a press conference to announce that a deal had been struck. It involved a restructuring of the stadium lease and a promise to build fifty skyboxes, with the team receiving 100 percent of that revenue. It was enough for Tose to shelve the plans of relocating.

Tose pulled the rug out from under Monaghan, but the Philly fans didn't care about that. Their team wasn't going anywhere, and that's all that mattered. I was still angry, however, and after the game—which the Eagles lost, 26–10—I went back to my hotel room and wrote a scathing column.

Philadelphia fans might be opinionated. They might be lacking in certain social graces, but they aren't stupid and they sure know right from wrong. Nothing makes them madder than some dandy in a three-piece suit patting them on the head, telling them how nice they are, then turning around and selling them out for a fast buck. That's what Leonard Tose did last week and no matter how many press conferences he calls, no matter how many times he crosses his heart and says it will never happen again, he will be written off as a hustler and not a very skillful one at that.

It is a matter of record, Eagles fans will put up with a lot. They will put up with bad drafts, lousy coaches and rotten weather. Most years they put up with all three at once. They grumble but they hang on because pro football is something they grew up with in their laps. They will put up with ticket price increases and parking increases and security guards patting them down for pocket flasks, but they won't put up with a man who rolls down his limousine window to spit in their faces.[7]

Two days later, Rozelle summoned Tose and Fletcher to New York for a meeting with the other owners. They would discuss what to do about this embarrassment in Philadelphia. Was the commissioner going to ask the other owners to float Tose a loan so he could pay off his debts? Or would they pass a motion to force him out?

A large contingent of Philadelphia media came to New York to cover the emergency session. We stood in the lobby of the Waldorf Astoria, watching the owners come through the revolving doors. They were stone-faced and silent as they filed past us on their way to the meeting room.

The hotel opened a room off the lobby to serve as a waiting area. There weren't enough chairs, so some of us sat on the floor. Paul Domowitch of the *Daily News* and I made a lunch run to the Stage Deli and came back with enough pastrami and corned beef to ease the pain of the long wait. After six hours, the owners emerged. Most were hustling to catch a flight home. They referred all questions to Rozelle.

The commissioner met with the press in a conference room down the hall. Tose stood next to Rozelle at the podium. Rozelle said he had appointed a committee to explore ways to refinance the Eagles and get the owner out of debt. He said the committee had forty-five days to study the matter and draw up a proposal. The commissioner assured everyone the Eagles would remain in Philadelphia. He also said Tose would be in charge, at least for the time being.

Rozelle and Tose did their best to make it sound like this was just another day at the office. No rancor, no outrage, just a lot of football guys talking shop. They convinced no one. OK, so maybe no one threw an ashtray at Tose, but no one was offering a vote of confidence either. We wrote down the quotes because that's why we were there, but we knew it was a lot of empty words.

In the next day's *Daily News*, I wrote:

> Tose goes before the NFL, IOUs sticking out of his pockets like chewing gum wrappers, and the commissioner reports, "No one was mad." Well, someone should have been mad. Tose and daughter Susan Fletcher have fumbled the ball in a very big and very public way.
>
> The Philadelphia Eagles are not exactly a run-down commodity. This is a blue-chip franchise with 50,000 plus season tickets and TV millions falling like snowflakes through the skylight. Tose took it over in 1969 and while the league enjoyed its most profitable decade and the Eagles went to the Super Bowl, the man in charge managed to lose his ruffled shirt and cuff links.[8]

We knew it was only a matter of time before Tose was forced to sell the team. He swore it would never come to that, but it was inevitable. Three months later came the announcement: Tose was selling the Eagles to a Florida car dealer named Norman Braman. The price was $65 million, a record amount for a sports franchise at the time.

Tose claimed that after his personal obligations were settled and taxes were paid, he would walk away with $10 million. For most people, that would have been enough to live on for the rest of their lives, but he went through it in less than five years. He left most of it on the blackjack tables in Atlantic City.

Braman vowed to keep the Eagles in Philadelphia. I'm sure it was part of the agreement he made with the other club owners when they approved the sale. They didn't want to lose the Philadelphia market, with its rabid fan base and monster TV ratings.

After the sale, the pundits weighed in on Tose and his legacy. Most of them cut Tose some slack, saying that in the end he did the right thing and kept the Eagles in Philadelphia. They said Tose could have sold a portion of the team, paid off his debts, and still remained majority owner if he had agreed to move the franchise. The fact that he didn't do it was somehow noble in their eyes.

I didn't think there was anything noble in the way Tose conducted himself. I thought it was shameful the way he threated the fans and shook down city hall. I wrote a piece that wasn't at all sympathetic:

> Like all sports figures, Tose hoped when the time came he would step down a hero. He tried to salvage some respect yesterday when he spoke of cutting the deal that will keep the Eagles in Philadelphia. Of course, no one ever thought about taking the Eagles away until he tried it three months ago.
>
> Like it or not, Leonard, that's your legacy. You'll be remembered not as the owner who took the Eagles to the Super Bowl but as the guy who tried to swipe this city's football team and got caught. It's not much, but it's what you deserve.[9]

The editor said I took this story personally. I suppose I did, but I felt no need to apologize. I was angry. I was a Philly kid who had grown up on the wooden benches at Franklin Field, surrounded by good people who saw the Eagles as family, but to Tose, the team was just another poker chip.

Early the next morning, my phone rang. It was Ed Wisneski, the Eagles' publicity director.

"Mr. Tose will be calling you," Wisneski said. "He's really upset about what you wrote."

I looked at the clock. It wasn't even 9 A.M. Tose must have grabbed the first *Daily News* that rolled off the presses. I had no sooner hung up from talking to Wisneski than the phone rang again. I knew who it was. Once again, he skipped the formality of "Hello."

"You son of a bitch," Tose said.

From there, the now-former owner of the Eagles launched into a profane rant about what a terrible person I was. After several minutes of yelling, Tose said, "If you ever see me coming, you'd better get the f—k outta the way."

He slammed the phone down, and we didn't speak for five years. I occasionally saw him at functions around town. He would glare at me and keep walking. We took the same elevator to Carmichael's retirement party. I nodded hello. Tose looked right through me.

In 1990, Ron Jaworski hosted a ten-year reunion of the NFC championship team at his South Jersey golf club. It was a private affair, but he invited me, which I appreciated. I knew Tose would be there, but I thought he would ignore me, as he had done before. This time, however, he was walking toward me.

I thought he was about to tell me to leave, but he didn't. Instead, he extended his hand. He said he wanted to bury the bitterness he had felt at the time of the sale. It wasn't going to change anything at this point, he said. He was tired of looking back and tired of grudges.

"I don't even remember what you wrote, it was so long ago," he said. "You called me a lot of names. . . ."

"Actually, you called *me* a lot of names," I said.

"Yeah, I was pissed off," he said, "but I remember you wrote a lot of nice things about me too, so it all evens out, I guess."

We shook hands, and that was that. We put the ugliness behind us and spent the rest of the night talking about the good times. There were plenty of those.

I reminded Tose about the time we were riding Amtrak to Washington for a Redskins game. He was in the club car with Jimmy Murray, Carol Vermeil, and their families. The media members were riding in coach. Tose sent Murray to find us and bring us to the club car. He had paid off the conductor so we could ride first class.

"Yeah and you wouldn't do it," Tose said.

"I couldn't do it," I said. "I couldn't have you paying my train fare."

"The other guys didn't have a problem with it," Tose said, referring to the media members who joined him in the club car. "It isn't like I was trying to bribe you, for Christ's sake. It was just a train ride."

"I wouldn't have felt right about it," I said.

"You were a real pain in the ass at times," Tose said.

"I'm a reporter, I'm supposed to be a pain in the ass," I said.

We both laughed.

I'm sure it sounds odd, the two of us talking like old friends after all the nasty stuff that had passed between us. The columns I wrote about him were very tough, and some people considered them vicious. He was angry and let me know it. But this is where the "complicated" part of Tose comes in.

Through it all, I never forgot his many charitable acts and his willingness to help people in need. That was the other side of the man, and I saw it firsthand. He broke Murray's heart when he fired him, but years later when Tose sued the casinos, who was with him every day in the courtroom? Jimmy Murray.

If you were in Tose's circle—and I was on the outer edge of it—you learned to roll with the punches.

He had a ferocious temper, and we all experienced it—Murray, Caroline, me, even Vermeil. But we all saw him do great things for other people. This is the stuff that had Nouri, the actor playing Tose, shaking his head that day at Franklin Field.

Movies are a lot easier to cast when you have good guys and bad guys. It is harder when the characters don't fit neatly into one box or the other. Tose was not a one-box kind of guy. As general manager, Murray spent as much time managing the owner as he did managing the football team. He did his best to put the good Tose on display and keep the other Tose out of sight. But when Tose was good, he was very good.

One afternoon, I was watching practice, and Tose came over with a copy of the *Bulletin*. He had read a story that said Philadelphia's public schools were cutting funding for extracurricular activities and that one of the things being cut was high school football. Tose said it was a terrible thing; kids who might have a shot at a college scholarship now were out of luck.

"Somebody ought to do something," he said.

He wrote a check for $79,000, and the Public League had a football season.

Another time, he saw a story about a young girl in North Philadelphia, a gifted pianist who was unable to get to her music lessons because of a transit strike. Tose ripped the story out of the paper, handed it to Murray, and said, "Take care of this." That afternoon, a new Steinway piano was delivered to the family's rowhome.

He bought bulletproof vests for the Philadelphia Police. He created a City All-Star football game to showcase the area's top high school players. For all the money he threw away on gambling, high living, and alimony, Tose also did a lot of good.

"He was excessive in many things," Murray said, "but I think the big thing he was excessive in was his generosity."

But as a newspaper columnist, what do you say when the excesses threaten to wreck a public trust like the Eagles? You can't look the other way. You have to be honest, and that's what I tried to be. He saw it as a vendetta, me against him. He blamed me for turning the fans against him. I told him he did that to himself.

In the 1970s, I wrote many stories about his generosity, especially his role in creating the Eagles Fly for Leukemia charity. It started with a fundraising effort to pay for the treatment of Kim Hill, the daughter of tight end Fred Hill. Tose pledged $1 million, and with Murray heading up the campaign, the Eagles raised enough money to build a new wing for Children's Hospital of Philadelphia.

It didn't stop there. Murray enlisted the support of Ray Kroc, the chairman of McDonald's, to build the first Ronald McDonald House in West Philadelphia. It was a home away from home for families with children undergoing treatment for leukemia. That one house on Walnut Street grew into more than three hundred houses in thirty-five countries around the world.

Murray drew up the blueprint, but Tose wrote the checks. That's part of his legacy too. It is two sides of the same story, really. He was always giving money away—sometimes in good ways, other times bad. He saw it too, but he never thought it would destroy him as it did.

"I made every mistake a person can make," he said. "I'm very disappointed in myself. I should've known better."

At NFL Films, we did a thirty-minute special on Tose. I worked on the show with fellow producer Chris Barlow. Tose agreed to an on-camera interview with Steve Sabol. Tose had known Sabol for years and trusted him. That connection was important, because obviously we would be covering some very sensitive ground. There is no easy way to ask a man to go on TV and talk about how he screwed up his life.

At this point, Tose had lost everything. He was living in the Warwick Hotel and getting by on Social Security and money from Vermeil, yet he continued to carry himself like Leonard Tose. He walked around Rittenhouse Square in expensive suits and monogrammed shirts. He still went to Le Bec-Fin, the elegant French restaurant on Walnut Street, and sent bottles of champagne to diners at other tables.

It was all about keeping up appearances, even if he was eating tuna sandwiches the rest of the week.

I sat off to the side, watching the interview. Tose was surprisingly honest, admitting to his mistakes and what he termed "sheer stupidity." Asked why he did it, he said he believed the good times would never end. He had millions of dollars and millions of friends. He was Leonard Tose.

When friends tried to slow him down, he said, he refused to listen. When he lost hundreds of thousands of dollars at the blackjack table, he still tipped the dealer at the end of the night. Some people compared it to driving off a cliff. Give him this much: If he drove off a cliff, at least he was driving a Rolls Royce.

Sabol said, "If I gave you a million dollars right now, what would you do with it?"

You could have heard a pin drop in the room. Everyone wanted to hear his answer.

"I'd probably go to Atlantic City," Tose replied.

He smiled slightly, but sadly. "It's the truth," he said.

After the interview, Tose and I sat together while the crew broke down the set. He asked how he did. I told him he did very well. He didn't duck a single question. He didn't make excuses. He said the casinos took advantage of him—which they clearly did—but he accepted the ultimate responsibility.

"I don't want sympathy," he said. "I don't want people saying, 'Poor Leonard.' That's bullshit. I had a helluva ride."

We talked about November 1978, when he was in a Houston hospital after open-heart surgery, listening to the Eagles-Giants game on the radio. That was the day Herman Edwards scooped up a Joe Pisarcik fumble and scored the winning touchdown. We know it as "the Miracle of the Meadowlands," but the real miracle is that Tose's heart didn't explode at that moment.

Murray called Tose from a pay phone in the visitor's locker room. Murray handed the phone to Vermeil, who shouted, "What did that do to your new valve?" The players took turns talking to him. Edwards, still giddy from the touchdown, said, "Is this a good time to talk about my contract?" Everyone laughed. It was one of those moments you never forget.

The next day, I flew to Houston to see Tose in the hospital. The nurses didn't want to let me in, but Tose said it was OK. We talked for more than an hour. Tose talked about his father, Mike, a Russian immigrant who settled in Bridgeport, near Norristown.

Mike was a peddler with a pack on his back. He eventually bought a truck, then another and another, until finally he had the largest fleet of trucks on the East Coast. He created a company called Tose Trucking that raked in $20 million a year.

"I wasn't born rich," Tose said. "I broke my ass working with my father and my brother. Yeah, I like nice clothes, I like travel and going first class. What's wrong with that? If I see a bartender working his ass off and I want to tip him $100, what's wrong with that? It's my money. If I can afford it, what's the problem?"

Of course, the problem came years later when he had lost all his money. He found himself broke and alone.

"When Leonard had money, he had a lot of friends," Vermeil said. "When the money was gone, most of the friends were gone."

Sadly, that was true.

After the show aired, Tose began calling me just to chat. He usually started by telling me he had heard from someone who saw the show and liked it. Then he would start talking about something from the past, and I realized that's what this call was about. It was a chance to reconnect and relive the days when he was hanging out with movie stars and taking twenty people to breakfast at Brennan's in New Orleans.

Now he would leave messages for those same people, and they wouldn't call back. He would call someone at the league office, and a secretary would say, "I'm sorry, he's in a meeting." It was that feeling of not being important anymore that hurt him most of all.

"They say a gambler never wants to know what he lost," Tose said. "Now I'm finding out. I lost people I thought were my friends."

So in his final days, Tose wound up talking to me. Who would have predicted that?

In one of our last conversations, Tose talked about a Hollywood producer who wanted to make a movie about his life. He was excited about it, even though he knew it wouldn't be all that flattering. He was OK with that, as long as it put him back in the spotlight.

There was talk that Alec Baldwin would play him in the film. Tose preferred Michael Douglas, but he didn't really care—just as long as the film was made. He was already jotting down ideas for the script.

"Remember when I almost brought the Super Bowl to Philadelphia?" he said. "I had nine owners who were willing to go along with me. I brought the Mummers to the owners' meeting that year. Remember that? I want that in the movie: the Mummers coming into that cocktail party. See the look on Rozelle's face. I laughed my ass off."

The Super Bowl never came to Philadelphia, and the movie idea fizzled on Hollywood's back burner. Like so many things in Tose's life, it ended in disappointment. He was right about one thing, though: It would have been a great movie.

On April 15, 2003, Tose died in his sleep in the hospice wing of St. Agnes Medical Center, less than a mile from where the Vet once stood. Jimmy Murray was there, along with Susan Fletcher and Bill Bergey.

A memorial service was held a few days later. The room was full of familiar faces, including John Fitch, his former limo driver who had stayed loyal to Tose even after the limo was gone. Vermeil delivered the

eulogy. He called Tose "an original piece of work." The mourners nodded and smiled. Yes, those words described him perfectly.

The *New York Times* obituary called Tose "a slim, suave man who
always dressed impeccably."[10]

Tose would have liked that.

My *Daily News* colleague Stan Hochman always had a soft spot for
Tose. When he passed away, Stan wrote, "Remember what you choose,
the weaknesses or the strengths, the reckless gambling or the funding
for the first Ronald McDonald House. Me, I hope Tose is somewhere
peaceful, elegantly dressed, his glass full of top shelf scotch, poured by
a pretty young woman with a genuine smile, sweet music playing in the
background."[11]

Ray's Tavern, my grandfather's bar on Woodland Avenue in Southwest Philadelphia.
(Author's collection)

My grandfather (second from the right) *and the Ray's Tavern bartenders.*
(Author's collection)

Mom and Dad on their wedding day in June 1945.
(Author's collection)

My father (back row, second from the left) *and crew with their B-24 bomber.*
(Author's collection)

Chuck Bednarik and me at Eagles training camp in Hershey, 1957.
(Author's collection)

Flyers president Bill Putnam (left) *with general manager Bud Poile, 1966.*
(Courtesy Comcast Spectacor)

My first job was writing news for the Delaware County Daily Times
in Chester, Pennsylvania.
(Photo by Bert Hodge)

Jack Wilson hired me to cover high school sports for the Philadelphia Bulletin *in 1969. One year later, he promoted me to the Eagles beat.*
(Photo by Maria Gallagher)

Fight night at the Blue Horizon.
(Photo courtesy of J Russell Peltz)

John Carlos (right) *on the medal stand at the 1968 Summer Olympics.*
When he and Tommie Smith raised their gloved fists to protest racial injustice
in America, it was front page news around the world.
(Associated Press)

Eagles coach Charlie Gauer took me inside the game.
(Author's collection)

Tim Rossovich ate glass and set himself on fire when he wasn't playing linebacker for the Eagles.
(Photo by Ed Mahan)

Interviewing NFL commissioner Pete Rozelle at his office in New York City.
(Photo by Mike Maicher)

Flyers owner Ed Snider (right) *toasts a playoff victory with* (from left) *general manager Keith Allen, player personnel director Marcel Pelletier, and Bobby Clarke.*
(Courtesy Comcast Spectacor)

The Flyers' first Stanley Cup parade drew two million fans to Center City.
(Courtesy Comcast Spectacor)

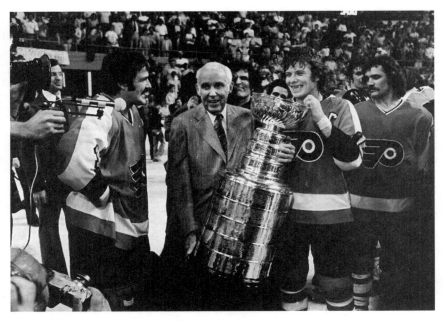

Bernie Parent and Bobby Clarke accept the Stanley Cup
from NHL commissioner Clarence Campbell, 1975.
(Courtesy Comcast Spectacor)

Eagles owner Leonard Tose (left) *with general manager Jim Murray at the 1978 wild-card game in Atlanta.*

(Photo by Ed Mahan)

Coach Dick Vermeil celebrates with wide receiver Harold Carmichael.

(Photo by Ed Mahan)

Eagles Hall of Famer Steve Van Buren (right) *congratulates Wilbert Montgomery for breaking his single season rushing record in 1978.*
(Photo by Ed Mahan)

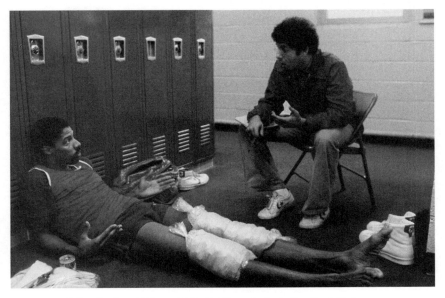

Julius Erving chilling with Daily News *basketball writer Phil Jasner.*
(Ted Spiegel/National Geographic Creative)

Interviewing Pete Rose at his first Phillies spring training, 1979.
(Photo by Mike Maicher)

It was a joy working with the great Stan Hochman
at the Philadelphia Daily News *and WIP Sports Radio.*
(Photo © Brad Nau)

I was writing on an oversized
computer at the 1984 Summer
Olympics in Los Angeles. That
is Daily News *colleague Rich*
Hofmann working behind me.
(Photo by Maria Gallagher)

*Mike Schmidt was the Most Valuable Player when the Phillies
won their first World Series title in 1980.*
(Copyright © The Phillies)

Interviewing Phillies Hall of Famers Mike Schmidt and Rich Ashburn in May 1995.
(Photo by Bob Laramie, *Philadelphia Daily News*)

Celebrating the Dick McCann Award with (left to right) *my daughter, Kathleen; my mother and my father; my wife, Maria; and my son, David.*
(Author's collection)

My boyhood hero Tommy McDonald asked me to be his presenter at the Pro Football Hall of Fame, August 1, 1998.
(Author's collection)

Dick Vermeil and his wife, Carol, at the screening of Vermeil: A Coach for All Seasons.
My co-producer Chris Barlow is on the far right with NFL Films president Steve Sabol.
(Photo by Maria Gallagher)

Hanging out with WIP Sports Radio teammates Ike Reese (left) *and Angelo Cataldi.*
(Photo by Cindy Webster)

*The Prof and R Diddy. Glen Macnow and I have been a
WIP Sports Radio team for almost twenty years.*
(Photo by Maria Gallagher)

The first Eagles Post-Game Live *cast: Michael Barkann* (left) *and Tom Brookshier
join me on the Comcast SportsNet set, October 1997.*
(Courtesy NBC Universal)

Andy Reid enjoys his first win as the Eagles' coach in 1999.

(Photo by Ed Mahan)

The Eagles Post-Game Live crew celebrates Ed Rendell's election as Pennsylvania's governor in 2002.

(Courtesy NBC Universal)

Eagles Post-Game Live was named Best Local TV Show by Philadelphia Magazine *in 2005. Michael Barkann and Vaughn Hebron made my job easy.*

(Courtesy NBC Universal)

Frank Bertucci and I attended the last hockey game played at the Spectrum on April 10, 2009. It was the Philadelphia Phantoms versus the Hershey Bears. These were the same seats we sat in when we saw the first Flyers game on October 19, 1967. The upper deck was empty that night, too.

(Photo © Brad Nau)

On the book tour with the New Eagles Encyclopedia, *2014.*
(Photo by Aaron Hamrick)

Dick Vermeil came to the opening night of Tommy and Me *in August 2018.*
He met with the cast after the show: (left to right) *Simon Kiley, Frank Nardi Jr., Vermeil,*
Tom Teti, Matt Pfeiffer, myself, and director Joe Canuso.
(Photo by Maria Gallagher / Theatre Exile's production of *Tommy and Me* by Ray Didinger,
directed by Joe Canuso, with the set designed by Thom Weaver)

Tommy and Me *played to full houses at the Media Theatre in August 2018.*
(Photo by Maria Gallagher)

*Eagles owner Jeff Lurie answers questions from the audience after
a performance of* Tommy and Me *in August 2019.*
(Philadelphia Eagles/Drew Hallowell)

Eagles Post-Game Live *at Super Bowl LII.* (Left to right) *Michael Barkann,*
Barrett Brooks, a smiling Seth Joyner, and Governor Rendell join me in the celebration.
(Courtesy NBC Universal)

My son, David, and me after Super Bowl LII.
The hug said it all.
(Courtesy NBC Universal)

Thumbs-up at Super Bowl LII.
(Photo by Michael Barkann)

10

Clown Show

I T WAS THE FALL OF 1984, and Mike Rathet, the *Daily News* sports editor, called me into his office. There wasn't a lot happening on the local sports scene. The Phillies were sliding toward irrelevance. The Eagles were listless losers. The Flyers and Sixers looked promising, but in the fall, who cares? Check back when the playoffs start.

Rathet said we needed something new and different to energize the sports section. The *Daily News* is a paper that relies on street sales. It isn't being dropped on thousands of doorsteps. It is a tabloid that has to sell itself every day, so it needs something sexy on the cover. John Felske and Marion Campbell weren't doing it, that's for sure.

"What do you know about wrestling?" Rathet asked.

"You mean like Hulk Hogan and Andre the Giant?" I said.

"It's the hottest thing going," Rathet said, "and we've never written about it."

"That's because it's not a real sport," I said. "It's a clown show."

"Well, it sells out the Spectrum and gets huge ratings on TV," he said.

I could see where this was headed. Rathet wanted me to do a deep dive into the world of professional wrestling. I wanted no part of it. I suggested letting the features department handle it. They wrote about TV and movies and all that make-believe stuff. That's what professional wrestling is—showbiz. In my opinion, it did not belong in the sports section.

Rathet insisted on doing the story in sports. As I feared, he wanted me to write it—and not just one story. He wanted a five-part series that the paper could promote.

He posted the schedule that afternoon, and there it was—Didinger, Wrestling. Stan Hochman saw it and laughed.

"Wrestling?" he said.

"Don't ask," I replied.

So that fall between NFL games, I traveled the wrestling circuit. It was the kind of thing newspapers rarely do anymore. Some papers called it enterprise reporting, and others called it investigative reporting, but it involved lots of time, travel, and money.

Most newspapers today don't have the budget or the space to devote to articles that run thousands of words. In the 1980s, big-city papers used these stories to set themselves apart. The idea was to bring magazine-style journalism to the daily newspaper.

As a writer, it was a sweet deal because you weren't faced with a daily deadline. You could take your time gathering the information and writing the story. If you had to spend a week or two out of the office, you did it. You checked in with the editor now and then just to let him know how it was going. Otherwise, you were on your own.

I did my share of these stories, but they were about real issues, such as minority hiring practices in the NFL and drug testing for Olympic athletes. But professional wrestling? Big John Studd versus Brutus Beefcake? I was supposed to take that seriously?

"Treat it like any other story," Rathet said. "Write what you find."

I quickly learned that the wrestling circuit wasn't anything like the NFL, where every media person needs a credential to get through the door. At most wrestling venues, I drove to the arena and bought a ticket. Once inside, I made my way backstage. If you acted like you belonged there, no one bothered you.

Most nights, I walked right into the dressing room. The wrestlers were usually engaged in friendly conversation. Guys who the fans thought despised each other were shooting the breeze and laughing like two guys in an office.

I remember walking into a dressing room at the Hershey Park Arena and seeing the Iron Sheik with his feet up, reading the *Wall Street Journal*, while Sergeant Slaughter pulled on his camouflage tights. In an hour, they would be tossing each other around the ring, but now, out of public view, they were just two guys getting ready for a gig. They were like Penn and Teller, only bigger.

The only media the wrestlers saw on a regular basis were the TV broadcasters and an occasional stringer for a wrestling magazine. Their faces were familiar. I was a stranger with no connection to the wrestling business, so I was viewed with suspicion.

The wrestlers' first question was usually "What kind of story are you doing?" I explained I was doing a story about the sport's growth and popularity. In 1984, pro wrestling was the number-one sport on cable TV. It outdrew college basketball 3-to-1 on the USA Network, and it clobbered college football on Ted Turner's Atlanta-based superstation WTBS. It was taking in an estimated $250 million a year in the United States alone.

At the time, the three biggest crowds in the Spectrum's history—and four of the top five—were for wrestling. In 1983, a dozen shows brought in 161,768 fans and grossed $1 million.

"Try to name a boxing match that would put that many people in the Spectrum," said Jimmy Binns, chairman of the Pennsylvania State Athletic Commission. "There isn't one. Say what you want about wrestling, it's entertaining. I know some people put it down, but I think the wrestlers put on a helluva show."

There was no question the wrestlers put on a show, but that was the whole point. It was a show, not a competition, and that made interviewing the wrestlers challenging. Some would talk; others would not.

One wrestler, David Schultz, who went by the name of "Doctor D," flew into a rage when I broached the question of whether wrestling was fake. He walked toward me with his fists clenched, saying, "I'll show you how real it is." The look in Schultz's eyes suggested he was not fooling around. Luckily, a security guard stepped in to defuse the situation.

A few months later, Schultz slugged TV reporter John Stossel for asking the same question. Stossel was knocked to the floor twice by Schultz and suffered partial hearing loss. Stossel sued the World Wrestling Federation (WWF) and won a $425,000 settlement. If that guard hadn't intervened that night in Hershey, I'm sure I would have wound up on the floor too.

The other wrestlers were generally cordial, but cautious. They feared getting in trouble with the people who ran the shows, so even if they did agree to talk to me, they were careful about what they said.

There was no players' association for wrestlers, so they could be fired at any time. If they said anything negative about the business or if they dared to suggest the matches were not on the level, there likely would be repercussions. As a result, they usually stuck to the script. I understood.

However, their description of the wrestling life—barnstorming from town to town, sharing rides with other wrestlers, including guys they had just finished slamming into a turnbuckle—was fascinating. I found myself agreeing with Rathet: It was a good story. It wasn't what I expected, but it was interesting on a human level.

SERGEANT SLAUGHTER was a pleasant fellow with a square jaw and a mustache. He was 6'5", with the thick frame of an NFL lineman. He traveled the WWF circuit in a camouflage car. He was a crowd favorite, but it wasn't always that way. He was a villain when he started wrestling, but his career changed one night in Allentown.

"We were taping a TV show," Slaughter said. "This was February of last year. I was scheduled for the next match but the [Iron] Sheik wouldn't leave the ring. He was up there chanting, 'Iran is No. 1.' I got ticked off. The promoter told me I couldn't go on, but I went on anyway.

"I told them to hit the music, and I went out. I told the Sheik, 'Let's go,' so we wrestled, and I won. The fans were chanting, 'U-S-A, U-S-A' the whole time. When I won, the crowd went wild."

The whole thing was scripted, obviously, like everything else on the circuit, but it worked beautifully. The career of Sergeant Slaughter took a screeching U-turn. Instead of putting the Cobra Clutch on good guys like Hogan, Slaughter began pummeling the Iron Sheik and Russian bad guy Nikolai Volkoff, and the fans were chanting his name.

The Sarge became the hottest draw in the WWF. He was so hot that he was stolen away by the rival National Wrestling Alliance (NWA). It was the same script, only with different players. Instead of Nikolai Volkoff, he was tossing around Nikita Koloff, the NWA's token Commie. The fans lapped it up.

"I don't know if anyone has gone from the top of the Most Hated list to the top of the Most Popular list that quickly," Slaughter said, "but I like it better this way. I walk to the ring now, and people shake my hand. They used to spit on me.

"I'm getting calls to do endorsements now. I'm the [TV] spokesman for a fundraising drive to restore the Statue of Liberty. They could've had anybody, but they called me. That would've never happened before. They gave me a great line: 'There is one lady in my life, and her name is Liberty.' I love that."

"So, everything has changed?" I asked.

"Not everything," he said. "I drive around in my camouflage car, and the fans used to tear it up because they hated me. Now they tear it up for souvenirs."

Hulk Hogan was a journeyman wrestler touring the Midwest when he was spotted by Vince McMahon, the czar of the WWF. McMahon saw potential in the 6'8", 310-pound former rock guitarist. He put him in a T-shirt that read "American Made" and matched him with every Iranian, Russian, and hooded assassin in sight. That's how "Hulkamania" was born.

"My phone never stops ringing," Hogan said during a promotional stop in Philadelphia. "The post office needs a separate truck just to deliver my mail. Some of it is fan mail, but a lot of it is from talent scouts in Hollywood. There has never been anything like Hulkamania."

Hogan's popularity reached new heights in March 1984, when he joined forces with Mr. T for a tag-team match with Rowdy Roddy Piper and Paul "Mr. Wonderful" Orndorff at Madison Square Garden. Not only did the match fill the Garden; it attracted thousands more to closed-circuit theater locations around the country. It was an indication that this sweaty slapstick, once thought to have just a cult following, had gone mainstream in a big way.

Hans Schroeder was a twenty-seven-year-old wrestler whose ring name was "the Undertaker." When I met him, he was backstage at an armory in Allentown, holding an ice pack on his knee. He would be climbing into the ring in an hour, his third match in as many nights in three different cities.

"You take a beating in this business," he said. "Look at this. . . ."

He pointed to his scalp.

"Twenty-eight stitches, that's from last week," he said. "I hurt my knee last night. People don't know how tough it is."

The matches are a charade. Punches miss by a mile. The wide-eyed mugging looks like it was lifted from a silent movie.

The promoters decide who will win; it is left up to the wrestlers to work out the choreography. The outcome is predetermined, but that doesn't mean it is not a bruising night's work. The flips, the falls, the body slams, they are all real.

The good guy is known as "the baby face." The bad guy is known as "the heel." Promoters decide who plays which role. As a heel, Schroeder usually got the worst of it.

"I've been hit with bottles," he said. "I've been hit over the head with metal chairs. A woman hit me with her handbag, and she had a brick in it. I got stabbed one time in Louisiana. I was on my way from the ring, and a guy pulled a knife on me. Luckily, I saw him coming, or it could've been worse.

"People spit on you. Little kids and old ladies call you names. You find the weirdest people at wrestling matches. I've wrestled all over the world. The fans in Europe are better behaved. In Germany, they wear tuxedos and evening gowns. Here, it's a tough crowd. They like the blood. They like the mayhem."

Tully Blanchard was another heel working in the Deep South. I caught up with him one night at the Greenville [South Carolina] Coliseum. He was a thirty-year-old former quarterback at West Texas State who had followed his father, Joe, into the wrestling business. Blanchard suffered more injuries in the ring than he did on the football field.

"I had cracked ribs, a compressed fracture in my neck, a cracked vertebra in my back, torn ligaments in my knee," he said. "Stuff that would've put me out for the season [in football], but I had to keep going [in wrestling], because if you don't work, you don't eat."

Blanchard came to the arena that night to tape a television interview with Ricky Steamboat, a popular baby face. The two exchanged insults and then walked away smiling while the announcer said, "You heard it, folks. There's bad blood between these two. You'll want to be there when they meet in Corpus Christi next month."

"You gotta give 'em color," Blanchard said. "These people aren't here to see a sport. This is showtime, baby, honky-tonk, USA.

"I laugh when people say wrestling is fake. When I get thrown out of the ring and fall seven feet to the concrete floor, that's not fake. Until they invent a way to put an air bag on my ass, there is nothing fake about it.

"Last month, a guy crushed a lit cigarette on my back in Richmond. An old lady got me with a nail file in Laredo. But we rile 'em up with bullshit like that [TV] interview, and that's what happens. We're putting on a show."

The appeal of wrestling was nothing new. Strangler Lewis filled arenas during the Depression. Killer Kowalski was a legend in the '50s. Bruno Sammartino was wildly popular in the '60s. They were old-school wrestlers. They were replaced by the likes of Gorgeous George, who blew kisses to the crowd.

Every match became a one-act morality play. It was predictable, but that's why it sold. Psychologists claim there is too much ambiguity in modern society. It is hard to tell the good guys from the bad guys. Wrestling lays it out, plain and simple.

"We deal in personality conflicts, people get into that," said wrestler Ron Shaw, who was in his second decade on the circuit. "Then there is the violence. People get into that too. What do they love to see in an auto race? A crash, right? In wrestling, there is a crash every thirty seconds, only there are no cars."

"Spectators relate to the action on more of a gut level than they do at baseball or football," said Bruce Robertson, a clinical social worker who came to the wrestling card at the Spectrum. "This is a sport, but it taps into an entirely different emotion. In other sports, you have the home team and the visitors. In wrestling, you have the good guys and the bad guys. It's like a John Wayne movie.

"Most of the time, we feel powerless. We were powerless during the [Iran] hostage crisis, and we're powerless whenever Russia flexes its muscles, but we aren't powerless when Sergeant Slaughter gets some Russian in the Cobra Clutch and chokes the daylights out of him. We aren't rooting for the wrestlers as much as we are rooting for ourselves. The fans are like participants. You don't find that in a baseball or football crowd, at least not to this extent."

Robertson gestured toward the Spectrum crowd, which was full of Sergeant Slaughter fans dressed in camouflage attire.

"The last time I saw this many people in battle fatigues," Robertson said, "I was catching a C-141 from Saigon."

Another thing driving the popularity of pro wrestling in the 1980s was the weird marriage of the sport and rock and roll. In July 1984, singer Cyndi Lauper managed wrestler Wendi Richter to the women's world championship. Richter defeated the Fabulous Moolah live on MTV, the Music Television network. Captain Lou Albano, a wrestling manager, appeared as Lauper's father in the music video for her hit song "Girls Just Wanna Have Fun." Rock fans became wrestling fans and vice versa.

————

NONE OF THE WRESTLERS would admit it, but the matches were play acting, with the wrestlers performing like stuntmen in the movies. The idea was to make it look real. Many matches ended with one or both wrestlers covered in blood. I assumed it was fake blood, but I wanted to find out.

When the next wrestling show came to the Spectrum, I decided to get a blood sample. My wife, Maria, was a *Daily News* reporter who covered everything from mob trials to street shootouts. She's not afraid of anything, so she worked her way to the front row. When Andre the Giant exited the ring, she swept his bloody arm with a handkerchief. The guards thought she was just a crazy fan getting a souvenir.

We brought the bloody hankie to a lab for testing. I thought they would find it was some kind of red dye or maybe chicken blood. But the report came back that it was human blood. So all this blood was *real*? I wanted to learn more about that, but I knew the guys on the circuit weren't going to share their trade secrets. I had to find someone who knew the business and would talk about it honestly.

It just so happened that two former wrestlers, Eddy Mansfield and Jim Wilson, were in the process of taking on the promoters. They wanted to unionize the wrestlers and clean up the sport, so they were willing to talk on the record. We agreed to meet in Atlanta.

Mansfield and Wilson arrived at my hotel room with boxes full of contracts, check stubs, newspaper clippings, and letters. We talked for hours. Mansfield recounted various things he did: tanking matches, cutting his forehead with a hidden razor blade so he would "bleed good" for the fans, acting like a star when he had just $5 in his pocket. He felt stupid for allowing himself to be used that way.

"No matter how badly a wrestler is being treated, he'll protect the business," Mansfield said.

"Why?" I asked.

"Because there is some promoter telling him to hang on because he's *this close* to making it big," Mansfield said. "You want so bad to believe it that you go along. I went into hock to pay for wrestling lessons. All my dreams were tied up in the business. Once I got in, I couldn't see any way out.

"You're afraid of what the promoters will do if you speak up. They'll cut you off; they'll tell other promoters not to use you. So, you hang in. But the whole time, you're embarrassed. I never wanted to tell anyone I made $35 for a show. I'd strut around like a big shot, and I might not have enough money to buy a hamburger at Hardee's.

"They're so quick to tell you about [the wrestlers] who are making big money. But there are a thousand guys who don't make diddly."

In the WWF at the time, a dozen wrestlers earned more than $100,000. Proven attractions like Hulk Hogan, Andre the Giant, and

Jimmy "Superfly" Snuka made twice that. They flew to the big cities and stayed in nice hotels. That's the major leagues.

The others—too inexperienced, too bland, or too rebellious—scraped out a living in the minor leagues. Mansfield—a Gulf Coast headliner who was demoted after a run-in with an Atlanta promoter—kept the pay stubs from his last tour in 1983. They read:

> April 14—Kansas City, $65.
> April 16—Fort Scott, Kansas, $50.
> April 17—Des Moines, Iowa, $85.
> April 18—Wichita, Kansas, $65.

Earlier, Mansfield recalled drawing a $65,000 gate in San Antonio. He was promised $5,000 plus a $1,000 bonus if he let his opponent cut his long blond hair in the ring. Mansfield, who wrestled under the name "the Continental Lover," agreed. They packed the house, and the promoter padded his profits by selling Mansfield's hair at the souvenir stand.

Mansfield's pay for the evening: $1,500, less than half of what he was promised.

"The promoter lied to me, but what was I gonna do, call a cop?" he asked. "As a wrestler, you have no union and no court of appeals. The man hands you an envelope and says, 'Here. Take it or leave it.' The bookers tell you, 'If you don't like it, quit.' Finally, that's what I did.

"I don't believe half the stuff about how rich these stars are. They'd like you to believe that. I can show you stories they put out on me when I was hot, saying, 'The Continental Lover has seven cars and lives in a $300,000 house.' It was all bullshit.

"I had an apartment in San Antonio, and I was driving an Olds Cutlass. The promoters use you every which way they can. They tell you how to act, what to wear, what to say, when to win, when to lose, even when to bleed.

"To get to the top and stay there, you have to sell your soul," Mansfield said. "I couldn't do that. I was treated like a piece of meat for seven years. That's long enough."

The active wrestlers insist they go all out. WWF heavyweight Ron Shaw gave me the company line. He said like a boxer, a wrestler needs to compile an impressive record to earn a title shot.

"Total bullshit," Mansfield said. "You'll get a title shot when they [the promoters] decide, then they will tell you whether you're gonna win or not. They're writing the story; you're just reading the lines."

I asked Mansfield about the blood. He produced a small razor blade, roughly the size of his thumbnail, which he hid in either his wristband or his trunks. During the match, he would use it to cut himself and satisfy the crowd's blood lust.

"That's the promoter's call too," Mansfield said. "He'll come in the dressing room and say, 'I want juice tonight.' That means blood. If he says, 'I want double juice,' that means the baby face has to use the blade too. I laugh when people say we use fake blood or blood capsules. It wouldn't fool anybody."

I told Mansfield about my wife getting Andre the Giant's blood on a hankie and taking it to a lab for testing.

"I could've saved you the trouble," he said. "Yeah, the blood is real; we cut ourselves. You look at most wrestlers, and they have a ridge of scar tissue right here [forehead]. All it takes is one nick in the right spot, and the blood flows like water.

"It's not hard to do. The baby face distracts the crowd by strutting around or talking to the ref. That gives me time to get the blade. He slams my head into the ring post. I shoot my hands up to my face, and, zip, I run the blade across my forehead. The blood spurts, and the crowd goes wild.

"I cut myself in the same spot seven straight nights. I hated it, but the bookers told me I was paying my dues. It sounds crazy now, but it made sense at the time. I had promoters tell me, 'No red, no bread.' What are you gonna do? I'd say, 'Aw hell, gimme the blade.'"

"That's sick," I said.

"No, that's the business," Mansfield replied.

He went on to describe how the matches play out. He said it was like a dance routine.

"The heel calls the match because he's the one who takes the bumps," Mansfield said. "I get baby face in a headlock, and everyone thinks I'm talking dirty to him, but I'm really saying, 'OK, one tackle, drop down, hip lock, arm drag.'

"We both know the moves, so we do them. I'll let him run me off the ropes [and] then put me into a hip toss. I'll feed him my arm so he can apply the [arm] bar. I'll say, 'OK, let me get some hair.' I'll get a good handful and pull. He'll yell and throw a punch. I'll stumble backward like he really clocked me.

"It's hard to have a game plan going in. You've got to see what the crowd is buying that night. If they want a lot of flips, you give 'em flips. If they want a lot of heads bouncing off the turnbuckle, that's OK too.

"The finish is set in advance," Mansfield said. "That way we know it will look good. We'll be in a hold, and I'll say, 'OK, let's go home.' I'll throw a flying elbow, he'll duck. I'll hit the floor, he'll cover me. One, two, three, good night."

The baby face doesn't always win. Sometimes the heel wins, usually with the aid of brass knuckles that somehow escaped the referee's attention. That sets up a grudge rematch, and those are big box office.

"Scott Casey and I worked a whole Texas tour like that," Mansfield said. "He'd win one night, I'd win the next night. We worked it out between ourselves. One night, I pulled off his cowboy hat and spit in it. He went on TV and said some kid who was dying gave him that hat, and he'd make me pay. It was a bullshit story, but people ate it up. I put a bounty on him. God, those people hated me.

"They set up a cowboy match between us. That's where the winner puts a saddle on the loser and rides him around the ring. Naturally, I lost, but while I was giving Scott a ride, I flipped him over [and] then whipped the hell out of him with the bridle. That set up a Texas bull rope match [the wrestlers are tied together with an eight-foot rope] the next week that drew an even bigger crowd. Then we went to the next town and started all over again."

Wilson, who accompanied Mansfield to the hotel, pulled out letter after letter, recounting his efforts to enlist support for his campaign to organize the other wrestlers. He was storming around the room, waving his arms and shouting. He was acting like one of those hyperventilating wrestlers on TV.

Mansfield pulled him in the bathroom and closed the door. He began shouting at Wilson, telling him to calm down.

"Jim, you're blowing it," Mansfield said. "You're scaring this guy. I can see the way he's looking at you. He thinks you're f—king crazy. You want to get our story out there, don't you? Well, get it together."

Mansfield was right: I did think Wilson was crazy. I didn't expect that. I had done some research on the two men before we met. Mansfield seemed to be the wild card with the whole Continental Lover routine. Wilson had the more impressive resume. He had been an All-American offensive lineman at the University of Georgia. He made the NFL All-Rookie team with Gale Sayers and Dick Butkus in 1965. He wasn't some kook, in other words.

He was a headliner on the wrestling circuit in the '70s—billed as "the All-American Boy"—and now he was married with six children. He was selling real estate in Marietta, Georgia. He quit wrestling after clashing with a promoter who, he claimed, scuttled his career. He said the promoter was gay and made sexual advances that Wilson rejected.

Almost immediately, Wilson claimed, his role was changed. He wasn't the headliner anymore, his pay was slashed, and the nightly script called for him to lose rather than win. It wasn't long before he was phased out entirely. He could have quit and devoted himself to real estate, but he was determined to bring change to the sport.

It seemed plausible enough, but Wilson's manic behavior concerned me. Mansfield seemed credible, but Wilson's ranting caused me to wonder whether I should just forget the whole thing.

When Wilson emerged from the bathroom, he apologized. He didn't intend to get so worked up, but he was just so frustrated. He had been on this crusade for a decade, and no one would listen. He wrote letters to everyone from Ed Asner, the head of the Screen Actors Guild, to President Reagan, and no one showed interest.

"I'm sorry for carrying on like that," he said, "but this shit is just wrong, and no one will listen."

One year earlier, Wilson had gone before the Georgia legislature and called the wrestling industry "an old plantation system, the most discriminating, most abusive business left in the state." He was joined by four former wrestlers. He told the politicians, "We speak for the silent majority, believe me."

In four sessions, Wilson told the state representatives about his career: how promoters had blackballed him and threatened his life. He told of hit men who were paid extra by promoters to deliberately injure wrestlers who didn't go along with the program.

What had come of it?

"Basically, nothing," he said.

Part of the problem, Wilson said, was that no one took professional wrestling seriously. Sports people saw it as low-brow comedy. Entertainment people saw it as a muscle-flexing freak show. Journalists and politicians would rather not have seen it at all. I could relate to that. I didn't want this assignment either.

"I've talked to a lot of sportswriters," Mansfield said, "and they say, 'It's not a sport. It's stupid.' Yeah, but it's corrupt. Shouldn't that matter?"

"It's easy to say, 'Wrestling is a farce,'" Wilson said, "except when it's your life and someone is squeezing it out of you."

Wilson wanted to establish a wrestling commission to regulate the sport and make sure the promoters paid the wrestlers what they were promised. He also wanted to organize a union for wrestlers similar to the players' association in football. It would provide medical insurance, a pension plan, and other benefits as well as protection from vindictive promoters.

"Security in this business is nonexistent," Wilson said. "A wrestler is dirt, a piece of meat, a dime a dozen."

To support his point, he pulled out a newspaper clipping with a quote from Eddie Einhorn, the president of the Chicago White Sox and a former wrestling promoter.

"I like a lot of things about wrestling," Einhorn was quoted as saying. "There is no union. If one of those blonde superstars gets hurt or retires, you can create another one and you don't even have to draft him. All you have to do is get a bottle of peroxide, come up with a name for him and the crowds love him."[1]

"In other words," Wilson said, "one monkey don't stop the show. You break down or get out of line, I'll get another monkey off the street."

I did not doubt Wilson's sincerity. He hoped my articles would make people sit up and take notice. He thought then the politicians would get behind him and force people like McMahon to make the necessary changes. He believed that my series in the *Daily News* would be the catalyst for change.

Unfortunately, my series began running the same day the story broke about Leonard Tose negotiating to move the Eagles to Phoenix. Instead of getting front-page headlines, my wrestling stories were buried under the Eagles coverage. The series did not make the immediate splash that everyone, especially Wilson and Mansfield, expected.

However, the Associated Press syndicate bought the series. Titled "Inside Wrestling," the AP offered it to subscribers, and almost two hundred newspapers picked it up. The NBC television network saw the series and decided to do a special on the subject. Bob Costas came to the *Daily News* office to interview me for the show. He also interviewed Wilson and Mansfield.

ABC's *20/20* followed with its own investigative piece. Unfortunately for Wilson and the would-be reformers, the only thing viewers remembered was the video of the enraged Schultz knocking reporter John Stossel to the floor. It certainly spoke to the craziness of the business, but the larger issues about the abuses and corruption were lost in the noise.

In April 1985, *Sports Illustrated* devoted most of one issue to professional wrestling. Hogan was on the cover with the headline "Mat Mania." The story dealt largely with the show-business aspects of wrestling and glossed over the ugly stuff.

Wilson and Mansfield were mentioned, but only in passing. Mostly, the story was a lightweight look at the bizarre world of wrestling, focusing on McMahon as a blustery P. T. Barnum who was giving fans what they wanted.

Wilson was disappointed that nothing more came of his efforts. There was occasional talk of better regulations, but, based on our conversations, nothing really changed. In 2003, Wilson wrote a book titled *Chokehold: Pro Wrestling's Mayhem outside the Ring.* It recounted many of the stories he had told me twenty years earlier. There was talk of making it into a movie, but that never happened. Wilson was still calling for change when he died in 2009.

I traveled the wrestling circuit on and off for three months. It was like living in a cartoon world. It was funny, but it was also scary. Behind the masks and the silly names, there was real darkness. It was clear by looking at their pumped-up bodies that many of the wrestlers were using steroids. With their grueling schedules, hopping from city to city and match to match, Wilson said many wrestlers were doing drugs just to keep going. I certainly believed that.

There was a disturbing pattern of wrestlers dying young, some from drug overdoses, others from heart attacks possibly brought on by steroid abuse. There also were a number of deaths by suicide, including former world champion Chris Benoit, age forty, who murdered his wife and seven-year-old son before hanging himself in the weight room of his Fayetteville, Georgia, home.

The stories are out there, yet men and women still sign up to join the circuit, and fans continue to watch in large numbers. Weekly TV shows, such as *Monday Night Raw* and *Smackdown*, pull in big ratings.

Undoubtedly, some wrestlers see the sport as a stepping-stone to a career in movies. Dwayne Johnson, one of the top box-office attractions in Hollywood, spent seven years in the WWF as "the Rock." Others, such as Hulk Hogan, Jesse Ventura, John Cena, and Steve Austin, have made the transition from the ring to the screen.

Tessa Blanchard followed her father, Tully, into wrestling and appeared in a 2018 film, *Fighting with My Family.* It was a story about—what else?—a family involved in wrestling. Art and life are the same in this bizarre world.

In 2008, Mickey Rourke starred in a movie called *The Wrestler*. It was a brutal look at the business through the eyes of a fading star reduced to working small-time matches in VFW halls and high school gyms. In one scene, Rourke's character and his opponent fall off a ladder onto a pile of bloody barbed wire. In another scene, an opponent uses a staple gun on Rourke's head. Apparently, the razor blade had become passé.

As I was leaving the theater, I heard someone say, "I'm sure it's not like *that*."

Yes, it is.

I recall a conversation I had with Sergeant Slaughter after the show in Hershey. He had finished signing autographs, so it was just the two of us walking through the deserted parking lot to his camouflage car.

"What's it like to be Sergeant Slaughter?" I asked.

"You've gotta understand," he said. "That's Sergeant Slaughter, it's not me. It's like Paul Newman. He's not Butch Cassidy; that was just a role he played.

"When I leave here, I'm Bob. I'm a regular guy. I like my privacy. I like to play golf and listen to music. My idea of a perfect evening is to cook a steak, build a fire, and relax. I wish I had more time to do that. Family is important.

"When I was a bad guy [in the ring], I wouldn't let my daughters watch. I didn't want them to see their father treated that way. Money don't make up for that.

"It's a hard life," he said, "but somebody's gotta do it, right?"

11

The Good Doctor

O F THE FOUR MAJOR SPORTS, basketball was my least favorite. I liked it, but I didn't love it, certainly not the way I loved football. I enjoyed baseball and hockey. Basketball, not so much.

It is funny because my parents loved basketball. The Eagles were number one, of course, but the Warriors were a strong second. The NBA played doubleheaders in those days. For one admission, you could see, for example, the New York Knicks play the Fort Wayne Pistons at 6 P.M., with the Warriors playing the St. Louis Hawks at 8:15. It was quite a bargain.

One night, my father decided on the spur of the moment to go see the Warriors play the Celtics. When we got to Convention Hall, the parking lot attendant told us the game was sold out. I don't know what made my father think he could walk up to the box office and buy tickets for a Celtics game right before tipoff. He was normally more practical than that.

We found ourselves parked on Thirty-Fourth Street with nowhere to go.

I had a suggestion. The Ramblers had a game that night at the Arena, which was just a few blocks away. I said we could go there. My father looked at my mother and sighed. "What do you think?" he said with a distinct lack of enthusiasm. Before she could answer, the parking lot attendant reappeared.

"I shouldn't be telling you this," he said, "but you see that guy over there? He's selling tickets."

My father sprinted over to the scalper and bought three tickets. They probably cost him a week's pay, but he was happy to spend it, knowing it saved him from sitting through another Ramblers game. I was the only one disappointed. I wanted to see the Ramblers.

It sounds crazy, but that's how I felt about basketball, at least back then.

When I was in high school, the Warriors moved to California, and one year later the Syracuse franchise relocated to Philadelphia. In 1966–1967, the team now known as the 76ers fielded one of the best lineups in NBA history and finished the regular season with a 68–13 record.

Future Hall of Famers Wilt Chamberlain, Chet Walker, Hal Greer, and Billy Cunningham led them to the NBA championship. They also had Wali Jones, Billy Melchionni, and Matt Guokas, all local college stars, in the backcourt. Even I became interested.

When I first got into the newspaper business, I had to cover the occasional basketball game. I found I liked the college game more than the pros. I liked the atmosphere at the Palestra, the cheering sections, and the rollouts. I enjoyed covering Rollie Massimino's Villanova team, mostly because he was such a character. I thought their upset of top-ranked Georgetown in the NCAA final in 1985 was one of the great sports stories in the city's history.

One thing I liked about covering basketball was how close we as reporters were to the action. With other sports, we were upstairs in a press box. In basketball, we were seated on the floor between the benches. We could hear the coach's instructions, and we could see the physical contact. A point guard driving down the lane isn't much different than a receiver going across the middle. It is not a game for the faint of heart. I saw that more clearly from courtside.

Also, the smaller roster allowed me to get to know the players. In football, there were so many players on the team that I could go through an entire season and not speak to everyone on the roster. In basketball, there were just a dozen players, so it is easier to develop relationships.

That was particularly true when Julius Erving joined the Sixers in 1976. More than anyone else, Doctor J made me a basketball fan. It was more about Erving himself than it was about the game. The Doctor was a unique talent, but he also was a unique personality. I'll give just one illustration from memory.

The 76ers' team bus was parked next to the Mecca, the basketball arena in downtown Milwaukee. The Sixers had just lost a playoff game to the Bucks, and the bus was waiting to take the team to the airport.

A young fan was standing on the sidewalk, holding a 76ers pennant and a pen. He was hoping to get a few autographs, but the bus driver shooed him away as the players filed past. The last one out of the locker room, as always, was Erving. He would not leave until he had filled every reporter's notebook.

"Let's go, Doc," the bus driver said.

Erving saw the boy standing there. Without saying a word, he took the pennant and signed it. Then he brought it on the bus and had the other players sign it. He returned it to the boy, who was so awed that he could only mouth the words "Thank you."

Erving could have walked right past the boy the way everyone else did, and no one would have thought twice about it. He was late, the team was waiting—people would understand. Instead, he took the time to reach out to a kid he didn't know. I asked why.

"You saw the smile on his face," Erving said. "That's why."

I have many memories of Doctor J—soaring dunks, windmill jams, one-on-one battles with Larry Bird—but the memory of him handing the pennant back to that wide-eyed kid in Milwaukee ranks with any of them because it was so genuine.

Stan Hochman called Erving "a mensch," a Yiddish term for a man with a good heart. Stan didn't use the term often—certainly not when discussing most of the athletes we dealt with, many of whom were churlish—but he saw those qualities in Erving. I did too.

When most people think of the Doctor, they think of him in flight, soaring down the lane to the basket, but the grace he displayed just walking through daily life set him apart. Even the other NBA players treated him with a respectful deference.

If he was the face of the league—which he surely was for a time— the other players were fine with it because they knew it was good for everyone. His image was a tide that raised every boat in the NBA's cluttered harbor.

"I've never heard anybody knock him or express jealousy," said Dominique Wilkins, a superstar in his own right with the Atlanta Hawks. "Never one negative word. I can't name you one other player who has that status."[1]

In 1986, the *Denver Post* polled media members from across the country to identify the "nicest" people in sports. Erving, then in his final season with the Sixers, won in a landslide. When Erving was saying his goodbyes to basketball, *Sports Illustrated*'s Frank Deford wrote about his legacy: "For all his talent and humanity, what has set Erving apart is the way he combined excellence and entertainment in sports. The Doctor was a gentleman and a scholar."[2]

Erving was bigger than his sport. Yes, he won an NBA title, but he also narrated *Peter and the Wolf* at the Philadelphia Zoo, read the Declaration of Independence at a Fourth of July celebration, and lit the Christmas tree in city hall's courtyard.

We have seen other great athletes, but few achieved his stature. People who weren't even sports fans knew him and what he was about. My wife, Maria, hardly an authority on basketball, had a parakeet, and the only thing she taught it to say was "Stuff it, Doctor J." That is how thoroughly he captivated our collective imagination.

Jack McMahon was an assistant coach with the Sixers. He spent a lifetime in basketball. He played with Bob Pettit and coached Oscar Robertson. He discovered Darryl Dawkins as a high school player, and he found such hidden gems as Maurice Cheeks and Andrew Toney on the backroads of college basketball. But he had never seen anyone quite like the Doctor.

"He was a guy everyone knew about but not many people had seen," McMahon said. "He went to the University of Massachusetts, which isn't exactly big time, and he played in the ABA (American Basketball Association), so he wasn't on TV, yet everyone in basketball knew about him. He was mythic. He was the Doctor."

We saw photographs of the lithe 6'6" forward with the lush Afro cradling the red, white, and blue ABA basketball in his oversized hands. We read stories about how he was changing the game, making it more artistic and expressive. So, when the Sixers purchased his rights from the New Jersey Nets, Philadelphia embraced him immediately.

When he was introduced at his Spectrum debut and public address announcer Dave Zinkoff rolled out his first "Julius Errrrrrrrr-ving," a season-ticket holder named Steve Solms ran onto the court and presented him with a doctor's kit. A fan base notoriously hard to win over put the Doctor on a pedestal that night and kept him there for more than a decade.

It wasn't always the smoothest ride. From the start, there was an expectation that he would bring the city an NBA championship. Many predicted it would happen the first year, when Erving joined a team with George McGinnis, Lloyd Free, Darryl Dawkins, Doug Collins, and

Joe Bryant. They were a colorful bunch and abundantly talented, but they were more of a floor show than a basketball team.

The Sixers went to the finals that season but lost to Portland in six games. The next year, they won fifty-three games in the regular season but lost in the second round of the playoffs to Washington. The front office saw the need to change, so McGinnis was traded to Denver for Bobby Jones. The Sixers drafted Cheeks to run the offense, and with Cunningham replacing Gene Shue as coach, things began to take shape.

"In the past, Julius, McGinnis, Free all wanted to be the main man," said general manager Pat Williams. "But if you have more than one money player, it doesn't work. So we decided to shape the team around Julius. Let him set the tone and take over."[3]

Traveling with that team was an experience. Chuck Daly, the assistant coach, said it was like traveling with the Rolling Stones. Wherever they went, there was always a crowd. Erving was the big draw, but people also came to gawk at Dawkins, the 6'11", 280-pound man-child who could fill a hotel lobby all by himself.

The Sixers had drafted Dawkins out of Maynard Evans High School in Orlando, Florida. They signed him to a seven-year contract worth $1 million. He had the size and strength to be a great NBA center—comparisons to Wilt Chamberlain were unavoidable—but he was just eighteen years old.

"Darryl loved the money, the action, the limelight, the whole scene," McMahon said. "He just never loved basketball."[4]

Dawkins was goofing around one day at practice. Cunningham chewed him out in front of the whole team. Dawkins vowed to do better. As the coach turned to walk away, Dawkins stuck out his leg and tripped him.

"It was so Darryl," Cunningham said.

Dawkins talked about living on the planet Lovetron. He assumed various identities: Chocolate Thunder, Dr. Jam, the Master Blaster, and Zandokan the Mad Dunker. He assigned names to his various dunks: the In Your Face Disgrace, the Spine Chiller Supreme, the Heart Stopper, and the Yo Mama. He referred to himself as Agent 0014, saying, "I'm twice as bad as 007."

He was a big kid, really, guileless in many ways. Once in an interview, he was quizzed on what he knew about Philadelphia. He was asked if he knew where they signed the Declaration of Independence. Of course, he knew.

"At the bottom," he said.[5]

He traveled with an enormous boom box. He wore headphones, but he played his music so loud that you could hear it across the aisle on the team plane. He had nicknames for everyone, even the writers. He called the *Bulletin*'s Mark Whicker "Biscuit Belly." He called me "Dillinger." I corrected him one time, and he shook his head. "No," he said, "you're Dillinger." I learned to live with it.

Early in his career, Dawkins was a teenager playing in a man's league. It wasn't like the NBA of today, where players are drafted after one or two years of college. The game of the '70s was dominated by veteran players and old-school coaches. Dawkins was raw and undisciplined, which made him an odd fit.

If he were to come into the league today, it would be an easier transition. As it was, he had trouble finding his way. He succeeded as a personality but fell short as a player. Erving, who functioned as a big brother for Dawkins, saw the goofy stuff like Lovetron as his way of hiding his insecurity.

"So much of what he says is a smoke screen," Erving said. "He wants to project that [aura of] confidence. When you are that big, everyone wants you to be The Franchise, but how many players could handle that at 18?"[6]

In the 1977 NBA finals, the Sixers and the Trail Blazers came to blows during Game 2. Dawkins and Portland's Bob Gross were fighting for a rebound, and Dawkins threw the smaller Gross to the floor. Maurice Lucas, Portland's 6'9", 230-pound enforcer, hit Dawkins from behind. The two men squared off, punches were thrown, and both were ejected from the game.

Dawkins was enraged when he went to the locker room. He ripped a partition out of the bathroom wall and bent the steel door in half. Al Meltzer, the local TV anchor, surveyed the damage and said, "It looks like Godzilla was here."

The Sixers won the first two games of the series, but when it shifted to Portland, the Trail Blazers turned it around. They won the two games on their home court, playing great team basketball while the Sixers reverted to a one-on-one game, forcing shots and turning the ball over. The Trail Blazers won Game 5 in Philadelphia and closed out the series in Portland.

After the last game, Erving sat on the locker room floor, his legs stretched out in front of him, an ice bag taped to each knee. He faced wave after wave of reporters, patiently answering every question, trying to explain how the Sixers had lost four straight games. He gave credit to the victors, especially Bill Walton, who had 20 points, 23 rebounds, 7 assists, and 8 blocked shots in the last game.

Erving was only irritated once, and it was when someone asked whether the Sixers had "choked."

"We didn't choke," he said. "They played better than we did."

Erving had played brilliantly throughout the series. He averaged 30 points a game and scored 40 in the final game. He was exhausted, but he found time for every interviewer. As he was packing to leave, a young reporter from a local paper appeared at his locker.

"I'm sorry," he said. "I know I'm late."

"It's OK," Erving said putting down his bag to answer another round of questions.

I saw that scene play out dozens of times over the eleven years Erving played in Philadelphia. Indeed, that's how I remember him: sitting on the floor, ice bags on his knees, talking to either a crowd of reporters or just one guy with a tape recorder.

He understood that he was an ambassador for his sport. It meant answering every question, signing every autograph, posing for every picture. It does not seem like much of a hardship until you travel with a team and see what it is like to face that responsibility on a daily basis. Every time you walk into a hotel or arena, someone is asking you to do something. They say it will only take a minute, but, of course, it always takes longer, sometimes much longer. Dealing with that day after day, the constant tugging on the sleeve, can wear on even the most patient person.

Of all the athletes I've been around, Erving and hockey's Wayne Gretzky handled it the best. During the 1987 Stanley Cup finals, the Edmonton Oilers flew commercial while the Flyers flew on a charter. What's more, the Oilers' players, including Gretzky, flew coach from Philadelphia to Edmonton. Gretzky would be in an aisle seat, trying to sleep, and people kept tapping him on the shoulder to ask for his autograph. He signed every one.

Erving was equally gracious. We shared a few meals on the road, and people were always coming by for a handshake or an autograph. Most were respectful, but some were not. There were the ones who just shoved a piece of paper in front of him and said, "Sign it to. . . ." I never saw him refuse or complain. He accepted it as part of being who he was.

In Erving's final NBA season, he received a telegram from Isiah Thomas, the Detroit Pistons' star, who said, "You have been an inspiration, a leader and a perfect role model for me and all other NBA players. You have made the path much smoother for us younger guys to follow."[7]

Few do, however. The culture of jock stardom has changed—starting really with Michael Jordan—with the superstars now shielded by handlers and bodyguards. Mike Trout sits with other Eagles fans at the Linc, but he is the exception. You want to grab a selfie with LeBron James? Shake hands with Tom Brady? Yeah, good luck.

There were cynics who saw it as phony, a salesman polishing his brand or, in Erving's case, selling another pair of sneakers. I can see how people might draw that conclusion. The Doctor's image was on a number of products in those days, from basketballs to soft drinks. But if you were around him enough, you saw moments like the one with the boy in Milwaukee when he wasn't trying to sell anything. He was just being himself.

That's not to say the Doctor was unaware of his image. How he was perceived was important to him, which is why it was so shocking in November 1984 when he got into a scuffle with Larry Bird during a game in Boston. He didn't start the fight; Bird did. The Celtics star was killing the Sixers, and on his way down the court, he threw an elbow. The Doctor responded by putting his left hand around Bird's throat.

Other players jumped in, punches were thrown, and Erving and Bird wound up being fined $7,500 each. In the *Philadelphia Daily News*, columnist John Schulian called the actions of Erving and Bird "demeaning." Wrote Schulian, "Royalty shouldn't behave like stewbums quarreling over the last drop of muscatel."[8]

When the teams prepared to meet again in December, this time at the Spectrum, the media built it up like a World Wrestling Federation grudge match. Erving did his best to put the whole thing to rest. He was not proud of what had happened in Boston.

"We did something that was an embarrassment to the league and to ourselves," he said. "We need a better image than that, as athletes and as gentlemen of the sport. That [night] was a setback. Maybe there was a full moon or something. I just know it was not professional."[9]

The December game went off without incident. Bird won the individual battle, scoring 34 points to Erving's 16, but the Sixers won the game, 110–107. Afterward, Bird shrugged off questions about the earlier dustup. He said he and the Doctor were friends. They also were business partners, with their names attached to a popular video game.

"Stuff like that happens in the course of a game," Bird said. "Guys are banging around, somebody catches an elbow. It's competitive out there. The Celtics and Sixers go on the court, it's going to be physical. It's going to get heated. But the Doctor and I have nothing but respect for each other."

For all his greatness, the Doctor would not have won his championship if the Sixers had not acquired Moses Malone. The Doctor spent seven years playing alongside Dawkins and Caldwell Jones, and while those teams filled highlight reels with their high-flying flamboyance, they came up short in the playoffs. They lacked the down-and-dirty toughness to win in the paint, and without that, you won't win an NBA championship.

Malone's arrival changed all that. At 6'10" and 240 pounds, Malone thrived on doing the dirty work other players abhorred. Asked to describe his game, he said, "I go to the rack," meaning he went to the boards and collected every loose ball and missed shot. He played six seasons in Houston and led the league in rebounds four times. His arrival completed the team the Sixers had been trying to build for years. Malone was, in many ways, the opposite of Dawkins. He was not quotable, and he was not colorful. He was never going to visit Lovetron or shatter a backboard. But he dominated the game every night. That was not true of Dawkins, who could be spectacular one night and invisible the next.

No one was happier to see Malone arrive than Erving. At thirty-two, his hair was flecked with gray. Time was running out for him to win an NBA title. He had been to the finals three times and lost each time, but with Malone on board, he knew the team was built to go the distance.

As personalities, the Doctor and Malone were very different. Where Erving was warm and outgoing, Malone was gruff and withdrawn. Where Erving would talk to anyone, Malone talked to no one. Erving enjoyed a good laugh, while Malone rarely smiled. He went about his business in such a workmanlike fashion that, to the fans, he seemed almost joyless.

As that 1982–1983 season wound down, the Sixers had the best record in the NBA, and Malone was a lock to win the Most Valuable Player Award. The *Daily News* sports editor, Mike Rathet, assigned me to do a profile on the big man. He wanted a piece that provided some insight into Malone's personality.

Malone was not the kind of guy to bare his soul to a writer, especially one he did not know. He hardly talked after games. He showered, grabbed his bag, and headed for the door. What were the chances he would sit down for two or three hours with me and tell his life story? Zero was my guess.

"Just ask him," Rathet said. "See what he says."

I went to practice the next day. I approached Malone in the locker room and told him what we had in mind. He shook his head.

"Got nothin' to say," he said. "Talk to somebody else."

"The story is about you," I said. "The people in Philadelphia don't know much about you."

"I was in Houston six years, they didn't know me there either," he said. "I like it that way."

"Why?" I asked.

"Just do," he said reaching for his bag. As far as he was concerned, the interview was over.

Rathet suggested calling Malone's agent, Lee Fentress. Surely, he could convince him to do the interview. Fentress said he would talk to Malone. He called back the next day. The answer was no. The next time I saw Malone, he glared at me. He didn't appreciate the call to his agent nor his agent's attempt to talk him into doing something he did not want to do.

"Lee Fentress works for me, I don't work for him," Malone said.

Rathet came up with another idea: He would send me on the Sixers' next road trip. Our beat writer, Phil Jasner, would cover the games; I would just shadow Malone. Get him for a few minutes here and there, talk to him at the hotel, sit next to him on the plane, pull up a chair in the coffee shop.

"Just get what you can," he said.

It was a typical March road trip in the NBA. Three games in four days: Indiana on Saturday, Milwaukee on Sunday, New York on Tuesday. I dutifully approached Malone each day, and he waved me off. By the time we got to New York, he wasn't even acknowledging me. He walked by as if I wasn't there.

Erving asked what I was doing. He knew I didn't normally travel with the team. I told him I was assigned to do a profile on Malone.

"How's it going?" he asked. The smile on his face suggested he already knew the answer.

"He won't even talk to me," I said.

"Moses is a good dude, but he is very private," Erving said. "He'll joke around with us, but when there are reporters around or people he doesn't know, he keeps to himself."

That afternoon, we got on the same hotel elevator. Doc and I exchanged hellos; Malone just stared at the floor. We rode in silence. Doc and Malone didn't say a word to each other, yet that night on the court, you would've thought they were best friends. They had almost nothing in common except what they shared on the basketball court, but that was enough. Indeed, it was sublime.

I returned from the trip and told Rathet what had happened. I thought he would scrap the whole idea, but he told me to do the piece anyway.

"Go to his hometown," he said. "Talk to his family, talk to the guys he grew up with. If you need more time, just tell me. But he's the f—king MVP. We're doing this story."

I flew to Petersburg, Virginia, where Malone was born. I went to the Heights, the area where he grew up. A guy named Johnny Byrd had a grocery store there. He was robbed and shot at so many times, he worked the counter with a .38 strapped to his hip. He talked about closing his store at night and seeing young Moses on the playground, working on his game.

"Kids in the neighborhood say Moses slept with his basketball," Byrd said. "Could be."

I set up an interview with Mary, Malone's mother, but on the day I arrived, she was taken to the hospital with what doctors feared was a heart attack. It proved to be a false alarm, but her doctor kept her hospitalized. I offered to interview her at the hospital, but she said no. She had told her son that I was in town, and he didn't want her talking to me.

"I'm sorry," she said, "but I have to do what he says."

The more I talked to people in Petersburg, the more I understood Malone's walled-off existence. He did not trust many people, and it was largely due to his background. He was a high school phenom recruited by dozens of colleges, but he chose to go straight to pro basketball because he wanted to give his mother a better life. He signed a $3-million contract with the Utah franchise in the ABA.

Malone was an eighteen-year-old African American, almost seven feet tall, living on his own in Salt Lake City. He was already a shy kid, but the experience of being alone in a strange place—and if you grew up in the Heights, it doesn't get much stranger than Utah—made him even more wary and withdrawn. He rarely left his apartment except to play basketball.

I talked to his best friend, David Pair, a classmate from Petersburg High School. He talked about Malone coming home in the off-season and playing in pickup games with the old gang. When Pair got married, Malone flew in to serve as best man. Pair laughed when I told him the Philadelphia media considered his friend aloof. Nothing could be farther from the truth, he said.

"He's just careful in his dealings with people," Pair said. "When he was young, he had so many people coming after him. Recruiters, scouts, agents. Everyone wanted a piece of him. He didn't know who to trust. He's still suspicious of strangers. He keeps his distance, but you should see him with the people here. He has a good heart, he's always helping out.

"Moses earned everything he's got. He came here [the playground] and worked every night on his game. I kept him company. That's how we became close. I was a big Wilt Chamberlain fan. I had a poster of him in my room. One time, Moses said, 'How come you like Wilt so much?' I said, 'Because he's the best.' Moses said, 'Someday I'm gonna be the best.' I said, 'When you're the best, I'll put your poster up.'"

Pair took me to his bedroom. There was a poster of Malone, signed by the man himself.

"The neighborhood kids come by to see it, like it's a shrine or something," Pair said.

I came back to Philadelphia and wrote the story. It ran the day the Sixers played Game 1 of the finals against the Lakers. There were no quotes from Malone—obviously—but the piece ran almost three thousand words. I saw Malone that night. Again, he walked by without saying a word. I still don't know whether he ever read the story. My guess is probably not.

Rathet liked the piece enough to enter it in the Keystone Press Awards judging. A few months later, he called me into his office to tell me the Malone story had won the award for top sports feature of the year in Pennsylvania. He believed that Malone's refusal to speak to me actually made the story better.

"If you had the quotes, it would've read like every other story," he said. "This way, you had to *write* it."

He believed that sportswriters lean too heavily on quotes. Often, they are nothing but clichés, but we string them together because we think that's what readers want. What they really want, he said, is a good story. By describing the Heights and talking about the grocer with the .38 on his hip and the poster in Pair's bedroom, we told the readers more about Malone than he ever would have said himself.

I think there is some truth to that.

I had an entirely different experience with Charles Barkley. He was as easy to deal with as Malone was difficult. In 1986, I was assigned to do a series on Barkley, who was already a star in just his second year with the Sixers. Again, the paper sent me to the subject's hometown—in this case, Leeds, Alabama—to meet with his family and friends.

Unlike Malone, who contacted people and told them not to cooperate, Barkley set up interviews with his mother and his grandmother. He gave me the names of guys he played ball with. He told me about Old Smokey's Bar-B-Q, where he ate lunch every day when he was in town.

"Ask for Diana," he said.

When I walked into Old Smokey's a week later, the woman behind the counter said, "You must be Ray. Charles told us you'd be coming. I'm Diana." She announced to everyone, "Ray here is from Philadelphia, and he's doing a story about Charles, so y'all be nice."

No one had to ask, "Charles who?" In Leeds, everyone knew.

"He sits at that corner table and talks to everyone who comes in," Diana said. "He doesn't act like a big shot. He's just as nice as can be. He told me, 'I'm gonna put Leeds on the map, and I'm gonna make you famous.' Now here you are talking to me, so I guess he was telling the truth."

Barkley had been written up in *Sports Illustrated* and *Inside Sports* earlier in the season. He had just filmed his first Nike commercial. He was known as "the Leaning Tower of Pizza," a reference to his 6'5", 270-pound frame. He had acquired many nicknames: "Boy Gorge," "Chuck Wagon," and, of course, "the Round Mound of Rebound."

His weight had always been an issue. As a junior at Leeds High, he was 5'10" and 230 pounds. He was called "Fat Boy," and the fans at other schools threw pizza boxes at him. He grew to 6'3" as a senior, so he carried the weight better, but he still was plus sized. He was awarded a basketball scholarship to Auburn, where he was named Player of the Year in the Southeastern Conference. The Sixers made him the fifth overall pick in the 1984 draft.

When general manager Pat Williams introduced Barkley to Philadelphia, he opened with a series of fat jokes. A sample: "Even his bathtub has stretch marks." Barkley shrugged it off as teasing. He was low-key. He addressed reporters as "sir." He was not the rollicking, irreverent presence he would later become. He was on a team with Erving, Malone, Cheeks, and other veterans, so he took a back seat, at least initially.

As a rookie, he played in all eighty-two regular-season games, but he came off the bench most nights. He still averaged 14 points and 8.6 rebounds per game. His second year, he started every game and averaged 20 points and 12.8 rebounds. The more Barkley played, the more he allowed his personality to show. He became a folk hero in Philadelphia, but he was an easy target for abuse in other cities, which troubled his mother, Charcey Glenn.

"I watch the games on TV, I hear the fans yelling at him," she said, sitting on her porch in Leeds. "I'm thinking, 'That's my child, what's wrong with you?' Charles tells me not to worry, but mothers always worry."

Charles and his mother were very close. They spoke all the time during the season, and once the season ended, he was back home, going to Old Smokey's, hanging with his friends, and watching TV. Glenn was a plain-spoken woman with both feet planted firmly in the soil of Leeds. She was a realist, which made her distrustful of what others called "celebrity."

"I told Charles long ago, when people started asking for his autograph and things like that, I said, 'Just remember, the only part of this that's real is you,'" she said. "You can't ever lose sight of that. We talk about that all the time. Stay true to yourself."

It was clear that Barkley got the message. We spoke in the locker room one day before my trip to Leeds, and he said all the things his mother would say later, almost word for word.

"That's not a real world I'm living in," he said. "I'm a success, but it could end any day. I could wreck my knee tomorrow, then what? I have one thing I can count on, and that's my family. They'll be there for me, win or lose. The rest of this is superficial. It's like wrapping paper. It looks pretty on the outside, but you can't see what's underneath. It might be nothing but an empty box."

At the time I interviewed Barkley, the Sixers were involved in a playoff series with Milwaukee, a series they would ultimately lose in seven games. The Milwaukee crowd was booing and shouting obscenities at Barkley. They threw coins at him during Game 5. Asked about it, Barkley snapped, "They can kiss me where the sun don't shine."

Williams told Barkley he was only inflaming the situation.

"Fine," Barkley said. "I won't talk at all."

Barkley talked to me because he had already agreed to do so, but he shut out everyone else. It was ironic given what I had gone through with Malone: I went from getting nothing to having an exclusive with the hottest story in the playoffs.

One day, we were talking about his image—how it had grown and how he had escaped the dual shadows of Erving and Malone. Williams compared Barkley to William "the Refrigerator" Perry, the Chicago Bears' rookie who was a breakout star that season. Perry was on talk shows and magazine covers. He was in demand for commercial endorsements. Williams said Barkley would be the next Refrigerator.

"Ain't happening," Barkley said.

Why not? The Fridge was making a fortune. He had deals with McDonald's, Kraft Foods, and Hasbro Toys that would pay him $3 million.

"There are two sides to being a celebrity," Barkley said. "The one side is what everybody sees, the money and the TV. The other side is dealing with ignorant people who think you're public property. I might learn to deal with the one side, but I won't ever learn to deal with the other.

"There are two things I hate. The first thing is losing. The second thing is people who don't treat us like human beings. They think we're machines or robots. They act like we have no feelings. I have feelings, the same as anyone else.

"It bothers me when people shout stuff. You should hear the things they call me. And if I get mad and I shout something back, the press writes what a bad guy I am. It's like they build you up just so they can cut you down."

After Malone was traded and the Doctor retired, Barkley became the centerpiece of the franchise. Unfortunately, the Sixers went downhill after the Malone deal, which still ranks as one of the worst organizational decisions ever made. The team's management swapped Malone and two first-round picks for a broken-down Jeff Ruland, Roy Hinson, and Cliff Robinson. It was a colossal mistake, and Barkley was left to clean up the mess.

He poured everything he had into restoring the Sixers to glory, but there were too many Armen Gilliams and Kenny Paynes on the roster. Despite his lack of height, Barkley led the league in offensive rebounds three years in a row. But the losing drained the fun from the game. The frustration caused him to melt down to the tune of 30 technical fouls, a league record, in the 1987–1988 season.

"Emotion is what fuels Charles's fire," said Jim Lynam, the Sixers' coach. "That's what sets him apart. But I told him, 'Don't let this thing that powers you be the same thing that destroys you.' Some people knock Charles for this and for that, but if I'm going to war, I want Charles Barkley on my side every time."

"My game is hard work," Barkley said. "There are guys in the league who are bigger than me, and there are guys who have more talent, but nobody outworks me. The other players know when they go up against me, they gotta be prepared to give as much as I give for forty minutes, and that's hard to do.

"I see the way they look at me sometimes, like, 'What's wrong with you? What are you trying to prove?' All I want to do is win, and anybody who don't like it can just get the hell out of the way. I want to win an NBA championship. Not a day goes by that I don't think about it.

"I'm gonna do it too," he vowed. "Either that or die trying."

Barkley never did win his championship. He played eight seasons with the Sixers, four with Phoenix, and four with Houston. He averaged 22.1 points and 11.7 rebounds for his career. He was only the fourth player in NBA history with 20,000 points, 10,000 rebounds, and 4,000 assists. Like Erving and Malone, he was voted into the Basketball Hall of Fame. He also made the NBA's All-Interview team every year. He is still one of the great interviews on any topic.

Doctor J, Moses Malone, and Charles Barkley. Three men, three different personalities. All three have their numbers hanging from the rafters at the Wells Fargo Center. All three have statues outside the Sixers' practice facility in Camden. Each carved out a unique place in the team's history.

Malone is gone, a victim of heart disease at age sixty. Barkley is still a visible presence with his role on the Turner Network Television post-game show. He is funny, outrageous, and unfiltered. In other words, he is still Sir Charles. Erving, now fully gray, doesn't come around that often, but he doesn't have to. He is—and will always be—the Doctor.

"I'm not insecure about my place in basketball history," he said. "No individual is bigger than the game. The game has a life of its own. I feel the respect I've garnered has been earned the old-fashioned way. I've earned it."[10]

12

Michael Jack

I'M OFTEN ASKED to rank the athletes I covered in my fifty years around Philadelphia sports. It is a tough question.

I covered dozens of athletes who are in various Halls of Fame. How do you compare athletes from different sports? How do you compare Bobby Clarke with Brian Dawkins? Julius Erving with Joe Frazier? Steve Carlton with Donovan McNabb? Allen Iverson with Bernie Parent? Bernard Hopkins with Smarty Jones?

It is impossible to compare them, but it doesn't stop people from asking.

I knew I couldn't write this book without addressing the question. These are the very debates that fuel sports fandom. Today, they call it "hot takes"—pundits like Stephen A. Smith and Skip Bayless voicing their opinions on TV—but it is nothing more than what I saw the regulars do every afternoon at Ray's Tavern.

If you are going to talk sports, "Who's the greatest?" has to be part of it.

I considered the entire who's who of Philadelphia athletes for the past half century. I studied the numbers, and while there was a lot of star power to consider, I kept coming back to one person—Mike Schmidt.

I wasn't influenced by friendship. I didn't know Mike Schmidt all that well. I knew Brian Dawkins and Reggie White because I spent more time around the Eagles. I got to know Bobby Clarke and Bernie Parent because our sons played youth hockey at the same rink in South Jersey.

I covered the Phillies as a columnist, and I was there when they won the World Series in 1980, but I did not travel with the team, so I didn't get close to any of the players. I wrote about Schmidt, obviously, and I interviewed him, mostly in groups, but he kept his distance—not just from me but from most people.

He would hit a game-winning home run and then stand at his locker and discuss it like "What's the big deal?" He would be standing right in front of you, but emotionally it was like he was on the other side of a moat. He was so aloof that *Daily News* columnist Bill Conlin called him "the Sultan of So What?" I once wrote that he led the league in Shrugging Percentage.

"What's that supposed to mean?" he asked.

I tried to explain. Shrugging, you know, like you just shrug it off.

He responded—no kidding—by shrugging.

So, I wasn't swayed by personal feelings in picking Schmidt as the best Philadelphia athlete of my time. I went purely by what I saw on the field, and what I saw was greatness. I saw him play eighteen seasons with the Phillies, earn three National League Most Valuable Player Awards, and basically rewrite the club's record book. He was a first-ballot Hall of Fame selection in 1995.

In covering sports, every so often it occurs to you that you might be watching the best *ever*. I felt that when I saw Wayne Gretzky play hockey. I felt it when I saw Michael Jordan on a basketball court. I felt it while watching the young Muhammad Ali.

I had that feeling about only two athletes I covered in Philadelphia. One was Reggie White; the other was Mike Schmidt. If I have to put one above the other, I'll go with Schmidt. With apologies to all the Brooks Robinson fans, I believe that Schmidt is the best third baseman who ever laced up a pair of spikes. That's my hot take, and I'm sticking to it.

Schmidt hit more home runs than any other third baseman in the history of the game (548). He won more Gold Gloves (10) than any other National League third baseman. He led the league in home runs a record eight times. He was voted into twelve All-Star Games, including the 1989 game after he retired.

Oddly, he was not a blue-chip prospect when the Phillies selected him in the second round of the 1971 draft. He received no scholarship offers when he graduated from Fairview High School in Dayton, Ohio.

He walked onto the team at Ohio University, and in three seasons, he batted .326 with 17 home runs.

Tony Lucadello, the Phillies' area scout, signed forty-nine players who made it to the major leagues, but Schmidt was the prospect who intrigued him the most. He was playing shortstop when Lucadello first saw him at Ohio University.

"He had great upper-body strength combined with fast hands," Lucadello said. "I knew we would have to be patient. I knew he would strike out a lot. But I believed once he adjusted to major league pitching, he could be a 40-home-run man. He was a big kid [6'2", 205 pounds] with bad knees, so I wasn't sure he had the range to play shortstop, but I thought he'd be a very good third baseman."

Lucadello convinced Paul Owens, the Phillies' farm director, to take a look at Schmidt. Owens came to one game—Ohio University versus Bowling Green—and saw Schmidt hit a monster home run off Doug Bair, who later pitched fifteen seasons in the majors. Owens was sold.

The Phillies signed Schmidt to a $32,500 contract with a $7,500 bonus. He looked overmatched in his first full major league season, batting .196 with 136 strikeouts in 367 at bats. Manager Danny Ozark said, "I'd trade Schmitty for a wagon load of pumpkins." Ozark wanted to send him back to the minors, but Owens argued against it.

"They didn't think he was ready," Owens said, "but I took the position that we had to get our young talent ready in a hurry. They were better off getting their feet wet against the Tom Seavers than they would be hitting against minor league pitching."

After the 1973 season, Schmidt played winter ball in Puerto Rico. There, he rediscovered his hitting stroke and his confidence. He had a breakout season in 1974, winning the first of three consecutive National League home run titles. He batted .282, with 36 home runs, 116 runs batted in, and 23 stolen bases.

Schmidt gave much of the credit to second baseman Dave Cash, an off-season acquisition from Pittsburgh. Cash gave the Phillies an experienced leadoff man, but more than that, he brought a new attitude to the clubhouse. His favorite expression was "Yes we can," and he drummed that message into his younger teammates, notably Larry Bowa, Greg Luzinski, and Mike Schmidt.

"Dave helped me tremendously," Schmidt said. "He patted me on the back and encouraged me. That's the hardest thing for a young player, staying positive. You always think your next 0-for-4 will be your last."

Schmidt had another big season—38 homers, 95 RBIs, 29 stolen bases—in 1975, as the Phillies topped the .500 mark for the first time in eight years.

Schmidt's first landmark game came on Easter Saturday in 1976, when he homered in four consecutive at bats at Wrigley Field. He knocked in eight runs to tie a club record in a wild 14–13 Phillies win.

"That day, Dick Allen was teasing me about losing the ability to have fun playing the game," Schmidt said. "He said he wanted to see a smile on my face. He said we were going to go out that day and have fun. He was throwing me passes [in infield practice] like a quarterback. We were cutting up and laughing, and I wound up hitting four homers. Maybe I should've done that more often."

Schmidt was a perfectionist, which is usually a good quality, except in a sport like baseball, where even a .300 hitter fails seven out of ten times. In my time around the Phillies, I couldn't help noticing how rarely Schmidt smiled. Go through his photo gallery and try to find one where he looks happy. It is very rare.

In some ways, that grim determination helped make him a great player, but it also took an emotional toll. He could hit the game-winning homer, but by the time he left the ballpark, he was already thinking about the next day's pitcher and how tough he was going to be. Guys like Dick Allen and Pete Rose tried to ease the pressure, and that day in Chicago was a prime example. Schmidt's four-home-run game sparked the club. The Phillies won fifty of their next sixty-three games and were off and running to the first of three straight National League East pennants.

While Schmidt piled up impressive numbers in the late '70s and the Phillies won more regular-season games than any other team in the division, there was something missing. The team always seemed to come up short in the postseason, and Schmidt was an easy target for the frustrated fan base.

The Phillies were swept by Cincinnati in the 1976 National League Championship Series, three games to none. Schmidt had no homers and 2 RBIs. The team lost the 1977 NLCS to Los Angeles, three games to one. Schmidt batted .063 (1 for 16). They lost the 1978 NLCS to the Dodgers, three games to one. Schmidt batted .200, with no homers and 1 RBI. He was roundly criticized for not being a clutch performer.

However, 1980 was a watershed year for Schmidt and the team. The Phillies won their first world championship, and Schmidt was the World Series MVP, batting .381, with 2 homers and 7 RBIs against the Kansas

City Royals. It was the culmination of a great season for Schmidt, who led the league with 48 home runs and 121 RBIs, both career highs. He won the first of his three National League MVP awards.

"I'm proud of the fact that I helped the team get to the World Series that year," he said, "and I'm proud of the fact that I came up big for the team when we finally got there. I got the job done in 1980, and after that I was able to face Philadelphia. I felt secure as a player for the first time in Philadelphia."

Schmidt carried that good feeling into the next season, and it appeared that he might be on his way to the best year of his career. In June, he led the National League in home runs, RBIs, on-base percentage, and slugging percentage, but then the players went on strike, and the season was shut down for fifty days. Schmidt finished that season with 31 homers to lead the league, but he was on pace to hit more than 50.

Two years later, the Phillies were back in the World Series against the Baltimore Orioles. Schmidt was coming off another great season; his 40 home runs led the National League for the sixth time. He had a stellar playoff series against the Dodgers, batting .467. He appeared poised for another big World Series. Instead, he went 1 for 20 with 6 strikeouts as the Orioles defeated the Phillies, four games to one.

After the final game, a dreary 5–0 loss, Schmidt stood at his locker for an hour answering questions. Of all his postgame interviews, that is the one I remember best, because he handled it so well. He talked honestly about the pain he was feeling. It was a different Mike Schmidt, more open and more human.

"Nobody in this city is more disappointed than I am right now," he said. "I'm sure the next couple days will be gut-wrenching. I'll spend hours reflecting on what went wrong."

A TV reporter asked Schmidt whether he felt "responsible" for the loss. The question was phrased so bluntly that I thought it might cause Schmidt to walk away. Instead, he took it head on.

"That's a hard question," he said. "If I had eight RBIs in the series, we might still be playing. The fact is I didn't. I probably tried too hard. I was pressing at the end, but that's nothing new. I just wasn't a good hitter this week, period."

Prior to Game 5, the story of the series was the dual slumps of Mike Schmidt and Baltimore's Eddie Murray. The two future Hall of Famers were a combined 3 for 32. However, Murray snapped out of it in the final game, hitting two home runs. I asked Schmidt what he was thinking as he watched Murray glide by on his home-run trot.

"I thought, 'That could have been me,' but it wasn't," he said. "All I know is Eddie could be 1 for 20, and the [Baltimore] fans would be chanting, 'Ed-die, Ed-die.' Here, I get booed, but Philadelphia is a different kind of town. This is a town where they put roses in your mailbox when you win, and they pull it down when you lose."

That was Schmidt's relationship with the Philadelphia fans: The highs were heady, and the lows were steep and painful. It is said that Schmidt was booed more than any athlete in the city's history. I don't know how you calculate something like that. Dick Allen was booed viciously in the '60s. Ryan Howard heard it even after winning a World Series. Ron Jaworski and Donovan McNabb were booed, and so was Charles Barkley.

But it is fair to say Schmidt got a rougher ride than he deserved. The national media talked about it all the time. Bob Costas once asked me, "What do those fans want? I don't get it." Costas began his broadcasting career in St. Louis, and he saw the way Stan Musial was revered in that city. He could not understand why the Philadelphia fans did not have Schmidt on a similar pedestal.

"I know that's your town, and you love it," Costas said to me, "but I'm sorry, that's just wrong."

You certainly couldn't question Schmidt's production. He hit 30 or more home runs a dozen times. As an offensive force, he ranks with the all-time greats. But he was aloof and inscrutable in a way that irritated the Philadelphia fans. This is a town where the fans want—no, insist—that their athletes show emotion. Schmidt didn't do that. It wasn't his personality.

On those occasions when Dallas Green would stand in the middle of the clubhouse and bellow, "Stop being so f—king cool," he was really addressing Schmidt. Pete Rose, a notorious needler, would sometimes walk past Schmidt and say, "Hey, Mr. Cool." Inside, Schmidt was wound tight, but he never let it show.

I once annoyed Schmidt by suggesting that he and Dodgers' third baseman Ron Cey switch teams. I was making the point that Schmidt would fit nicely in Los Angeles and Cey, with his stubby body and penguin waddle, would be a fan favorite in Philadelphia. Cey finished every game with a dirty uniform because he had to dive for every ground ball. Schmidt could have played a doubleheader in a top hat and tails.

When I presented the scenario to Schmidt, he shot back, "So you think Ron Cey is better than me?"

That's not what I was saying at all. Schmidt was superior in every aspect of the game. That wasn't even debatable. My point was that if you cast it like a movie, Cey and Schmidt were each better suited to playing in the other guy's town. It was a matter of styles. I must not have explained it well, because Schmidt walked away, shaking his head.

"You guys are unbelievable," he said.

Schmidt occasionally talked about the media—he once said Philadelphia is a place where athletes experience "the thrill of victory and the agony of reading about it the next day," a very funny line—but he was careful not to criticize the fans, no doubt believing it would only make matters worse.

However, in 1985, when the Phillies were mired in fifth place, and Schmidt was batting .237 and playing out of position at first base, his frustration boiled over. He did an interview with a Montreal writer in which he called the Philadelphia fans "uncontrollable" and "beyond help."

"Whatever I've got in my career now, I would've had a great deal more if I played in Los Angeles or Chicago," he said. "You name a town, somewhere where they were just grateful to have me around. I drive in 100 runs a year and hit 40 home runs; I would have been on more winning teams over the course of my career than most guys. It's a damn shame to have negative fan reactions tied to it."

Schmidt's words became headline news in Philadelphia. No one knew what to expect when the team returned to the Vet. The next home game was July 1 against the Cubs. More than twenty-three thousand people came to the park, and most of them were there to dump on Schmidt.

"I was scared out of my mind," he said.

Pitcher Larry Andersen, the team jokester, kept a fright wig in his locker. He suggested Schmidt wear it onto the field for pregame warm-ups. He believed that a good laugh might defuse the situation. Schmidt took the wig and borrowed shortstop Steve Jeltz's sunglasses when he took the field. The fans didn't know what was going on at first, but then they realized Schmidt was having fun with them. Instead of booing, there was laughter and even some cheers.

"It was the last thing people expected," Andersen said. "Schmitty was almost robotic in his approach to the game. The sight of him in that wig cracked people up. All these years later, people still bring that up: 'Remember the night Schmitty came out in the wig?' It showed another side of him, which was good."

After the game, Schmidt tried to explain his feelings.

"Sometimes it makes you want to be in Steve Carlton's shoes as far as the media is concerned," he said, alluding to the fact that Carlton did not talk to reporters for much of his career. "I regret saying what I said, but I don't deny saying it. Anything I've ever said about the fans was to try and make it more of a hometown environment [at the Vet] and make it more comfortable to play."

Those were tough times for the Phillies. The nucleus of the 1983 World Series team was gone, and the team was backsliding under manager John Felske. By 1987, there was only one compelling storyline, and it was Schmidt's pursuit of career home run number five hundred.

He went into the season needing five homers to join the select club, which at the time had only thirteen members. The *Daily News* planned a forty-page pullout to celebrate the milestone. Mike Rathet gave me the choice assignment of interviewing all the living members of the 500 Home Run Club.

I've talked about other assignments I dreaded—the wrestling series for one, the Moses Malone piece for another—but this one I embraced. I had a chance to interview ten of baseball's immortals: Hank Aaron, Willie Mays, Frank Robinson, Harmon Killebrew, Reggie Jackson, Mickey Mantle, Ted Williams, Willie McCovey, Eddie Matthews, and Ernie Banks.

I traveled coast to coast to do the interviews. Aaron, Killebrew, Williams, and Matthews were in Florida for spring training. Mays, Robinson, Jackson, and McCovey were doing similar duty in Arizona. I met up with Mantle and Banks at card shows. Every interview was enjoyable. Even Williams, who had a reputation for being surly and unapproachable, was a delight. We sat in the dugout for more than an hour, talking about his dual passions: hitting and fishing.

The 500 Clubbers had the utmost respect for Schmidt and were happy to welcome him into their ranks. Even those who never met him admired him. Killebrew was awed by his ten Gold Gloves. Killebrew was a third baseman early in his career but never dazzled anyone with his defense. Said Killebrew, "Schmidt plays the position better than some guys who were strictly glove men."

Mantle was impressed by the way Schmidt worked to improve every year.

"He used to chase more bad pitches than he does now," Mantle said. "He looks more relaxed at the plate. I hope he doesn't tie himself in knots thinking about 500. I know it affected me. That's all the newspaper guys wanted to talk about. I started pressing, wanting to get it over with. I wound up in a slump [4 for 33] until I finally hit the f—ker [no. 500], [and] then I was able to relax."

At the time, Aaron was the all-time home-run leader, with 755. He was fifty-three and working for the Atlanta Braves as the director of player development. We met at his office in West Palm Beach. Aaron had come to Philadelphia the previous summer for a ceremony honoring Schmidt. They talked at length about the adjustments a power hitter must make in his later years.

Aaron had three 40-plus-home-run seasons after the age of thirty-five. He broke Babe Ruth's career home-run record when he was forty. He said it was all about letting the mind pick up where the body leaves off.

"I didn't realize Schmidt was such a student of hitting," Aaron said. "He told me what he had done, moving up to the plate so he could pull the ball more. I told him that when I got older, I dropped my hands so I could get them around quicker.

"I wished him luck going for 500. He seemed to have it in its proper perspective. He said he wanted to enjoy the chase, and that's the right attitude. You can't let all the hoopla distract you.

"I've always liked Schmidt," Aaron said. "I thought he was a real big leaguer. By that, I mean he played the game very well in all phases, and he carried himself with a lot of class. I didn't think he got the credit he deserved until the Phillies won the World Series. That MVP was huge for him."

McCovey agreed when I caught up with him at the Giants' spring-training facility in Scottsdale, Arizona.

"Schmidt took a lot of abuse," McCovey said. "I went through the same thing in San Francisco. I came in as a rookie and moved Orlando Cepeda, the favorite son, off first base. It was a big controversy: Who should stay? Who should go?

"When Cepeda was traded, the press wanted to know why it wasn't me. The fans took sides. It got so bad, I looked forward to road trips so I could get away. But you hang on long enough, and things turn around. I left San Francisco for a while [and] then came back, and I was like a landmark. Schmidt has gone through the same cycle: hero, anti-hero, back to hero. The fans love him now, right?"

The fans certainly loved him that season, as he hit five homers in the first two weeks to arrive at the magic number. He hit number five hundred off Pittsburgh's Don Robinson on April 18, a two-on, two-out shot in the ninth inning to lift the Phillies to an 8–6 victory. It was a no-doubt-about-it rocket that left Three Rivers Stadium so quickly that Harry Kalas didn't have time for his trademark "That ball is outta here" call.

Instead, Kalas said, "Swing and a long drive. There it is, number five hundred. Career five-hundredth home run for Michael Jack Schmidt."

Schmidt did a fist-pumping happy dance as he began the biggest home-run trot of his career. It was an unusual show of emotion for Schmidt. He had a smile on his face as he reached home plate, where his teammates waited to greet him. He had threatened to kiss home plate on number five hundred, but when the moment came, he thought better of it.

"There were two reasons I didn't kiss home plate," he said. "One was that all my teammates were standing there. The other was that plate looked kind of dirty."

Schmidt hit the landmark home run on a Saturday. The *Daily News* doesn't publish on Sunday, so our special section did not hit the streets until Monday. My story on the 500 Home Run Club filled eleven of the forty pages. I rewrote the lead a dozen times. Finally, I settled on this:

> We stand in awe of The Slugger. He is part man and part myth. He is the heavyweight champion of our national pastime, Paul Bunyan with a 36-ounce switch. He swings hard, he hits hard and even when he fails, he fails hard.
>
> The Mighty Casey, now there was a Slugger. He struck out and they still wrote a poem about him. Roy Hobbs, The Natural, was another. Did you ever notice there aren't any literary classics devoted to singles hitters? It is always the man who carries the big stick. That's because The Slugger is a special breed. We can all close our eyes and make a lucky catch. Given enough chances, we can all throw a strike. But we can't all hit a baseball over the roof at Yankee Stadium.[1]

In my interviews, all the greats talked about how the 500 Home Run Club is the prestige address in Cooperstown, New York, an executive suite within the Hall of Fame itself. Jackson explained it well when he described the home run as the ultimate sports analogy.

"When people want to describe a great feeling," Jackson said, "they don't say, 'It was like making a hole in one.' They don't say, 'It was like serving an ace at Wimbledon.' They say, 'It was like hitting a home run in the World Series.'"

Two years after Schmidt hit that mammoth home run in Pittsburgh, he was thirty-nine and hitting .203 for a last-place team. He booted a routine ground ball in a game at San Francisco and stood for a long time staring into his glove, looking bewildered and embarrassed.

It was time to leave the game; he knew it. He told manager Nick Leyva about his decision on the flight to San Diego that night, and he announced it at a news conference the next day. It caught everyone— his teammates, the media, and the fans in Philadelphia—by surprise.

"The fire that I had in me for seventeen years has gone out," Schmidt said, wiping away tears. "I didn't like going out on the field without being aggressive. When I stood out there on third base, I knew I wasn't the player I should be. It was not me or the way I played the game for all those years. I just didn't have the same feeling.

"There were no plans [to retire], nothing staged. I made the decision after the first game in San Francisco, but I didn't have the guts to go through with it. The same thing happened after the second game. I just knew it was time. Unless you've been through it, no one can understand a decision like this."

Schmidt's words evoked memories of author Roger Kahn, who wrote in his classic book *The Boys of Summer*: "Unlike most, a ball player must confront two deaths. First, he perishes as an athlete."[2]

It is a reality that faces even the greatest athletes, even those in the 500 Home Run Club. Willie Mays finished his career stumbling around the outfield for the New York Mets. Schmidt, who was a Mays fan as a boy, vowed that would never happen to him.

"I don't want to leave this game ungracefully," he said.

I'm sure he meant it at the time, but he found himself doing the same thing. It is hard to walk away from something you love, even when you know it is the right thing to do. Joe Namath once told me he knew it was time to quit football when he was at practice one day and found himself feeling bored.

"I thought, 'I don't belong out here anymore,'" Namath said. He retired at the end of the season.

As the 1989 season wound down, the paper assigned me to do a piece on Schmidt in retirement. Did he miss the game? Did he regret his decision to walk away? I was pretty sure I knew the answer to that one. The Phillies were a last-place team playing out the string in an empty Vet. Schmidt had just finished judging the Miss America pageant. Where would you rather be: in the National League cellar or in the front row at a beauty pageant?

We set up a midweek lunch at the Rose Tree Inn in Media. Schmidt came with his wife, Donna, looking very relaxed in his golf shirt and jeans. It was two o'clock on a September afternoon, and the Schmidts had nothing planned, no appointments to keep. It felt good, Schmidt said. Different, but good.

"This is the time I used to leave for the ballpark," he said. "I'd already be thinking about the game and the pitcher we were going to face. The butterflies would be starting up in my stomach. I'd get so pumped up, I couldn't wait for the game to start. But it wasn't like that the last couple years. I'm glad I made the decision to get out when I did. This is a whole new lifestyle. I'm enjoying it."

"No second thoughts?" I asked.

"None," Schmidt said. "I wanted to move on with my life. It was time."

Four months had passed since the press conference in San Diego, time enough for regret to set in, but Schmidt wasn't feeling it. If anything, he felt liberated. He was enjoying the freedom. He was like Dick Vermeil when he stepped away from football and saw the colors of autumn for the first time. He found there was another world out there, and he was exploring it with Donna and the kids.

"A few weeks ago, Von [Hayes] called to congratulate me on the blue marlin I caught," Schmidt said, referring to the 470-pound fish he landed off Cape May, New Jersey. "Von was on his way to the ballpark. They had a doubleheader that night, and they were something like 22 games out. There I was, sitting on my boat, soaking up the sun. I thought, 'You made the right call, Mike. You're right where you should be.'"

Schmidt wasn't lacking for things to do. Golf tournaments, speaking engagements, card shows—the phone never stopped ringing. He was one of a half dozen baseball stars invited to the White House to meet President George H. W. Bush.

"I found out the president actually picked *his* favorite players," Schmidt said. "I was very flattered."

In July, he became the first player in major league history to be voted into the All-Star Game after he retired. He received 729,249 votes in the fan balloting, finishing well ahead of runner-up Chris Sabo of Cincinnati.

"It was like the ultimate curtain call," he said. "I never expected it."

The best thing about retirement, he said, was it gave him more time with his family. In the past, his children, Jessica and Jonathan, had to share their father with the autograph seekers around the Vet. Now they had him all to themselves as the family relaxed at home and vacationed in Bermuda and Avalon, New Jersey.

"This was the first time Mike attended their piano recitals," Donna said. "He was always either on the road or playing a night game."

"This was something I looked forward to," Schmidt said. "I knew having children later in life would allow me to be around for their formative years. Most players have their children early in their careers, and the kids are grown and gone by the time [the player] retires.

"Look at Bob Boone. His sons are in college, and Bob is still playing. I'm glad that didn't happen to me. I want to spend as much time with Jonathan and Jessica as I can. You know what might have been the best thing about this summer? Going to Jonathan's Little League games and sitting in the stands like a regular parent.

"I didn't have to watch from the car or sneak around in a Groucho Marx mask. The kids and parents got used to seeing me. It was great."

Schmidt became so involved with the Little League that he threw his gardening tools in the car one day and went to work on the field. He spent three hours mowing the grass, raking the infield, trimming the base lines, and leveling the pitcher's mound.

"I was all by myself," he said. "It must have been ninety-five degrees. I didn't intend to make a project out of it, but once I got started, I couldn't stop. You know me, I'm a perfectionist."

He also took a turn as hitting instructor for his son's team. Nice idea, bad results.

"I was watching the kids take batting practice one day," he said, "and the coach said, 'We could use your help.' I didn't want to step on anybody's toes, but the coach said, 'The kids would love it.' I said OK."

Schmidt took each boy aside and worked on his stance and his grip. The kids, naturally, were in awe. This was the great Mike Schmidt sharing his secrets of hitting. Jonathan's team was leading the Media Little League at the time and scoring runs in bunches, but after Schmidt worked with them, nothing.

"I sat there the next game, watching all these kids strike out," Schmidt said. "The parents were looking at me as if to say, 'Nice going.'"

"Oh, Mike," Donna said, "it wasn't that bad."

"Yes, it was," he said. "The good news is the kids got themselves straightened out eventually. I didn't do any permanent damage."

Who would have guessed it: Schmidt turned out to be a better groundskeeper than a coach. Crazy game, baseball.

Schmidt did not go to the Vet very often that summer. The Phillies were a mess, so that was part of it. He didn't want people asking him what was wrong and who to blame. He believed that it was best if he kept a low profile. On the occasions when he did go to a game, he had one rule.

"I don't boo," he said. "I'll *never* boo. I know how it feels."

The TV behind the bar was showing highlights from the previous night's game. Schmidt glanced over and returned to his salad. He didn't seem at all interested.

"You really don't miss it?" I asked.

"Yes and no," he said. "I don't miss the life. I don't miss the travel. I don't miss the interviews. I don't miss the rain delays and all the stuff that comes with losing. But I still get the urge to hit. I'll be watching a game on TV, and I'll grab a bat and put myself in the hitter's shoes. I love that challenge. I love that feeling. Hitting is the one thing I miss.

"I just have to accept the fact it's over. It's not the end of the world; it's just time to try something new."

Schmidt knew, of course, that in five years he was eligible for induction into the Baseball Hall of Fame. There was no suspense involved; he was a slam dunk to go in on the first ballot. What he did not know was when he went to Cooperstown in 1995, he would be joined by his good friend Rich Ashburn, who finally would be inducted into the hall after a thirty-year wait.

The Philadelphia fans made a pilgrimage to upstate New York that summer and filled the gallery with red Phillies caps and #20 jerseys. It was one of the biggest and most enthusiastic crowds in the hall's history.

The *Daily News* marked the occasion with a special tribute section honoring the two Phillies icons. Again, Rathet assigned me to do the lead piece, a Q&A with Schmidt and Ashburn discussing their careers, their friendship, and their shared love of baseball.

We set up the interview for May, when the Phillies were in Miami to play the Marlins. Ashburn was on the trip as part of the broadcast team. Schmidt had a home in nearby Jupiter, so we met at Joe Robbie Stadium. We did the interview in an empty football locker room. We talked for more than an hour. It was great fun, with the two men telling stories and occasionally jumping up, bat in hand, to make a point about hitting.

I'm a reporter, but I'm also a sports fan, so to spend an hour with the men who ranked one-two in Phillies history for games played, at bats, and hits was a fascinating trip back in time. Hearing Ashburn talk about the 1950 Whiz Kids and watching Schmidt re-create his first at bat against Nolan Ryan was wonderful.

I never saw Schmidt looser or more engaged than he was that day. All the doubt and worry he had carried around in his playing career was gone. His legacy was in place. His Hall of Fame plaque was being engraved. The fans he once called the worst in baseball now embraced him. He, in turn, was finally opening up.

I asked Ashburn if he had a theory about why the Philadelphia fans were so tough on Schmidt.

"I always felt that no matter how well Mike did, the fans thought he should have done better," Ashburn said. "He had streaks where he carried the ball club, but there was always that feeling [among fans] it was going to disappear. A lot of times you couldn't do any better than he did."

I went to a lot of Phillies games as a kid, and I never heard Ashburn booed, not once. You can't say that about many Philadelphia athletes. Doctor J maybe. But it was true of Ashburn. When I said it, Ashburn agreed. Schmidt had a theory.

"The perception was different, because we were different kinds of players," Schmidt said. "I could go two or three games and not do anything [exciting]. But Richie always drew his walks, dove into some bases, ran down fly balls. He was like a point guard in basketball, doing something all the time. His job was to get dirty, and in Philadelphia, that's the guy they love. I'm the guy they love one time, hate the other. Love, hate, love, hate."

Ashburn was his usual puckish self, needling Schmidt even as he praised him. At one point, I asked Ashburn whether Schmidt was the best third baseman he had seen in his many years around the game.

"The best third basemen I've seen are Mike, Brooks Robinson, and Billy Cox of the [Brooklyn] Dodgers," Ashburn said. "But I never saw anybody make as many great plays as Mike. Offensively, he was a better hitter than either Brooks or Cox. He wasn't a better hitter than Eddie Matthews but he was a better fielder."

Schmidt appeared blindsided. Eddie Matthews, a better hitter?

"Hey, that's a rip," Schmidt said.

"No, it's not," Ashburn said. "Did you ever see Eddie Matthews hit? I played against him a lot of years and let me tell you, he was a great hitter. You hit more home runs, but I'll bet he had more total hits."

"I don't think so," Schmidt said.

I pulled out the stat book and looked it up. Ashburn was right. Matthews had 2,315 career hits to 2,234 for Schmidt. He also hit for a higher average (.271 to Schmidt's .267). Schmidt asked to see the numbers for himself.

"Whaddya know, he did have more hits than me," Schmidt said.

Ashburn smiled, clearly pleased with himself.

"All-around though Mike was the best," Ashburn said. "Put it all together—defense, speed, base running, power—Mike is number one. Put it this way: There's no third baseman I would've rather had on my team. I'd play with Mike Schmidt any day."

"You never told me that," Schmidt said.

"Well, I'm telling you now," Ashburn replied.

Schmidt appeared genuinely touched.

"Thanks, Rich," he said. "That means a lot."

The two men shared a smile. It was a Hall of Fame moment.

13

Butterflies and Raging Bulls

I WATCHED A LOT OF BOXING over the years. The Friday Night Fights were always on the TV in my grandfather's bar. Dick Tiger, Bobo Olson, Emile Griffith, and Gene Fullmer were as familiar to me as the big names in baseball and football. I read *Ring Magazine* as faithfully as I read *Sports Illustrated* and the *Sporting News*.

I went to see my first live fight in December 1964. My grandfather bought tickets for the middleweight title fight between Philadelphia's Joey Giardello and Rubin "Hurricane" Carter at Convention Hall. Our seats were in last row of the balcony, so the view wasn't the best, but it was still exciting to see the local champion, then thirty-four, outbox and outpoint his younger opponent.

I saw a few more fights at the Arena and the Blue Horizon on North Broad Street. The Blue Horizon was hailed by *Sports Illustrated* and *Ring Magazine* as the best boxing venue in the country. It was basically a row house that was converted into a fight club by local promoter Jimmy Toppi. He renamed the building the Blue Horizon, but the fight crowd just called it "the Blue."

It didn't look like much from the outside, but when you climbed the steps to the second floor, it was like going back in time to the old fight clubs with the cigar smoke rising to the ceiling and spectators sitting on folding chairs. It wasn't like the casinos in Atlantic City, where the cocktail waitresses delivered drinks to ringside. The Blue was old school and proud of it.

The Blue was closed for a while in the '60s. J Russell Peltz, my Temple classmate, talked about reopening the place and promoting shows there. He was studying journalism and working at the *Temple News*, but he really wanted to be a boxing promoter. We didn't take him seriously. He was this rich kid from Lower Merion. How was he going to make it in the cutthroat world of professional boxing?

"You'll see," he would say, pointing down Broad Street to the Blue. "Right there."

On September 30, 1969, one year after graduation, I was standing in line at the box office to buy a ticket for Russell's first show at the Blue. The main event was Bennie Briscoe taking on Tito Marshall. Russell's father and mother were working the window selling tickets. General admission was three bucks, and ringside seats cost five.

Even though we were old friends, I had to pay for my ticket. There were no comps at Peltz Boxing, Inc.

"It's a business, Raymundo," Russell said.

Russell jammed 1,600 people into the Blue that night. It was a good show, too. Briscoe, a veteran of the Philly gym wars, knocked out Marshall. Two young fighters with real promise—Bobby "Boogaloo" Watts and Eugene "Cyclone" Hart—scored impressive wins on the undercard.

The sellout crowd was thoroughly entertained. It was a great opening night for Russell, who was dubbed "the mustachioed boy promoter" by *Daily News* columnist Tom Cushman.

Frank Bertucci, our fellow classmate, also came to the fight. On the way out, Frank and I stopped by the office to congratulate Russell on his big night. We found him tallying up the night's receipts. It was not a good idea to be alone with all that cash, especially in that neighborhood.

Russell was so busy counting that he didn't hear us come in. Frank nudged me and whispered, "Watch this." He jabbed his index finger into Russell's back.

"Stick 'em up," he said.

Russell threw up his hands. We started laughing, and he looked over his shoulder. He saw it was us.

"Don't *do* that," he said. "You want to give me a heart attack?"

"You want to get robbed?" Frank said. "Lock the door, why don't you?"

When Frank and I came to the next show, the office door was locked. Russell had learned.

The boy promoter is still in the fight game more than fifty years later. He moved on to promote shows at the Spectrum, the Arena, and the Atlantic City casinos. He booked dozens of world champions, including Thomas "Hitman" Hearns, Matthew Saad Muhammad, Roberto Duran, Marvin Hagler, and Michael Spinks. He was inducted into the International Boxing Hall of Fame. Russell was right all along; he did belong in the fight game.

I WENT TO SEVERAL CLOSED-CIRCUIT TELECASTS at the Spectrum, including the first Joe Frazier–Muhammad Ali fight in March 1971. The fight was at Madison Square Garden, but it was broadcast on a TV hookup to movie theaters and arenas around the world. The Spectrum was sold out, and it was buzzing.

I expected the crowd to be pro-Frazier since he was a Philly guy, but there was a lot of support for Ali. That was because the event had become politicized. Ali wasn't just fighting Frazier; he was fighting the U.S. government. With his refusal to enter the draft, he had become part of the protest against the Vietnam War. By the time Ali and Frazier climbed into the ring, it was a fight for America's conscience as much as it was for the heavyweight title.

It was not the typical fight crowd. There were a lot of college kids drawn to Ali as a symbol of their political ideology. There were more women in the audience, and they, too, seemed to favor the handsome and charismatic Ali. There also were the hard-core fight fans, faces I recognized from the Blue, and they were solidly behind Frazier, who was like royalty in the city's boxing community.

I was sitting in the upper deck with Ted Beitchman, who worked with me at the *Bulletin*. He was rooting for Ali, and I was rooting for Frazier. When the fighters appeared on the screen, the cheers were almost equal for each man. I sensed there were more Frazier fans in the building, but the Ali fans were more animated. They were on their feet, chanting, "Ali, Ali, Ali" as he played to the crowd. Frazier, typically, was all business.

There was a palpable tension, something you felt in the pit of your stomach as we awaited the opening bell. If it was like that in the Spectrum where we were watching on a fuzzy movie screen, I can only imagine what it was like at the Garden. My *Daily News* colleague Stan Hochman was ringside, and he said he never experienced anything like it.

Frank Sinatra was there, taking photos for *Life Magazine*. Richard Burton and Elizabeth Taylor were there, along with Hugh Hefner, Diana Ross, and Michael Caine. Hubert Humphrey and Ethel Kennedy provided the political backdrop, while '60s radical Abbie Hoffman led the counterculture cheers for Ali. Eagles owner Leonard Tose and John Taxin, the owner of Bookbinder's, were there rooting for Frazier.

Typically before a big fight or a big game, you have a sense of how it is likely to unfold. You have some idea based on past performance how one side is likely to win or the other side is likely to lose. But we never had seen either Ali or Frazier lose. They were a combined 57–0 as professionals. They had each won a gold medal at the Olympics. It was impossible to imagine either man losing, yet we knew that tonight one of them would.

Thirty million people watched the closed-circuit telecast. Richard Nixon had it beamed into the White House. The Garden issued 760 press credentials and turned down 500 more requests. Don Dunphy, the venerable boxing announcer, called the action, with actor Burt Lancaster in the unfamiliar role of color analyst. Lancaster later said it was the most nervous he had ever been in his life.

Mark Kram Sr., a boxing writer for *Sports Illustrated*, was among those at ringside. Norman Mailer was there covering the fight for *Life Magazine*, and Budd Schulberg, who wrote the screenplay for *On the Waterfront*, was covering it for *Playboy*, but no one captured the moment as well as Kram, who wrote of Ali:

> He has always wanted the world as his audience, wanted the kind of attention that few men in history ever receive. On Monday night it was his, all of it, the intense hate and love of his own nation, the singular concentration and concern of multitudes in every corner of the earth, all of it suddenly blowing across a squared patch of light like a relentless wind.[1]

Ali-Frazier I was the rare event that not only lived up to the hype but exceeded it: Ali on his toes, dancing and peppering Frazier with lightning-fast combinations, while Frazier bobbed and weaved and closed the distance between them. Once inside, Frazier pounded Ali with left hooks to the body.

In the early rounds, Ali shook his head and waved to the crowd as if to say, "He can't hurt me." But as the fight wore on and the hooks kept coming, Ali stopped showboating. His cocky smile became a grimace then a wince. He realized perhaps for the first time what he was dealing with in Joe Frazier.

In the days prior to the fight, Ali scoffed at those who suggested Frazier could win. Ali's game plan was always the same: Float like a butterfly, sting like a bee. In Frazier, he saw a stocky, thick-legged plodder who would be an easy target for his snake-quick jabs and counters. In Ali's view, this was a bullfight, and he was the matador.

Ali told friends, "Joe Frazier ain't never fought nobody like me," which was true. But it was also true that Ali never fought anyone like Frazier, a relentless buzz saw who kept moving forward, taking punches, and firing back.

Early in the fight, they were in a rare clinch, and Ali said, "You know who you messing with? I'm God." Frazier replied, "Well, God, you're in the wrong place tonight."

It sounds like Ali, brash and boastful. It also sounds like Frazier, determined and fearless.

Who could forget how the night ended, with Ali bouncing off the canvas in the fifteenth round, the tassels on his shoes twirling, after catching the most famous left hook in boxing history? He was in the wrong place, indeed.

Frazier's hook, Stan Hochman wrote, "came whistling out of Beaufort like the Suncoast Limited, screeching on invisible tracks, sending sparks into the night. Only the wail of the whistle was missing. And it crashed into Ali's handsome head just like the locomotive it resembled. . . . The legend of Muhammad Ali came tumbling down."[2]

Frazier won a unanimous decision. They met twice more, with Ali winning both times, once in a sluggish rematch at the Garden, and then at "the Thrilla in Manila," where the two men pounded each other until they could barely stand. When it was over, their names were linked forever.

When you talk about the great rivalries, there is Wilt Chamberlain and Bill Russell, Bjorn Borg and John McEnroe, Arnold Palmer and Jack Nicklaus, Larry Bird and Magic Johnson, Tom Brady and Peyton Manning, but Muhammad Ali and Joe Frazier occupies a place all its own. You can't mention one without the other. You can't think of one without the other.

That is the irony. Ali and Frazier didn't like each other, yet they made each other. On their own, each would have been a great fighter and champion, but together, they were legendary. Ali could say he was "the Greatest," but he needed Frazier to prove it. The two men punished each other, but at the same time, they defined each other.

Ali was a showman; Frazier was a blue-collar worker. Ali spouted poetry; Frazier labored in a slaughterhouse. Ali was political and outspoken; Frazier was not. His fight was inside the ropes. They were vastly different, yet fate put one man directly in the path of the other and let them sort it out over forty-four memorable rounds.

A few years later, Jack Wilson, the *Bulletin*'s sports editor, sent me to Ali's training camp in Deer Lake, Pennsylvania. Ali was prepping for another fight. Our boxing writer, Jack Fried, didn't feel like making the long drive, so the editor asked me to cover the workout, get a few quotes, and report back to Fried so he could write a story.

Deer Lake was not an easy place to find. It was a dot on the map, tucked away in Schuylkill County just off Route 61 near Pottsville. In the days before GPS technology, you needed very good directions and a little luck to find it. The camp consisted of a dozen log cabins on six acres of wooded hills.

Ali liked running the trails on Sculps Hill Mountain. He liked the rustic setting. It was a good place to get away from distractions and focus on training. But Ali was a lousy hermit. He craved attention and adulation; it was his oxygen. He needed it on a daily basis, so his handlers had no choice but to allow the press and the public in to watch his workouts.

Dozens of celebrities passed through Deer Lake. Elvis Presley, Michael Jackson, and Andy Warhol all came by. Frank Sinatra and Sammy Davis Jr. dropped in one day. Journalists came from all over the world. Four writers and a TV crew were expected the day I was there, but I was the only one who showed up. The others probably got lost. That happened a lot at Deer Lake.

A staffer walked me to Ali's quarters and announced, "Hey, Champ, I have a writer here from Philly. You got a couple minutes?"

Ali opened the door. My first reaction was, "Wow, he's bigger than I thought." He looked like an NFL tight end. He was 6'3", and with his broad shoulders and thick chest, he looked at least 15 pounds heavier than his listed weight of 215. What I remember most were his hands. They were enormous. When he made a fist, it looked like a cannonball.

He looked sleepy, like he had just rolled out of bed. He waved me inside, and we sat at a small table. He was not the boisterous showman

I saw so often on TV. He spoke softly and spent a great deal of time gazing out the window.

"Pretty up here, ain't it?" he said.

"It's so quiet," I said.

Ali laughed.

"Except when Howard Cosell is here," he said, "then it's not so quiet."

I mentioned the large rocks I saw on the trail. Each one was painted with the name of a former champion. Ali said he did that. Each day when he did his roadwork, he looked at the names for inspiration: Jack Dempsey, Archie Moore, Joe Louis, on and on.

I asked Ali whether he had a favorite. He said Jack Johnson, which did not surprise me. Johnson was the first black heavyweight champion, and, like Ali, he fought the establishment. In his case, it was the corrupt lords of boxing who sought to strip him of his title because of his race.

I told Ali I had seen *The Great White Hope* on Broadway. It was a Pulitzer Prize–winning play based on Johnson's life. James Earl Jones won a Tony Award for his portrayal of the embattled champion. Ali said he was offered the lead but turned it down. I asked why. Ali loved being on stage, and there is no bigger stage than Broadway. I would have expected him to jump at the chance.

"I had my reasons," he said.

Later, I was told Ali had turned it down because the script called for his character to make love to a white mistress. As a highly visible figure in the Nation of Islam, he did not feel comfortable doing that.

Ali spent the next twenty minutes talking about Johnson's career and how he was one of the great fighters of all time. That started a long discussion about boxing history. Ali talked about fighters from all eras, every weight class. His depth of knowledge surprised me.

Most football and baseball players don't know the history of their sports and, frankly, don't care. Vince Coleman once said of Jackie Robinson, "I don't know nothing about him." Robinson merely broke the color barrier in baseball and paved the way for Coleman and other minorities to earn millions in the big leagues. Coleman didn't care.

Ali was different. He was curious by nature and always eager to learn. He believed that there was something to be gained by studying other great fighters. I brought up the name of Joe Frazier. Ali asked me if I had seen their first fight. I said I had seen the closed-circuit telecast.

Ali leaned across the table.

"Who was you rooting for?" he asked.

I was caught completely off guard. I knew what he wanted me to say, but. . . .

Ali leaned in closer until his nose was inches from mine.

"I'm sure you was rooting for somebody," he said. "Who was it?"

I couldn't tell whether he was kidding or not. He was staring at me with no trace of a smile. A million thoughts flashed through my mind. The smart thing to do, obviously, was to say I had rooted for him, but I couldn't do it because it wasn't true. He asked me an honest question, and I felt I owed him an honest answer.

"I was rooting for Joe Frazier," I said.

Ali rocked back in his chair. He appeared more shocked than angry.

"Why was you rooting for Joe Frazier?" he asked.

"I'm from Philadelphia," I said. "I was rooting for the home team."

Ali stared at me for what felt like a very long time. Finally, his scowl softened.

"You know something?" he said. "I respect you for telling me that."

On the drive back to Philadelphia, I replayed our conversation in my mind. What did he mean—respect? Respect what? That I wanted Joe Frazier to beat him? It didn't make sense.

But I thought about what I saw at Deer Lake, all the people who surrounded Ali and did nothing but pat him on the back and say, "That's right, Champ, whatever you say." It was such an echo chamber that Ali may actually have found it refreshing to have someone give him a straight answer, even if it wasn't what he wanted to hear.

Calvin Coolidge once said, "It is difficult for men in high office to avoid the malady of self-delusion. They are always surrounded by worshippers. They are constantly, and for the most part sincerely, assured of their greatness. They live in an artificial atmosphere of adulation and exaltation which sooner or later impairs their judgment."[3]

In Ali's case, it was the worshippers who kept him fighting long after he should have retired. It was sad to see him turn old before our eyes the night he lost to Larry Holmes. It was sadder still to see him years later, hands trembling from the effects of Parkinson's disease, as he lit the torch at the Atlanta Olympics.

At one time, he was arguably the most recognizable man on the planet. He was mobbed on the streets of Manila and in the villages of Zaire. He was feted by kings and queens.

At the end, Ali could barely speak, and the light in his eyes was gone. But if you were ever in his presence even once, you remember.

I NEVER SAT RINGSIDE until January 1972, when I was assigned to cover Frazier's first title defense. His opponent was Terry Daniels, a twenty-five-year-old former football player from Southern Methodist University. It was a mismatch—everyone, including Daniels, agreed on that—but it was booked for New Orleans the night before Super Bowl VI.

The editor didn't want to send the boxing writer all the way to New Orleans for what figured to be a nothing fight, so since I was already there to cover the Super Bowl, I was assigned to cover the fight. My seat was right at the ring apron. I was so close to the action that I finished the night with blood splatters on my shirt.

Frazier had not fought since his win over Ali ten months earlier. His manager, Yank Durham, wanted a soft touch for Frazier's first fight back. The unknown Daniels fit the bill. Frazier weighed in at 215 pounds, 20 pounds more than Daniels. The challenger entered the ring, wearing a pink robe and a look of terror.

In the first round, Frazier shoved Daniels into the ropes right above me. He did that bob-and-weave move where he ducked his head and slipped a punch. He was still in a crouch when he uncoiled with a vicious left hook to Daniels's rib cage. The punch sounded like an axe splitting a piece of rotted wood. I had never heard anything quite like it before.

Daniels's legs quivered all the way down to his shoes. The fight was over at that point. Daniels stopped throwing punches; he was just hanging on. The referee stopped the slaughter in the fourth round.

That night I saw for the first time how truly brutal the sport was. All the fights I saw on TV, all the fights I saw from the upper deck, none of them looked and sounded like this. Until you are ringside, you can't appreciate the knee-buckling power of a Joe Frazier hook, a Thomas Hearns overhand right, or a Marvin Hagler combination.

In the movies, the punches land in slow motion and the sweat flies, but it is nothing like the real thing. The real thing is scary and savage. Even the preliminary bouts—the four-round fights that precede the main event—are that way. The skill level isn't the same, but the punches carry the same intent and land with the same heavy, skull-rattling thud.

I was ringside on June 20, 1980, when Sugar Ray Leonard fought Roberto Duran for the first time. The bout was held at the Olympic Stadium in Montreal, where Leonard had won his gold medal as part of the U.S. team at the 1976 Summer Games. There were 46,317 fans in the stands, many sitting so far away that they needed binoculars to see the ring.

Leonard was unbeaten in twenty-seven professional fights. Duran, the legendary "Hands of Stone," was 71–1, with 56 knockouts. I interviewed Leonard prior to the fight. He was confident, almost cocky. While we talked, he doodled a misshapen, bug-eyed little man on a piece of paper. When he finished, he wrote "Duran, after the fight." He talked about his upcoming appearance on *The Tonight Show.* He seemed more interested in meeting Johnny Carson than he did in meeting Duran.

Duran, on the other hand, was laser-focused. He wasn't always that way. He often frustrated his trainers, Ray Arcel and Freddie Brown. He worked hard some days and goofed off other days, but he was all in for this fight.

Duran didn't respect Leonard. In Duran's view, the gold medal, some slick marketing, and a carefully plotted path through the welterweight ranks accounted for Leonard's success. The fact that Leonard was earning $9 million for the fight while Duran was taking home just $1 million merely added to his rage.

Duran taunted Leonard when they came face to face in Montreal. He called him a sissy and worse. It wasn't surprising—Duran was crude that way—but this time there was a method to his bad manners. He wanted to make this a fight about Leonard's manhood. He wanted to goad Leonard into a slugging match, which clearly would favor Duran.

The strategy worked. Leonard ignored the pleas of trainer Angelo Dundee and went toe-to-toe with Duran. He did not use his superior speed and boxing ability. Instead, he chose to fight Duran in close quarters. It was exactly what Duran wanted.

In his other fights, Leonard had danced away from trouble and finished the night without a mark on his boyish face. After five rounds of trading shots with Duran, Leonard's eye was swollen, and blood was streaming from his nose. I heard a commotion behind me and turned to see Leonard's wife, Juanita, surrounded by security guards and medics. She had passed out.

The fight went the distance, with Duran winning a unanimous decision. There never was any doubt that there would be a rematch. This time, however, it was Leonard who had the fire in his belly. He also had a plan.

Duran returned home to Panama to celebrate his victory. Leonard knew Duran would party 24/7 and not set foot in the gym, so he wanted to schedule the rematch as soon as possible. They set the date for November, just five months after the first fight.

Duran didn't have much time to get in shape. He had gained thirty pounds, so he had to starve himself to make the welterweight limit. When he arrived in New Orleans, he did not look like the same fighter. He was puffy and sluggish, and the rage was gone from his eyes. In his workouts, he spent as much time leering at Christie Brinkley, who was there as a celebrity photographer, as he did hitting the heavy bag.

Leonard and Duran weighed in the morning of the fight. Duran made weight, but he wasn't the same rock-hard 147 pounds he had been in Montreal. An hour after the weigh in, I walked past the hotel coffee shop, and there was Duran, devouring a huge plate of eggs and potatoes. A short time later, I saw him walking through the lobby, eating an ice cream cone.

That night, we watched in disbelief as Duran quit in the middle of the fight. With sixteen seconds remaining in the eighth round, Duran uttered the famous words "No mas," which meant "No more," and walked to his corner, where a wide-eyed Arcel shouted, "What are you doing?"

High rollers who had paid $1,000 for ringside seats were on their feet, demanding a refund. Thousands of Duran's countrymen who had made the trip from Panama looked on in horror. Duran quitting? It was the last thing anyone expected.

Duran said he quit due to stomach cramps, and, after watching him stuff his face, I could almost buy that. But I believe that it was something else, something more painful than stomach cramps. I think he was embarrassed by the way Leonard dominated him. At times, Leonard made Duran look foolish, and that is the worst sort of pain for a bully.

In the first fight, Duran won the psychological battle; this time, it was Leonard. He got Duran to agree to the early rematch, and then he came in with a different game plan. Instead of fighting on the ropes, Leonard stayed in the center of the ring, where he could use his superior hand speed to land jabs and combinations. In short, he did all the things he should have done in Montreal.

The seventh round was the turning point. Leonard was so totally in command that he began taunting Duran. He dropped his hands to his sides, stuck out his chin, and pointed at it. Duran threw a wild right hand. Leonard pulled back and watched the punch sail harmlessly by.

Leonard began cranking up his right arm, bringing it around in a circle, twice and then three times. It looked as though he was loading up to throw a bolo punch. Instead, he flicked a left jab that hit Duran flush on the nose. He could not have humiliated Duran more thoroughly if he had reached over and pulled down his trunks.

When things did not improve in the next round, Duran quit.

Arcel, the eighty-one-year-old trainer, had worked with fighters for more than fifty years, honing the skills of big names from Benny Leonard to Larry Holmes. He thought he had seen it all, but he wasn't prepared for what he saw that night. We found him pacing the hall outside the locker room. He was still fuming.

"This is terrible, it's a disgrace," Arcel said. "I've handled thousands of fighters, and I never had one quit on me. I think he [Duran] needs a psychiatrist more than anything else."

It still bothers Leonard that when people talk about his second fight with Duran, they talk more about Duran quitting than Leonard winning.

"I don't want to hear that," Leonard said. "I beat him fair and square. I know it, and he knows it."

––––––––

IN 2009, MY WIP RADIO PARTNER Glen Macnow and I collaborated on *The Ultimate Book of Sports Movies,* a fun project in which we selected and ranked the one hundred greatest sports films of all time.

The book generated a lot of discussion—former Pennsylvania Governor Ed Rendell still thinks we had *Field of Dreams* too low at number eleven—but most people agreed on the films near the top. We had *Rocky* at number one, which was a popular choice, especially in Philadelphia, and we had *Hoosiers* at number two. We put *Raging Bull* third.

The late Roger Ebert, one of America's foremost critics, called *Raging Bull* the finest American film of the 1980s. Martin Scorsese directed, and Robert De Niro won an Oscar for his portrayal of Jake La Motta, the former middleweight champion. Vincent Canby of the *New York Times* called De Niro's performance "the best of his career, a titanic character, a furious original."[4]

In the film, La Motta is a brute, in and out of the ring. He assaults his wife and brother as viciously as he does his opponents. He is the anti-Rocky, unlikeable and impossible to root for, but whereas Rocky was a fictional character imagined by Sylvester Stallone, La Motta was a real person. He was living in New York, pretty much forgotten, when De Niro stumbled upon his autobiography, written in 1970, and decided to bring it to the big screen.

Raging Bull was nominated for eight Academy Awards, and it earned De Niro his second Oscar. The film also brought La Motta, then sixty, back from obscurity. He began touring the country, dusting off a stand-up comedy routine he had once performed in night clubs around New York. People who had never heard of La Motta before now were curious and wanted to see the real Raging Bull.

On a frigid February night in 1983, La Motta did a one-night stand-up appearance at Palumbo's in South Philadelphia. Palumbo's was a landmark in the neighborhood near the Italian Market. In the 1940s, Benny Goodman and his orchestra performed a live radio concert there. Frank Sinatra, a frequent guest, referred to it as his "black-tie saloon." Frank Rizzo hung out there when he was mayor.

By the 1980s, the big names had stopped coming, and Palumbo's was in decline. Landing La Motta, even for one night, as an opening act for singer Jimmy Darren was something of a coup. I called that morning and asked the bartender who answered the phone if La Motta would be available for interviews.

"How the hell would I know?" he said. "Come down here and ask him yourself."

I went to Palumbo's that night and paid the cover charge to get in. The room was almost full, so I wound up at a table in the corner. La Motta's stand-up was lame. Sample joke: "I fought Sugar Ray Robinson so many times, it's a wonder I don't have diabetes." But the audience laughed on cue and gave La Motta a nice hand when he finished his thirty-minute set.

I followed him down the hall to his dressing room. I was surprised to find Gene Seymour, another writer from the *Daily News*, waiting at the door. He was a city side reporter assigned to write a story about the show. I was there to write a column for sports. The news desk and sports department had not bothered to consult with each other, so Gene and I were both there.

We went into the dressing room, which was small and cluttered with framed photographs of headliners who had passed through, from Louis Armstrong to Jimmy Durante to Bobby Rydell. I sat across from La Motta, who seemed pleased to have two reporters at his show. Gene wanted to talk to La Motta about how his life had changed since the release of *Raging Bull*. I was more interested in his opinions on the current state of boxing.

"The movie has done great things for me," La Motta said. "I tell people I lost my title in 1951, and I won it back when *Raging Bull* came out. People come up to me now and call me 'Champ.' It's a nice feeling to be back on top after all these years. I had people approach me tonight and say, 'Jake, I saw you fight so-and-so at the Garden.' They remember better than me sometimes."

I pointed out that the movie was hardly flattering. It shows De Niro as La Motta battering Vikki, the second of his five wives, and going to prison for pimping out teenage girls at his seedy nightclub in Miami Beach.

"I did a lot of bad things, things I'm not proud of," La Motta said. "I always felt the world was against me, so I lashed out. I mistreated people, people I cared about. I know people see the movie and think I'm a terrible person. I just think I'm a person who made a lot of mistakes. I can tell you, I'm not that guy anymore. I'm older and smarter, I hope.

"When they had the premiere, Vikki was there. We're still friends, even after all these years. I said to her, 'Was I really that bad?' She said, 'No, Jake, you were worse.' I can't go back and change that, but I'm not gonna run from it either. I'm sure there are people who see the movie and hate me, but most of them shake my hand and say, 'Glad you're back.'"

La Motta had 106 professional fights. He won eighty-three and lost nineteen, with four draws. He estimates he earned $2 million in his career. His biggest payday was $75,000 for his sixth and final match with Robinson, where he lost the middleweight title on a technical knockout. In the movie, Scorsese shows it as a blinding flurry of Robinson punches, with a defenseless La Motta hanging on the ropes, covered in blood. Even if you've seen the film multiple times, you still turn away because it is so horrific.

"Yeah, seventy-five thousand," La Motta said. "Just about covered my medical bills."

La Motta turned pro in March 1941. He had twenty fights the first year. He had five fights in April alone. He fought three guys—Stanley Goisz, Lorne McCarthy, and Monroe Crewe—in eleven days. He fought Robinson twice in three weeks. He had two more fights in the three weeks after that. He takes pride in the fact that he came up the hard way.

He went eight years and eighty-eight fights before he finally got a title shot. Even then, he had to throw a fight to Billy Fox to satisfy the mobsters before they would give him a crack at the championship. It is one of the film's most wrenching scenes: La Motta, who defied the mobsters for years, finally giving in and allowing Fox to pummel him. In the locker room afterward, De Niro weeps on the shoulder of his brother Joey, played by Joe Pesci, wailing, "Why? Why? Why?"

That night at Palumbo's, I asked La Motta if that's really what happened.

"Hell yes, that's what happened," he said. "I didn't want to do it, but what choice did I have? I beat all the top guys, but they [the mobsters] held all the cards. They decided who fought for the title and who didn't. I wanted to make it on my own, but they told me it wasn't gonna happen unless I did what they said.

"It made me mad, but what was I gonna do, keep getting my brains beat out for nothing? I wasn't getting any younger. They told me, 'You do this for us, we guarantee you a shot at the title.' I didn't want to do it. I could've beaten Fox with one hand tied behind my back, but I said, 'If this is what I have to do to get a shot at the title, I'm gonna do it.'

"And you know what?" La Motta said, "I'd do it again."

La Motta stopped Marcel Cerdan in ten rounds to win the middleweight crown. He had one successful title defense and then lost the belt to Robinson. I asked La Motta if he agreed with the boxing historians who considered Robinson the greatest fighter who ever lived.

"I have to go along with that, Ray beat me five out of six [fights]," La Motta said. "He was smart, fast, and tough. We had some great fights. We brought out the best in each other. Put those six fights together today, and we could make $100 million.

"Trouble with the sport today is the kids are being brought along too fast. They don't fight all the four-rounders and six-rounders like we did. They don't serve that apprenticeship. That's why I can't compare today's fighters with fighters forty years ago. This kid Leonard is a good fighter, but he ain't no Sugar Ray Robinson."

Listening to La Motta reminded me of Johnny Hayes, one of the regulars at my grandfather's bar. He was a squatty little guy with a flattened nose and misshapen ear. I had never heard of a cauliflower ear, but that's what he had. My grandfather told me Hayes was once a professional boxer, a tough Philly lightweight who fought in the local clubs for seventeen years.

"He fought a guy named Billy Petrolle at the Arena," my grandfather said. "Billy Petrolle was one of the toughest guys around. They called him 'the Fargo Express.' Johnny lost, but he put up a heckuva fight, toe-to-toe the whole way."

I asked Hayes about it the next time I saw him. He had a raspy voice, no doubt the result of catching too many punches in the throat. He remembered the Petrolle fight. It was his first main event, the first time he was on the top of the card. Petrolle was tough, he said. He had a chin like a cinderblock.

"Best guy I ever fought," said Hayes, who had 107 professional fights. "It was a big night. First time my name was on the marquee. The Arena was packed. Crowd was on my side. Petrolle was just a little too tough. He stopped me in the fifth round. First time I was ever knocked out."

I asked if he remembered how much he had earned that night.

"Forty bucks," he said.

Forty bucks? For a main event?

"My manager got his cut [and] then there were taxes," Hayes said. "I walked out of there with forty bucks in my pocket. There were a lot of nights I fought for half of that. This was the '20s [1927 to be exact], so there wasn't much money. I had to fight twice a month just to pay the bills.

"Back then you paid your dues," he said. "Your manager would get you two fights in a week sometimes. You just did it. It's a tough racket."

La Motta agreed, but he had no complaints.

"Boxing was good to me, it was good to a lot of guys," he said. "I use the example of me and Rocky Graziano. We grew up in the same neighborhood on the Lower East Side. It was a tough place. We had to steal to get by. People hear that we went to reform school and say we were bad kids. Shit, we were just trying to survive.

"But we turned to boxing, and look what happened. We both won the middleweight championship, we had movies made about our lives [Graziano's life story was called *Somebody up There Likes Me*, starring a young Paul Newman]. We still live a block from each other uptown. We've done OK.

"I look back on where I came from," La Motta said, "and I see where I am today, and I can't say too much bad about boxing. Let these people in Washington, the ones who want to abolish the sport, talk all they want. They don't know nothing. Rocky and me, we can tell them a few things."

14

Saviors

J EFFREY LURIE leaned across the table.
"I have to ask you something," he said.

He lowered his voice so no one else could hear.

"Did they really throw snowballs at Santa Claus?" he asked.

I laughed.

"Welcome to Philadelphia," I said.

Lurie had just purchased the Eagles, which meant the Philadelphia fans now were part of his extended family. He had heard the stories about the 700 level at the Vet, the fights in the stands, and, of course, the snowballs. He wondered how much of it was true. That's why we were having lunch—he wanted to know.

"Yes, they threw snowballs at Santa Claus," I said.

Lurie thought it was an urban legend, one of those stories that starts as a joke and then gets repeated so often that people accept it as fact. But in this case, it was fact. I was there that day—December 15, 1968—when the snowballs flew at Franklin Field.

"Oh wow," Lurie said.

I understood his concern. He had just paid $185 million for the Eagles, and here I was, telling him he had acquired a fan base that was the tailgating version of Hell's Angels.

I tried to put it in context. I explained it was the final home game of a miserable season, one that saw the Eagles win two games, which was just enough to blow the first pick in the draft, which would be O. J. Simpson. Team owner Jerry Wolman was bankrupt, and the city was in open revolt against coach Joe Kuharich.

Put that many angry people in a frigid stadium filled with snow, factor in another dismal performance—a 24–17 loss to Minnesota— and a halftime show featuring a shabby Santa Claus with a sack of cheap candy canes, and what do you think will happen? A snowball barrage, that's what.

You can say the fans were misguided—certainly, Santa wasn't to blame for what had happened that season—but the sense of outrage was understandable. I didn't throw a snowball—my parents wouldn't let me, even though my mother bought a "Joe Must Go" button on her way into the stadium—but I totally got why other people were throwing them.

They threw so many snowballs at Santa that he ran for cover.

No one knew it would become the narrative that would define Philadelphia for generations. Fans have thrown snowballs and worse in other NFL stadiums. I once got hit with a beer bottle at Kezar Stadium in San Francisco. I looked at the guy who threw it. He said, "I was aiming for Brodie," meaning John Brodie, the 49ers quarterback. "You got in the way."

Oh, I see. It was my fault.

I had a beer poured on my head in Schaefer Stadium in Foxboro, and I had my windshield smashed in the parking lot of Giants Stadium after an Eagles game. The security guard saw the damage and shrugged. "That's what you get for coming here with Pennsylvania tags," he said. I drove home in an ice storm and learned that windshield wipers work much better when you have a windshield.

Clearly, bad behavior isn't limited to Philadelphia fans, but the image is out there, and, sad to say, it isn't likely to change. I had many verbal battles with journalists around the country about Philadelphia fans. They say Philly fans are the worst. I say they are the best. It doesn't matter what I say, though. It always comes back to Santa and the snowballs, and no other city has *that*.

I tried to assure Lurie he had hitched his wagon to the best fan base in sports. It was the first chance I had to meet him. He invited me to lunch to pick my brain. I had covered the Eagles for twenty-five years at that point, and as a kid I went to the games and spent my summers at training camp, so I was as steeped in Eagles lore as anyone. Lurie hoped I could provide some perspective.

He was a different sort of owner. He was an out-of-towner, for one thing. The previous owners going back to Bert Bell in 1933 had Philly roots. Jim Clark was active in city politics. Frank McNamee was the fire commissioner. Wolman was born upstate but hitchhiked to Philadelphia to see games at Connie Mack Stadium. Len Tose was from nearby Bridgeport. Before Norman Braman had a villa on the French Riviera, he lived in the Cobbs Creek section of Philadelphia.

Lurie was from Boston and grew up rooting for the Red Sox, the Celtics, and the Bruins. When the Eagles were winning the NFL championship in 1960, he was watching Babe Parilli quarterback the Boston Patriots in Fenway Park. Lurie was a movie producer, a Ph.D., and the heir to a publishing fortune. It was an impressive resume, but there was nothing about it that said "Philly."

He was a smart guy, obviously, but he needed some educating on the ways of Philadelphia. That's where I came in.

We met at Morton's. Lurie was still new in town, so he didn't turn any heads when he walked into the dining room. He was forty-two and prematurely gray with a mustache. When I told him he was the first Eagles owner with a mustache, he was surprised. I told him about Ed Khayat, the coach who had ordered everyone to shave in 1971. It would have been interesting to see Khayat try to enforce that rule if the owner had a mustache.

Lurie didn't see the logic in it.

"This is football, it's not the Army," he said.

He seemed like a sensible guy, more soft-spoken than I expected, given his wealth and his background as a movie producer. His grandfather had founded the General Cinema Corporation theater chain. He earned a master's degree in psychology from Boston University and a doctorate in social policy from Brandeis. He taught at Boston University before moving to Los Angeles to make movies.

One thing was obvious: Lurie was a huge football fan, far more than Braman, the previous owner. Lurie talked about how much he loved the NFL draft and how he gathered with his buddies in his man cave in Beverly Hills to watch the draft on ESPN. He had notebooks full of observations he made while watching the bowl games on TV. He was Mel Kiper without the pompadour.

"If it were up to me," Lurie said, "the NFL draft would be a national holiday."

He had tried to buy his hometown Patriots but lost out in the bidding to Robert Kraft. That was his dream, really. He loved the Patriots.

He went to the games at Schaefer Stadium and sat behind the family of quarterback Steve Grogan. Grogan's mother thanked Lurie for sticking up for her son during those bleak seasons when other fans were booing him.

Lurie told friends his goal was to one day own an NFL team, and when he heard the Eagles were on the block, he was the first in line. My only concern was that Lurie might be *too* into the game. The way he talked about the draft, I had visions of him going to the NFL scouting combine with a stopwatch and a whistle around his neck. It was refreshing to have an owner who cared about the game, but when an owner starts meddling in personnel decisions, it usually spells disaster.

The people who knew Lurie best—those who worked with him in academia and the film industry—said it would not be a problem. I interviewed Jeff Kanew, who directed the film *V. I. Warshawski*, which Lurie produced in 1991. The film starred Kathleen Turner as a Chicago private eye. It was savaged by the critics and flopped at the box office.

"You learn more about people when things go badly than when they go well," Kanew said. "The film was a disappointment. Usually when that happens in Hollywood, the finger pointing starts. This person blames that person, the producer blames the director, the director blames the cast, all the way down the line.

"Jeffrey's not that way. To use a sports analogy, he's a team player. He's totally supportive. He was on set all the time, and the only thing he wanted to know was, 'What can I do to help?' It didn't work out, but we're still friends. I can tell you that's not how it goes, usually."

"Relationships are important to me," Lurie said. "I want to have the kind of relationship with our players that allows them to give 100 percent because they know their owner is backing them 100 percent."

Philadelphia welcomed Lurie with open arms, but Philadelphia always welcomes its football owners with open arms. That's because the fans are so glad to be rid of the previous owner that the new guy is seen as a savior, regardless of who he is. The fans always throw bouquets in the beginning, but in the end it's, well, snowballs.

Wolman was a fan favorite when he bought the team in 1963, a self-made millionaire from Shenandoah who went from working in a paint store to building apartments. At thirty-six, he had amassed enough wealth to buy the Eagles for $5.5 million. He was an enthusiastic young guy who laced up a pair of cleats and played catch with the receivers at training camp.

Wolman walked the sidelines at Hershey, personally thanking the fans who came to watch practice. He got into a fistfight with some Washington fans who were heckling the Eagles at a scrimmage. Several coaches rushed into the melee and dragged the bantamweight owner to safety. Wolman wore his swollen lip as a badge of honor.

My parents and I were in the bar at the Cocoa Inn, the hotel in Hershey, watching the College All-Star Game on TV. A guy came in with a stack of pizzas and announced, "Compliments of Mr. Wolman." Wolman dropped in an hour later and picked up everyone's tab. Who wouldn't love a guy like that?

But the fans soured on Wolman when he signed Kuharich to a bizarre fifteen-year contract in 1965. Then his construction empire crumbled along with the high-rise he was building in Chicago, and, suddenly, he was staring at bankruptcy. He was forced to put the team up for sale in 1969.

Tose bought the club for $16 million. The fans were elated, because the first thing Tose did was fire Kuharich and bring in Pete Retzlaff, one of the most popular players in franchise history, to run things. Tose was flush with money, so all the worries about what could happen to the team under a bankrupt Wolman were gone.

The fans toasted the flamboyant Tose, who flew around town in a private helicopter with Eagles wings painted on the sides. At training camp, the team stopped practice to allow the helicopter to land on the field. Tose would emerge from the swirling dust, resplendent in his custom-made suit, and wave to the cheering crowd. It was quite a scene.

When Tose lost his fortune in the casinos, he tried to move the Eagles to Arizona. That made him public enemy number one in Philadelphia. When he sold the team to Braman, the fans were elated. The day the sale went through, I went to a bar in Delaware County, the Green Lantern, to see what people were saying. Billy Grossman, the owner, spoke for the entire region when he said, "We finally have an owner we can trust."

Braman put on a show at his introductory press conference, unfurling a T-shirt with "Eagles Super Bowl '86" in sequined letters. He looked into the TV cameras and said, "This is a dream come true. The Eagles belong to Philadelphia. I'm here to restore this team to the glory days of the past."

He told a heartwarming tale of hanging out in his father's barbershop and playing basketball on the playgrounds in West Philadelphia.

He talked about how his mother walked a mile to save a nickel on a dozen eggs. He said he was "shocked and in despair" when he read reports about the Eagles possibly moving to Arizona.

"It was as though my very, very best friend was passing away," Braman said.

He was the most popular man in town. That lasted four months, right up to the time the doors at training camp opened to reveal that most of the veterans were not there. That's because Braman informed the players who were looking for new contracts that they were out of luck.

"These players must realize I'm for real," Braman said. "Things will be done my way."

The team that took the field that day was missing its top rusher (Wilbert Montgomery), its top draft pick (Kevin Allen), its best receiver (Mike Quick), both offensive tackles, and three of the four starting linebackers. The Eagles had more Pro Bowl players out of camp (three) than in camp (two). They led the league in empty bunks and unrest.

Braman talked about bringing the Eagles "back to the Bert Bell era." I wrote a column suggesting it was Braman saying he wanted to go back to paying players $50 a game, which was how things worked in the 1930s.

He had the lowest-paid coaching staff in football. He slashed the budget for scouting, training camp, and travel. He talked about "belt-tightening" throughout the organization, but at the same time, he was giving the *New York Times* a tour of his estate in Florida, with its art collection and world-class wine cellar that contained four thousand bottles, including a magnum of 1890 Lafite-Rothschild.

He told the *Times*, "I open a bottle every night, even if it is just for my wife and I, even if I don't finish it. I don't care if the wine is worth $1,500."[1]

It never occurred to Braman that such a statement might anger some people, especially when he was pinching pennies with the coaches and players.

On the day training camp opened, Braman spoke to the team. He spelled out his agenda as the new owner. He thought the talk went well. The players had a different opinion.

"I know he wants to make changes," cornerback Roynell Young said, "but at the expense of getting the team embarrassed on the field? I don't know where he's coming from."

I wrote a column for the *Daily News* pointing out the obvious disconnect between the owner and the players. When Braman gushed about the first practice—"The players were hustling, the coaches were exhilarated, it was fabulous"—I suggested his nickname should be "Pasadena" because he was viewing everything through rose-colored glasses.

Braman took me aside the next day to tell me that my column was "chicken shit." Our relationship went downhill from there.

When the team played its first preseason game, I passed Braman in the press box. He was walking with another man. I said hello. Braman ignored me. As they passed, I heard Braman say to his companion, "That's the one I was telling you about." I can only imagine what he said.

Braman was highly successful at selling luxury cars in Florida, but he thought the car business and the NFL operated out of the same playbook. He thought replacing three starting linebackers was the same thing as replacing three BMW salesmen. He thought all employees were interchangeable. They are not.

"Braman's strategy is bold and imaginative," wrote Stan Hochman. "So was General Custer's."[2]

Initially, Stan liked Braman. He gave the new owner high marks for his first press conference. He described Braman as resembling "a thin Rod Steiger," and he chided other media members, including me, for asking impertinent questions. Stan said Braman "made a splendid first impression."[3]

It wasn't long before Stan saw Braman for what he was: a greedy narcissist who had no feel for the team or its fans. He ripped Braman when the team gave Quick, the great receiver, an empty golf bag as a retirement gift. He began referring to the owner as "Bottom Line Braman," and the name stuck.

Braman liked the power and the money that came with owning an NFL franchise. He was a smart businessman, which put him on the fast track of league owners. He chaired most of the big committees, including NFL Properties, where his marketing skills tripled the revenue almost overnight. He slapped the NFL logo on everything from T-shirts to bedspreads. For "Bottom Line Braman," the cash register never stopped ringing.

As for the game itself, Braman was indifferent. He talked about wanting to win, but if he really wanted to win, he would not have let so many good players walk away. He visited the locker room after games, and it was amusing to see team president Harry Gamble whispering the players' names in his ear so he could congratulate them. Otherwise, Braman would not have known Ben Smith from Antone Davis.

Coach Buddy Ryan viewed Braman as an absentee owner and dilettante. The rift between the two men began in 1987, when the players went on strike. There were other strikes in other seasons, but this time, the owners brought in "replacement" players and kept the season going. It was like Halloween, with guys off the street dressing up in NFL uniforms. It was a shameful strategy, and Braman was among its most fiery advocates.

I never thought they would go through with it. I thought they would bring in these guys and practice for a few days to make it appear they were going to play a game, but in the end, they would not do it. How could they? To field a team of scabs and play games that actually counted in the standings would make a mockery of the league.

I thought it was a bluff, but I was wrong.

The NFL went ahead and played the replacement games. They were ugly everywhere, but especially in Philadelphia, a strong labor town where the teamsters, the roofers, and hundreds of other union members came to the Vet to support the striking players. They stood at the gates, intimidating and in some cases assaulting fans who came to see the Eagles' replacement team play the Chicago Bears' replacement team.

Only 4,074 fans made it inside to see the pitiful game, which the Eagles lost, 34–3. Ryan made no attempt to hide his disdain for the phony games. He basically refused to coach the replacement team. It showed on the field, as the Eagles could hardly line up, much less run a play. Ryan said it was the sorriest bunch of players he ever saw. Braman believed that Ryan was deliberately trying to embarrass him, which he probably was.

The owner was seething when he met with reporters after the game. I asked the first question: "What was accomplished by playing this game?"

Braman glared at me. He was well aware of my feelings. I had trashed the replacement games all week in the paper and on the radio. I didn't blame the replacement players—they were guys chasing a dream—but I blamed the owners for creating this sham in an effort to break the players' union.

Braman said by playing the game, the owners proved they would not be intimidated. They proved the striking players would not shut down the NFL.

"We'll continue playing football," he said, "with them or without them."

Indeed, there were two more weeks of replacement football. The Eagles' stand-ins lost all three games and, in the process, blew any chance the real team had of making the playoffs. When the strike ended and the replacements were kicked out the door, Braman showed his appreciation by informing them that if they tried to keep their jerseys, their paychecks would be docked.

The fans turned on Braman over the next few years as he allowed star players to leave with the advent of free agency. He refused to pay the big money to retain Reggie White, Keith Jackson, Seth Joyner, Eric Allen, Clyde Simmons, Keith Byars, and others. His dismissal of Ryan and the decision to replace him with Rich Kotite was another strike against him.

Then in 1992, the NFL's financial records were made public as part of the league's antitrust suit. Roger Noll, a Stanford economics professor, said his research indicated Braman paid himself a salary of $7.5 million in 1990. The salary was recorded as general expenses when it could have been counted as profit for Braman.[4]

Noll found other owners did the same thing. Buffalo's Ralph Wilson pocketed $3.4 million, and Arizona's Bill Bidwell scooped up $1.1 million, but no one else dipped into the vault as deeply as Braman. Noll told the jury, "A $7.5-million salary to the president of a company that earned $45 million is not justified."

This is the same guy who charged his players for tape and sweat socks if they exceeded their allotted amount. While the fans and media howled, Braman shrugged. "I was accused of running the Eagles like a business," he said. "I plead guilty to that."[5]

In the years from 1987 through 1992, the Eagles were one of the NFL's worst teams in terms of signing players. In those years, the Eagles had fifty-four veteran players miss 988 days of training camp because they were holding out for more money. Meanwhile, the financial records showed that over the same period, the Eagles were the league's most profitable team, clearing $28.7 million.[6]

Money that could have been used to keep Reggie White in Philadelphia instead was reinvested into Braman's wine cellar.

By 1994, the team was sinking, and the criticism was mounting. *Daily News* columnist Rich Hofmann wrote, "No pro sports owner in this town—and no owner in the NFL—is as reviled in his city the way Braman is hated here."[7]

Tired of the grief, Braman put the Eagles up for sale. Lurie jumped right on the opportunity, paying the highest price ever for a professional sports franchise.

Like his predecessors, Lurie was instantly embraced. A billboard went up on I-95 with the message: "Welcome Jeffrey. Let the Eagles Fly." Mayor Ed Rendell threw a party for Lurie in city hall's courtyard attended by two thousand guests, including city officials, former players, and a string band. A sign was unfurled across from city hall that read: "The Plague Is Over."

Lurie hit all the right notes at his city hall event, saying, "It has always been my feeling that a sports franchise should be integrated and should take a leadership role in the community. I had no idea that the Eagles were as divorced as apparently they have been in certain ways."

He was referring to Braman's management style, which was chilly and detached. Tose, for all his faults, had a human touch. If a former coach or player needed tickets for a game, he could call the office and either Tose or Jim Murray would pick up the phone. Under Braman, those same people were made to feel like strangers.

"It immediately became a priority to do things like reestablish tradition," Lurie said. "It doesn't take a rocket scientist to figure that out. I had the alumni association for lunch, and I told them I bought the Eagles franchise and that they built it. That's the truth.

"With me, there's very little separation from the fan aspect and the owner aspect. I can't sit here as an owner and divorce myself from being a fan. It's in my heart, it's in my mind. Every decision I make is as if I'm one of the most passionate fans. I can't just divorce that passion. That's how I think of myself—as a fan, slash, owner."

There was something in the way Lurie spoke that resonated with the Philadelphia fans. They believed him. Even though he was from Boston, even though he had a framed photograph of the parquet floor in Boston Garden hanging in his office, he connected with Philadelphia. He was authentic in a way Braman never was.

He hired Joe Banner, a boyhood friend, and installed him as the team's chief operating officer. Initially, some NFL executives dismissed Lurie and Banner as amateurs who were in over their heads, but the perception changed as Banner took control of contract negotiations. He mastered the salary cap in a way that allowed the Eagles to gain a competitive advantage on the rest of the league.

The team went 7–9 in Lurie's first year, losing its last seven games, which led to Kotite's firing. Lurie almost hired Dick Vermeil to replace Kotite, but Vermeil had been retired for thirteen years and wasn't ready to come back, although he did return to coaching the following year with the St. Louis Rams and won a Super Bowl.

Lurie decided to give the fiery Ray Rhodes a chance. At forty-four, Rhodes had won five Super Bowl rings as an assistant coach with San Francisco. He was the first African American head coach in Eagles history and only the third in the NFL's modern era, following Art Shell in Oakland and Dennis Green in Minnesota.

Rhodes had come up the hard way. He had been a tenth-round draft choice of the New York Giants and played four seasons there before finishing with the 49ers under coach Bill Walsh.

"Ray caught my eye as a player," Walsh said. "It was clear right away that he had an excellent football mind. I felt with his total dedication and focus, he'd be an excellent coach."

Walsh made Rhodes the assistant secondary coach under George Seifert and then put him in charge of the secondary when Seifert moved up to defensive coordinator. Rhodes was credited with developing the 49ers' young defensive backs, including future Hall of Famer Ronnie Lott.

"In the game of football, there will always be ways to intimidate somebody," Lott said. "As long as Ray is coaching the emphasis is going to be on punishing the other guy. He wanted you to instill fear. He said fear was half the battle."[8]

Rhodes talked about fear a lot. He said that's how he went through life: imagining there was a loaded .38 pointed at his head.

"You want to get to the Super Bowl?" Rhodes said. "You play like someone is threatening your life. You have to succeed or else."

For Rhodes, it was more than mere words. He truly felt that way. Perhaps it was how he had grown up as a poor black kid in a small Texas town; maybe it was the fact that at 5'10" and 180 pounds, he had to fight to survive as a player. He was driven, almost frightfully so, when he took over the Eagles in 1995.

He gulped down antacid tablets like they were M&Ms. He kept smelling salts in his pocket and waved them under his nose to jolt him into some higher level of concentration. After games, there were dozens of ammonia capsules littering the bench area.

Rhodes surrounded himself with people who were similarly driven. His first hire was Jon Gruden, a thirty-one-year-old football savant Rhodes met in San Francisco. He started as an intern with the 49ers, breaking down film, but he was hungry in the same way Rhodes was hungry. When Rhodes got the Eagles job, he hired Gruden to be his offensive coordinator.

No one had heard of Gruden, so the *Daily News* sports editor assigned me to write a profile. When I met him for the first time, I was taken aback. With his blond hair and boyish face, he looked like a teenager. The previous night, when he ordered a beer, the waitress had asked to see his ID.

"They carded me," he said. "Do you believe that?"

I did believe it. He could have passed for a college kid on spring break. He certainly didn't look like an NFL coach.

I asked Gruden whether we could schedule an interview. He made a face—now famously known as "the Chucky face"—and said, "I don't know, man, I'm really busy."

I assured him I didn't need much time—thirty minutes, tops.

"OK," Gruden said. "Four o'clock tomorrow."

"See you then," I said, heading for the door.

"You know, that's 4 A.M.," he said.

I laughed. Cool, I thought, the guy has a sense of humor.

"I'm not kidding," Gruden said. "I get here at 4 A.M. You want to talk, it's gotta be then. Once I put the tape on, man, I'm grinding."

I arrived at the Vet the next morning right on time. Gruden was already at his desk with his playbook open.

"You said thirty minutes, right?" he said. "OK, you're on the clock. Let's go."

He wasn't kidding. I had thirty minutes to get Gruden's life story. It was more than enough. When Gruden talks, it is a machine-gun burst of words, which served him well as a TV analyst. He was whip smart, that was obvious right away. He understood where I was going: Boy coordinator, looks like Doogie Howser, is he up to the challenge? He answered most of my questions before I even asked them.

"Youth is something that people associate with inexperience and immaturity, especially in pro football," he said. He assumed the raspy voice of a veteran coach: "'Shoot, we can't put that guy in the game, he's just a rookie.' How many times have you heard that? All the time, right?"

Gruden didn't wait for an answer. He kept going.

"Age is not the issue: The issue is, 'Can you do the job?'" he said. "I was concerned when I went to Green Bay and was told I'd be coaching Sterling Sharpe and Mark Clayton. Those are two pretty good receivers, All Pros, but we got along great.

"I'm over that apprehension now. I'm not one of those guru kind of guys who thinks he has all the answers. I'm just a guy who tried to learn as much football as he could in hopes that someday I'd get a chance to use it. This is my shot."

Gruden talked about growing up in a football family. His father, Jim, was a college coach, working his way up the ladder from Heidelberg College to Notre Dame. He went to the Tampa Bay Buccaneers as an assistant coach and moved into the personnel department.

Gruden had been a high school quarterback, but at 5'10", he knew he wasn't going to make it to the NFL as a player. He set his sights on coaching, and, after graduating from the University of Dayton, he got his break with the 49ers. He interned under offensive coordinator Mike Holmgren and was on the practice field every day with Joe Montana and Steve Young. He wasn't making much money—he rode a bike to work—but he believed that soaking up all that knowledge was more valuable.

Gruden had a difficult task that season, trying to educate Cunningham, the ultimate ad lib quarterback, in the ways of the West Coast offense. Under Ryan, Cunningham was given free rein to run around and use his boundless athletic ability to make plays. It worked to a point: Cunningham did some remarkable things—like leading the team in passing *and* rushing four years in a row—but he came up short against the better defenses in the postseason.

Gruden's challenge was to get Cunningham to buy into the short-drop, quick-throw style of offense that worked so well for the 49ers. Cunningham did not have the patience or the discipline to adapt. He drove Gruden crazy.

The team got off to a 1–3 start, which included a 48–17 drubbing in Oakland. Rhodes and Gruden made the decision to bench Cunningham and start Rodney Peete at quarterback. Peete didn't have Cunningham's arm, and he certainly didn't have Cunningham's legs, but he could run the West Coast offense. With Peete in the lineup, the Eagles turned their season around, winning seven of the next eight games.

On a blustery December day, the Eagles met division-leading Dallas at the Vet. The Eagles were 8–5, and the Cowboys were 10–3. With a win, the Eagles would establish themselves as a viable playoff contender. The night before the game, Rhodes delivered a memorable speech, laced with profanity and graphic imagery, comparing the Cowboys coming into the Vet to vandals coming into your home, robbing you, raping your wife, and sodomizing your children.

"It was more street talk than pep talk," guard Guy McIntyre said, "but Ray put it to each player: 'What are you gonna do about it?'"

It was beyond politically incorrect, but it worked: The Eagles played inspired football. The score was tied 17–17 late in the fourth quarter.

Dallas had the ball, fourth down and less than a foot to go for a first down at their 29-yard line. Coach Barry Switzer decided to go for the first down rather than punt.

"I wouldn't do this," said Fox TV analyst John Madden.

The Cowboys went with their best short-yardage play: a handoff to Emmitt Smith, running left behind fullback Daryl Johnston, tackle Mark Tuinei, and guard Nate Newton. The defense, led by tackle Andy Harmon and linebackers Bill Romanowski and Kurt Gouveia, stopped Smith in his tracks.

Over the roar of the crowd, Eagles radio analyst Stan Walters could be heard saying, "Uh oh, the officials are talking. We might have a problem."

Referee Ed Hochuli ruled the clock had ticked down to the two-minute warning before the ball was snapped. Therefore, it was a dead ball, no play. Switzer was handed a reprieve. He had seen his gamble blow up in his face. Surely, he wouldn't try it again—but he did. Not only did Switzer go for it again; he told quarterback Troy Aikman to run the same play.

"You would've thought we'd have an emotional letdown after stopping them and having the play waved off," said defensive end William Fuller, "but we were fired up. We were saying, 'C'mon, bring it on.'"

Aikman handed off to Smith again, and Harmon, Romanowski, and Mike Mamula stopped him cold. The Eagles took possession and won the game on a 42-yard field goal by Gary Anderson. The 20–17 win helped the Eagles finish the regular season with a 10–6 record and sent them into the NFC playoffs as a wild-card team.

Their opponent was the Detroit Lions, who rode into the postseason on a seven-game winning streak. They had the league's number-one offense with a pair of receivers, Herman Moore and Brett Perriman, who combined for 231 catches and 23 touchdowns. Barry Sanders rushed for 1,500 yards and 11 touchdowns. The Lions had outscored their last four opponents, 132–34.

I flew to Detroit that week to write a piece about the Lions. I went to the Wednesday practice at the Pontiac Silverdome. I was planning to do an article about Moore and Perriman, but when the locker room opened, they were nowhere to be found. I figured they were in the shower or the training room, so I waited by their lockers. I noticed a group of writers gathered around Lomas Brown, the Lions' Pro Bowl tackle. I decided to listen in while I waited for Moore and Perriman.

The first thing I heard Brown say was, "Any oddsmaker who doesn't pick us is doing himself a great disservice."

Say what?

"There is no question in my mind that we're going to win this game," Brown said. "It's just a matter of how much are we going to win it by and how long is it going to take."

I pulled out my notebook and started writing. I forgot all about Moore and Perriman. Brown, bless his heart, was writing my story for me.

"I'm serious about this," he said. "You need players who will talk like this. You need guys who will say, 'Hey, by the end of the first quarter, we want to have this game over with.' And that's how it should be.

"I'm not being boastful, I'm just very confident. I have no doubt we're going to beat this team. If they [the Eagles] want to take it like I'm being overconfident, fine, they can take it that way. I know the talent on our team. We have an offense that nobody can stop."

I called the *Daily News* to let the editors know they wouldn't be getting that Moore and Perriman story.

"I have something better," I said.

I wrote the story, and the editors played it on page 1. By noon, Rhodes had it posted on the locker room's bulletin board. He talked to the team before practice, telling the players that Brown "guaranteed" a Lions' victory. That wasn't really true. Brown had never used the word "guarantee," but Rhodes thought it made for a better rallying cry. He was right. The Eagles were fired up for the game, and so were the fans.

The Eagles jumped on the Lions early and built a 51–7 lead en route to a 58–37 victory. Peete, a former Lion, threw three touchdown passes, and Ricky Watters ran for two more scores as the Eagles amassed the third-highest point total in postseason history. As the clock ticked down, the fans chanted "Lo-mas, Lo-mas." On the radio, Walters chuckled and said, "Lomas, where are you?"

It was the first time something I had written actually played into the game itself. It was just luck, really. If either Moore or Perriman were at their lockers when they were supposed to be, none of this would have happened. Brown's voice would not have carried beyond the Detroit suburbs. But I just happened to wander by at the right moment, and Lomas did the rest.

After the game, Rhodes pulled me aside.

"I owe you a game ball," he said.

I told him I couldn't accept it, but I had a suggestion.

"Send it to Lomas," I said.

Rhodes laughed.

"I may just do that," he said.

Rhodes won NFL Coach of the Year honors that season, and when the Eagles started 7–2 the following year with a rousing 31–21 win over the Cowboys, it appeared they were on their way to great things. Then, with stunning swiftness, it all fell apart.

They lost four of the next seven games and limped into the playoffs, where they were quickly dispatched by the 49ers. They fell to 6–9–1 the next year and bottomed out at 3–13 in 1998, setting a franchise record for losses in a season.

So where did it all go wrong? Instability in the front office was part of the problem. The Eagles had three different scouting directors in Rhodes's four seasons. Rhodes asked for and got more power in person- nel matters—"I don't want to go to war with somebody else's soldiers," he said—but he made a mess of it. His drafts were poor, and his free- agent signings were worse.

By the end, all the black coffee and ammonia capsules in the world couldn't keep him going. When Lurie fired Rhodes, it was almost mer- ciful.

"This is a day where, as an owner, I hate it," Lurie said. "It's an uncomfortable situation. This is a friend of mine, somebody I gave his first chance to be a head coach. But production is the key in this busi- ness. We're making a change, but this is a tough one to make."

Later in his office, the owner was still feeling the pain.

"So hard," he said, talking about letting Rhodes go. "But when I bought the team, I said my goal was to bring a Super Bowl champion- ship to this city. That hasn't changed. I really thought we were close, but we'll keep going. We'll get there, I still believe that. We'll get there."

15

Tell Me a Story

WHEN I WAS A KID, I opened the daily newspaper, turned to the sports page, and read the columns by Sandy Grady, Larry Merchant, and Stan Hochman. When we went to Eagles training camp, I saw the *Bulletin*'s Hugh Brown watching practice and taking notes. I thought, "That's what I want to do."

I never wanted to do anything else. I never thought about being anything else. I wanted to write for a newspaper. I loved the idea of seeing my column in print. When my fifth-grade teacher said I should be a writer, it wasn't a surprise. I was thinking that too.

When I was hired by the *Bulletin*, my grandfather clipped my stories from the paper and taped them on the mirror behind the bar. He could not have been prouder if I had been the mayor of Philadelphia.

I spent almost thirty years in newspapers, starting at the *Delaware County Times* and then working for the *Bulletin* and later the *Daily News*. I was writing about the teams I grew up with. I thought I would do it forever, but sometimes things happen that you can't foresee.

In 1995, I was invited to an event at the Ritz Five in Old City. Steve Sabol, the president of NFL Films, was speaking at a symposium with filmmakers from around the world. The topic was how NFL Films had changed sports on television.

Sabol and his father, Ed, started the company in Philadelphia in 1962. Together, they built the most honored sports television empire in the world. They took a violent game and turned it into an art form, a ballet performed by hulking men in helmets and pads. Oscar-winning directors Ron Howard and Oliver Stone were among those influenced by the cinematic style of NFL Films.

Steve and I had met in 1970, when I was covering the Eagles and he was sharing an apartment with Tim Rossovich. They were an odd couple—Steve was an artsy straight arrow, and Rossovich was a wild man who ate glass and set himself on fire—but they threw great parties.

Steve and I shared a love for football and a love for movies, so when he invited me to the symposium, of course I accepted. But when the event rolled around, I was coming off a long road trip, and I was worn out. I considered just climbing into bed, but my wife, Maria, reminded me we had RSVP'd.

"We really should go," she said.

So, we got in the car and headed downtown.

Steve's talk drew a big crowd of international artists. They knew very little about American football, but they were fascinated by what they saw on the screen—a football spinning in slow motion, a wide receiver flipped in the air. Ninety percent of them wouldn't know Jerry Rice from Jerry Lewis, but it didn't matter. You didn't have to be a football fan to appreciate such great cinematography.

A question and answer period followed. Steve was asked if there were any new projects on the horizon. He said he was working on a film called *Football America*. He wanted to take the NFL Films cameras to the sandlots, the high schools, even the prisons—anywhere the game was played. It would be a film about everyday football heroes who live next door, bag your groceries, and play for the sheer joy of it.

Maria whispered, "You'd love to work on something like that."

"Yeah, it's a great idea," I said.

"Why don't you talk to Steve?" she said. "See if you can get involved."

"Involved how?" I said. "I'm not a filmmaker."

"Just talk to him. See what he says."

There was a reception afterward, but Steve was surrounded by film critics. I didn't want to intrude, and I wasn't sure what I would have said to him anyway. I gave up and went home. But Maria wasn't ready to let it drop. She called Steve the next day and told him of my interest in *Football America*.

"Tell him to come see me," he said.

A week later, I met with Steve and Phil Tuckett, the producer in charge of *Football America*. Phil was a former receiver with the San Diego Chargers. He had written an article for *Sport Magazine* about making the team as a free agent titled "How I Earned My Lightning Bolt." Ed Sabol liked it so much that he hired Phil as a producer even though he had no experience in filmmaking.

Over the next thirty years, Phil established himself as one of the most versatile people in the industry. He was an accomplished cameraman, film editor, writer, and director, with an office full of Emmys. He had crossed over into music and produced rock videos for Journey, Def Leppard, the Black Crowes, and Jon Secada.

But at heart, Phil was still a football player, and he loved the idea of *Football America*. The thought of returning to the grassroots of the game really appealed to him.

When we met, Steve explained that *Football America* was still just a concept. They had a vision of what they wanted the film to be, but they had to find the individual stories that would provide the narrative. What they needed, Steve said, was a researcher, someone who could find those stories.

"If we gave you a month, do you think you could come up with a dozen stories?" he asked.

"Give me a month and I'll come up with a hundred," I replied.

I worked the phones, calling every writer I knew to ask a simple question: "What's the best football story in your area?" It could be anything, I said. It could be a high school team, a college team, peewees, flag football, whatever. I was looking for good human-interest stories that we could follow through the 1995 season.

After three weeks, I had 108 story ideas. I brought them to Steve and Phil. Over the course of three days, we narrowed them down to ten stories that became the heart of *Football America*.

We found Bob Blechen, a sixty-five-year-old man still playing semi-pro football in California. We found Gene and Dot Murphy, a husband and wife coaching a junior college team in Hinds, Mississippi. We found a high school team in Juneau, Alaska, that was coached by a bush pilot and played its games on 100 yards of volcanic ash.

We found the smallest high school in America with a football team. Guthrie (Texas) High School had just fourteen students—eight boys and six girls. They played six-man football, a game created for the small schools in rural America. They had *Friday Night Lights*, but on a much smaller scale.

The last piece was the most challenging, and that was filming inside the walls of the State Correctional Institution in Graterford, Pennsylvania. It is a maximum-security prison thirty miles north of Philadelphia. There was a time when Graterford had a team in the Delaware Valley Semipro Conference, but they were expelled in 1985, after one of their games ended in a brawl. No teams would come to Graterford after that.

So, the prison created an in-house rough-touch league where the inmates were the coaches, the players, and even the referees. They held a draft every year and formed six teams that played on Saturdays.

I talked to the prison authorities about filming the games. They were reluctant. They feared the cameras would ratchet up the intensity and the games might get out of hand. There also was the issue of bringing our crews into the prison. What if something happened? Can you imagine if there was a riot and the NFL Films crew was taken hostage? It would be national news.

Finally, the warden agreed to let us in, but he made it clear that if there was an incident of any kind, he would pull the plug.

It took more than an hour to get our gear through security that first Saturday. Every trunk, every camera case, every roll of film had to be inspected. The guards were not happy. We were just one more thing for them to worry about.

"Shouldn't you guys be filming the Eagles?" a guard asked.

"That's tomorrow," Phil said. "Today we're here."

"Yeah, but why?"

"Because it's football," Phil said, lifting his camera to his shoulder.

It was an eerie feeling to walk through the cell block on our way to the prison yard. We were all in our NFL Films gear, pushing carts loaded with equipment past men who stared at us through the bars, not saying a word.

But once the game started, it was like football anywhere. There were big plays, end-zone dances, high fives, and laughter. It was enough to make you forget about the thirty-foot-high walls and guard towers, at least for a few hours. The prisoners took it very seriously.

I interviewed one of the players after the game. He was a husky guy in his twenties, a former high school star now serving a life sentence for murder. I asked what football meant to the men inside.

"When I'm running with the ball, man, there are no walls," he said. "It's the only time I feel free."

Moments like that—powerful and poignant—convinced me that *Football America* had a chance to be a very good show. My involvement was supposed to end when I delivered the story ideas to Steve and Phil, but I became emotionally involved in the project. I wanted to see it through.

I asked sports editor Mike Rathet if I could have a one-year leave of absence from the *Daily News*. That would give me enough time to write the script and work on the final edit. The two-hour special was scheduled to air on Turner Network Television in September 1996. I would come back to the *Daily News* after that.

Rathet took my request to upper management, and it was denied. If I wanted to work on the film full-time, I would have to leave the paper. I was surprised and disappointed. I didn't think it was an unreasonable request, but no matter. The answer was no.

Now I had to make a tough decision. I had worked in newspapers for twenty-eight years. It was all I had ever done. If I quit, I would have to look for another job when the film was completed. At fifty years of age, it was a scary proposition.

I talked it over with Maria. She, too, was a reporter for the *Daily News*, so she saw it from both sides. She asked, "What do *you* want to do?"

I said I was all in on *Football America.*

"Then you should do it," she said.

"But what about after?" I replied.

"We'll figure it out," she said.

So, I said goodbye to the newspaper and started working full-time on *Football America.* I set up shop in the corner of Phil's office and began traveling with the crews. I helped with the interviews while I gathered information for the script. I sat with film editor Jeff Hillegass as he sifted through more than five hundred hours of footage.

The writing proved more challenging than I expected. I had spent almost thirty years writing about football for newspapers. How different could it be to write about football for television? As it turned out, it was very different.

In newspapers, it is all about the words. It takes hundreds, even thousands of them to fill a page. In TV, there are so many elements—talking heads, radio calls, crowd noise, and, of course, music—in addition to the words. A writer's job is to fill the empty spaces—a few seconds here and there—with pieces of information that move the story along.

The idea is to say more with fewer words. At the newspaper, I wrote pieces of one thousand words or more. I could paint with a broad brush. In writing for TV, I felt like I was dispensing words with an eyedropper. I also had to write in shorter sentences. Long paragraphs full of descriptive imagery may be lovely on the printed page, but they leave narrators gasping for air.

"You don't have to write about the blue sky and the sun-drenched field," Steve said. "This is TV—the viewer can see it."

TNT poured a lot of money into the project. We logged more than a quarter million air miles filming the various stories, which stretched from coast to coast. NFL Films composers Tom Hedden and Dave Robidoux wrote original music for the show and recorded it with the London Symphony.

Delivering *Football America* on schedule required a team effort. Steve enlisted producers Chris Barlow, Greg Kohs, Suzanne Morgan, David Swain, and Bob Angelo to work on various segments in addition to their usual NFL duties. Phil locked himself in an editing suite for weeks at a time.

I was entrusted with writing the script. It was my first time writing for TV, and here I was, writing a two-hour prime-time network special. I felt even more pressure when Phil told me that James Coburn would be our narrator. James Coburn, the Oscar-winning actor, would be reading my words? Are you freaking kidding me?

Phil and I flew to Los Angeles to record the script. We met Coburn at a studio in Beverly Hills. The film was already cut, and there were specific holes that Coburn had to fill. I timed each one—five seconds for this line, eight seconds for that line, and so on. The narrator had to hit each one perfectly.

Coburn had done this many times before. He was doing more voice-over work than acting because he had severe rheumatoid arthritis. He was very limited in what he could do with his hands, and it greatly restricted what he could do on camera. However, his voice was as strong as ever, so he made a nice living by reading commercials and narrating documentaries.

It helped that Coburn was a football fan. He understood the terminology. Best of all, he got the concept. Grassroots football. Small-town America. Love of the game. He was born in rural Nebraska, so under that silk shirt and Malibu tan beat the heart of a cornhusker.

"This is going to be fun," he said as he settled into the recording studio with my script and a cappuccino.

Phil and I watched from the control booth. We started recording, and Coburn nailed every line. His timing, his tone, his energy—it was all perfect.

Several times, Coburn read a line and said, "Let me try something." Then he would read the line again—a little slower, perhaps, or with a slight change in inflection—and it would be even better. He took each line and polished it until it sparkled like fine crystal.

It was a new experience, hearing my words read aloud. My teacher, Sister Clare Ursula, did it in the fifth grade. Jack Giampalmi, our high school class president, did it when I wrote his speech for graduation night, but it was nothing like hearing James Coburn read the script for *Football America.*

"It's a game played with the exuberance of youth."

Dramatic pause, then. . . .

"It's a game played with a warrior's heart."

Coburn looked up and smiled at me through the glass.

"This is beautiful writing," he said.

I felt goosebumps rising on my arms.

TNT launched *Football America* with a premiere at the Waldorf Astoria Hotel in New York. Several hundred VIPs were there, including NFL executives and several participants from the film, as well as superstar quarterbacks Jim Kelly and Brett Favre. Coburn flew in from California to host the event along with Steve and Phil.

There were critics from the *New York Times,* the *New York Daily News,* the *Washington Post,* the *Boston Globe,* and other major papers in the audience. An old friend from the *Bulletin,* Alan Richman, who was winning James Beard Awards as a food writer for *GQ,* came by to lend moral support.

"Ignore the critics," he said. "They're miserable people. They hate everything."

"But you're a critic," I said.

"See?" he said. "I rest my case."

As it turned out, the reviews were glowing. John Martin of the *New York Times* called it "the best sports documentary of the year." Mike McDaniel of the *Houston Chronicle* wrote, "It is one of the best sports specials I've ever seen." Milton Kent of the *Baltimore Sun* called it "wonderful." Dusty Saunders of the Scripps Howard News Service said, "*Football America* is one of the most compelling programs fans will see during this or any other season."

Larry Stewart of the *Los Angeles Times* found the true heart of the film, saying, "You want to save this and show your kids. It shows football can be more than point spreads and uncivilized behavior and that there is still some purity left in sports."

Anthony Newman, a safety with the New Orleans Saints, saw the film and was so moved by the story of the Juneau High School team that he bought them new uniforms and equipment.

After the show aired, I figured my work was finished, and I'd be off to find my next job. I was packing up when Steve called me into his office. He asked if I would like to stay on as a producer. I didn't expect that. I still didn't know the fine points of filmmaking.

"You know football, and you know how to tell a story," he said. "The rest, we can teach you."

How could I say no? If you love football, there is no better place to work than NFL Films, and there was no better boss than Steve Sabol. I accepted his offer, but it was not without concern.

When I changed newspapers—going from the *Daily Times* to the *Bulletin* and then to the *Daily News*—I was changing addresses but not professions. It was emotional, especially leaving the *Bulletin*, where I got my start in sportswriting, but the paper was sinking financially. Going to the *Daily News*, with its circulation soaring, was an easy call.

This was an entirely different situation. Rather than pursue another job in newspapers, I was going to make films, something I had never done. I had learned a few things while working on *Football America*, but my role was mostly writing and researching. To be a producer, I had to learn how to operate an editing machine and cut a film. What if I couldn't do it?

Steve kept coming back to the same point: It is all about storytelling. He liked to quote an old proverb: "Tell me a fact and I'll learn. Tell me a truth and I'll believe. But tell me a story and it will live in my heart forever." NFL Films was in the storytelling business. No one in sports TV did it better.

It was proven again when the Sports Emmy nominations were announced. NFL Films earned seven nominations, including four for *Football America*. At the awards dinner in New York, *Football America* walked off with the top prize: Outstanding Edited Sports Special. We were up against tough competition: *100 Years of Olympic Glory* (TBS), the *Wide World of Sports 35th Anniversary Special* (ABC), and the *Sports Illustrated Olympic Special* (NBC). Yet we won.

Phil accepted the award, saying, "We wanted to make a movie that wasn't just about football, but about America." The National Academy of Television Arts and Sciences made it official: We had succeeded.

When I came home with my Emmy, Maria put it on the kitchen table, and we stared at it. She said, "Do you remember the night at the Ritz? You didn't want to go."

I remembered.

"If we didn't go," she said, "none of this would've happened."

She was right. I never would have known about *Football America*. I never would have gone to work at NFL Films. And there wouldn't be an Emmy on our kitchen table. Funny isn't it, how things work out?

I was at NFL Films for another twelve years and worked on some great projects. I co-produced three HBO specials: one on Johnny Unitas, another on pro football in the 1950s, and a third on Super Bowl I. I worked with Jeff Hillegass, who won an Emmy for editing *Football America*, and Steve Seidman, who has a Ph.D. in film from UCLA. Working with the Doctor was literally an education in filmmaking.

I also worked closely with Chris Barlow. Together, we produced ESPN specials on George Allen, Dick Vermeil, and Jim Brown. We did another special on the 2000 induction weekend at the Pro Football Hall of Fame. We had the chance to interview more than a hundred Hall of Famers. I sat across from Paul Hornung and watched his eyes fill with tears as he talked about Vince Lombardi. I listened to Raymond Berry talk about being in the huddle with Unitas when he led the winning drive in the '58 championship game. I saw Franco Harris's eyes light up when I asked about "the Immaculate Reception."

Those moments stay with you.

A funny thing happened during my time at NFL Films: I became a fast writer. When I was writing for newspapers, I was painfully slow. It would take me six or seven hours to write a column that another writer would dash off in half the time. I was locked inside every NFL stadium at least once. I scaled fences and outran guard dogs, all while carrying a typewriter. They don't teach that in journalism school.

Bill Lyon was a fine columnist for the *Philadelphia Inquirer*. He could write a column in thirty minutes. He had that gift. For me, it was a struggle. We sat next to each other many nights in the Vet Stadium press box. One night, he was packing to leave, and I still had not written a word.

"Don't wait for inspiration," he said. "Just start the damn thing."

It was excellent advice. I just couldn't do it. Writing was slow torture for me.

When I became a full-time producer, Steve asked me to serve as a script doctor. It meant looking over other scripts and tweaking a line here and there. But sometimes Steve would call in a panic and tell me to get to the studio right away. He would hand me a script and tell me to rewrite it while the narration was going on.

I would be writing new lines and handing them to the narrator while he was recording. The narrator would be reading one line and literally reaching for the next. I would be sitting next to him, writing as fast as I could. It was like working on an assembly line, just with words instead of nuts and bolts.

I found, to my amazement, that I could do it. I could write fast. Who knew?

Phil and I teamed up again on a project called *Lost Treasures*. It came about by accident. I was looking for a shot of Ron Waller, the interim coach in San Diego in 1973. Phil suggested pulling the film cans from the games Waller had coached. All game films are stored in the vault at NFL Films, dated and filed by year. It is better organized than the Library of Congress.

We opened the can for the San Diego–Denver game of November 11, 1973. It was Waller's first game as head coach. Sure enough, there were several good shots of Waller. OK, mission accomplished. But Phil also found a shot of Denver's Floyd Little walking off the field, with his jersey ripped and hanging off his shoulder pads. It was a great shot, and it had never been used.

"It makes you wonder how many other shots like that are in here," Phil said.

He got that "Hey, I have an idea" twinkle in his eye. He suggested a new show: *Lost Treasures of NFL Films*. We would go through the vault and unearth all the great shots that had never made it to the screen.

Initially we planned to produce one sixty-minute special, but we found so much great stuff that *Lost Treasures* became a twenty-two-episode series that aired on ESPN. I produced several pieces, including one about the demolitions of Three Rivers Stadium in Pittsburgh and Memorial Stadium in Baltimore.

The show, *There Used to Be a Ballpark*, was my idea, so Phil said I should take it all the way. I directed the shoots, wrote the script, selected the music, and edited the film. It was the first time I had done an entire show by myself. When I showed him the rough cut, Phil smiled and said, "Congratulations, you're a filmmaker." It was like receiving my diploma.

I stayed at NFL Films through the 2008 season, but by then, the NFL Network had taken over. New people were calling the shots. Phil surprised everyone by leaving the company after forty years to take a teaching job at a junior college in Utah. I decided to move on too.

I already was doing talk shows on 94WIP Sports Radio in Philadelphia and doubling as a football analyst on a new cable TV network,

Comcast SportsNet. We did a live postgame show after every Eagles game. Michael Barkann was the host, and Tom Brookshier and I broke down the Xs and Os.

Comcast SportsNet launched in 1997. The network scheduled the Eagles postgame show for ninety minutes, which I thought was crazy since, by league rule, we were not allowed to show highlights. It would just be the three of us, sitting at a desk talking. I mean, who was going to watch that?

The program director was Tom Stathakes. I knew him from KYW, where I had produced commentaries during the newspaper strike in 1985. I told him I didn't think the show had a chance of succeeding. We were up against live games on other channels. Our show was like C-SPAN. Why would fans watch us when they could watch a live game?

Stathakes agreed the format might not work in most cities, but Philadelphia wasn't most cities. In Philadelphia, the fans can't get enough Eagles coverage. He believed that people would switch from other games to watch us. They want the analysis, the interviews, the coach's press conference, all of it, win or lose.

Comcast SportsNet went on the air in October 1997, which meant we were five weeks late jumping into the NFL season. Ratings were strong from the start. Fans got in the habit of grabbing the remote when the Eagles game ended and switching over to SportsNet. Stathakes was right. People were watching.

The studio was in what was then known as the CoreStates Center, home of the Flyers and the Sixers. The TV studio was still under construction. There were cables everywhere, and wires were hanging from the ceiling. The restrooms weren't finished, so you had to run outside to the port-a-pots. That was no fun on a cold December day.

The brass invited then-mayor Ed Rendell to the first postgame show to give the new network his blessing. It was supposed to be a quick guest appearance, but the mayor—an Eagles season-ticket holder and total sports junkie—stayed for the entire show. He was so into it, talking football and trading good-natured barbs with the panel, that they decided to make him a regular.

Political columnists got all huffy and asked if the mayor didn't have more important things to do than spend his Sundays second-guessing Ray Rhodes. He responded by saying city hall was a ghost town on Sundays, so it wasn't as though he was missing anything. And even the most skeptical fans had to admit the mayor was no football poseur. He knew his stuff and was not afraid to voice his opinion.

268 • Ray Didinger

Leading up to the 1999 draft, he openly campaigned for the Eagles to draft University of Texas running back Ricky Williams. The other option was Syracuse quarterback Donovan McNabb. The mayor was all over television and radio saying he wanted Williams. When the Eagles took McNabb, he said it was a mistake.

McNabb, of course, came in and played very well. The mayor admitted he was wrong and became one of the quarterback's most vocal supporters. McNabb was asked what he thought of Rendell as a football analyst. He replied, "I think he's a very good mayor." It was a funny line, and the mayor laughed along with everyone else. He never took himself too seriously, even after he was elected governor in 2002.

In December 2010, the NFL postponed an Eagles-Vikings game because the weather forecast called for snow. There was no snow on the ground, but the forecast was for a foot or more late in the day. The city said the decision was made in the interest of public safety. The governor criticized the postponement. He said it was further proof that we were becoming, in his words, "a nation of wusses."

His comment sparked a debate in the national media—he wrote an op-ed piece that ran in the *Washington Times* titled "The Wussification of America"—but that is what made him such fun to work with. You never knew what he was going to say. He and I lived one block apart in East Falls, so I drove him home after every show. At the governor's urging, we usually stopped for a hoagie on the way.

The analyst role on the show changed several times. Johnny Sample, a former New York Jet, came aboard in Year 3. Vaughn Hebron, a former Eagle, joined us after winning two Super Bowls with Denver. Tra Thomas and Ike Reese did the show as well. Each former player brought his own perspective, and the ratings continued to climb. For fans, we were like their postgame tailgate party.

In 2006, *Philadelphia Magazine* picked *Eagles Post-Game Live* as the best local TV show for its annual "Best of Philly" issue. Eagles Hall of Famer Brian Westbrook joined us for three seasons, and now we have the fiery Seth Joyner and Barrett Brooks breaking down the game. In February 2018, we all sat together in Minneapolis and watched the Eagles win their first Super Bowl.

I combined my TV duties with appearances on WIP. Sports talk was a novelty when a team of investors, including Flyers president Ed Snider and Tom Brookshier, bought the station in 1988 and introduced the all-sports format. I thought it would run out of steam in a year or two. Again, I was wrong.

WIP became one of the top stations in the market. It made a smart decision by hiring an all-star lineup of local sportswriters to serve as talk show hosts. Angelo Cataldi, who wrote for the *Inquirer* and was a Pulitzer finalist for his Eagles coverage, anchored the morning drive with fellow *Inquirer* alum Al Morganti and Rhea Hughes, who worked her way up from producer to co-host. Together, they set the table for the city's sports conversation.

Glen Macnow and Mike Missinelli were two more *Inquirer* writers who left the newspaper to work at WIP. Stan Hochman continued to write for the *Daily News*, but he became a regular contributor to the station. I came aboard as well. The program director put Stan and me together on Saturday mornings. He called the show *The Morning Sports Page*, which made sense since we were still working for the *Daily News*.

We talked sports for four hours every Saturday. It was a blast. I had read Stan's columns every day when I was riding the subway to Temple. I had the utmost respect for him. Every time we worked together, I learned something.

Stan had a vacation house at the Jersey shore and decided he would rather spend his Saturdays sitting on the porch with his wife, Gloria, than sitting in a studio with me. I can't say I blamed him, but WIP wanted to keep the *Sports Page* theme going, so they paired me with another *Inquirer* writer, Don McKee. We worked together for a few years, and then they paired me with Glen Macnow.

We had met in the press box a few times, but I didn't know him that well. He was a former political writer who came to the *Inquirer* from Detroit to write about sports business. He was a good writer, and he made a seamless transition to radio. He was smart and funny, with an insatiable appetite for barbecued ribs and Netflix.

Happily, it could not have worked out better. We're now the Prof and R Diddy. Glen taught a journalism class at St. Joseph's University, so that's how he became "the Prof." An e-mailer to the *Eagles Post-Game Live* show gave me the nickname "R Diddy," which Vaughn and the governor found hilarious. I don't mind it. I see the irony.

Glen and I don't agree on everything. He loves the Beatles, I favor the Rolling Stones. He likes Sheryl Crow, I'm partial to Linda Ronstadt. He has cats, I have a bulldog. When we collaborated on *The Ultimate Book of Sports Movies*, we had opposite views of *Rudy*: Glen hated it, I liked it. He is sure it is because my wife went to Notre Dame. I tell him that's not true, but, whatever, we've gotten past that.

We have worked together for almost twenty years and become close friends. When I celebrated my seventieth birthday, Glen surprised me by turning our entire show into an R Diddy tribute with friends and some of my boyhood heroes—former Phillies pitcher Jack Baldschun, for example—calling in. He even had Dick Vermeil call in from his winery in California. I was truly touched.

It has been a great partnership, and I hope it continues for a long time. It is nice to hear listeners say they look forward to our weekend shows. They listen while they are jogging, running errands, or taking the kids to Little League. They say it sounds like we're having a good time, and that's because we are.

It was a challenge in the spring of 2020, when the coronavirus swept across the land and the world as we knew it ceased to exist. Professional sports locked its doors, the NCAA basketball tournament was shut down, and everything went dark. It was a tough time for everyone, but especially for those who worked in sports talk radio, because there was literally nothing going on.

Concern about the pandemic forced Glen and I to work apart. He did the show from his home in Havertown, and I went to WIP. All those years when we worked together, either in studio or on location, we communicated through winks, nudges, and hand signals. But how would it work when we could not see each other?

I thought we would be like two guys stumbling around in the dark, but it wasn't like that at all. We had worked together for so long that we were like two old jazz musicians who knew each other's rhythms. Physically, Glen and I were miles apart, but it sounded like we were sitting next to each other, just like always.

Glen came up with the idea of doing long-form interviews with well-known people—Flyers Hall of Famer Bernie Parent, Villanova basketball coach Jay Wright, former heavyweight champion George Foreman, ring announcer Michael Buffer, and Olympic hockey captain Mike Eruzione, among others. They would come on the show and basically tell their life stories. It was fascinating to learn that Heisman Trophy winner Herschel Walker was bullied to the point of tears in elementary school. Every interview had a surprise like that.

Three weeks into the pandemic, a man named Bill called the show to say thanks.

"You guys are helping a lot of people get through this," he said.

The truth is those same people were helping Glen and me get through it too.

16

Time's Yours

When Jeffrey Lurie was looking for a coach to succeed Ray Rhodes, there was no shortage of candidates. Mike Holmgren was ready to leave Green Bay. Brian Billick was a hot name after resurrecting Randall Cunningham's career in Minnesota. Jim Haslett, the defensive coordinator in Pittsburgh, was a rising star.

But Lurie surprised everyone by hiring Andy Reid, an unknown position coach from the Packers. The reaction among fans and media was: "Andy who?"

Reid was forty-one years old, which made him the second-youngest head coach in the NFL. He was making the jump from position coach to head coach. No one had done that since Art Shell with the Oakland Raiders ten years earlier. Usually the progression is position coach to coordinator to head coach. Reid was skipping a step.

He had no head coaching experience. He had coached at four different colleges—San Francisco State, Northern Arizona, Texas–El Paso, and Missouri—always as an assistant. He spent seven years as an assistant in Green Bay. Now he would be running the show in Philadelphia.

Lurie had gone the same route with Rhodes, and we saw how that ended. Why did he think this time would be any different?

I looked up Reid's bio on the Green Bay website. He was the tight ends' coach, then assistant line coach, and finally the quarterbacks' coach. That meant trying to harness the wild stallion that was the young Brett Favre. I saw Reid's photograph, and something clicked.

"Oh, *that* guy," I said.

Let me explain. . . .

I was working at NFL Films, so I went through a lot of footage. The most entertaining stuff was what our sound cameras got in the bench area: coaches and players plotting strategy or just goofing around. The Packers' bench was particularly lively because of Favre. He drove coaches crazy.

I always saw this big guy with a moustache standing next to him. He often looked annoyed because Favre didn't do what he was told. The coaches would send in a play, and Favre would do something entirely different.

Sometimes it worked in spectacular fashion—that's how Favre won three Most Valuable Player awards—and sometimes it didn't. When it didn't, Holmgren, the head coach, would lose his mind.

Without fail, every time Favre screwed up, the big guy would take the bullet. Holmgren would come over fuming. The big guy would step forward and say it was his fault. Favre would hide behind him, grinning like a kid who had pulled one over on the teacher.

We had Favre wired for sound in a preseason game. He was told to run a certain play, but he ran something else. The result was a sack and a fumble. Holmgren came over, and the big guy stepped in, his hand raised like a cop stopping traffic.

"That's on me," he said. "I sent in the wrong personnel."

"What the hell, we went over this last night," Holmgren said.

"I know," the big guy said tapping his chest. "My fault."

"Well, damn it, get it together," Holmgren said.

Only after the head coach stormed off did Favre appear. He put his arm around the big guy's shoulders.

"I love you, man," Favre said.

"Yeah, I can tell," the big guy said with a sigh.

I never knew the assistant coach's name until the Eagles hired him. It was Reid.

He dwarfed Lurie when they walked into their first press conference on January 11, 1999. The owner was smiling; Reid was not. After all those years as an assistant coach, this was his first time in the spotlight. He was stiff and uncomfortable.

Unlike most newly hired coaches, Reid didn't try to charm the media. When asked to discuss his plans for rebuilding the team, he offered no particulars, just a gruff "You have to trust me." It was asking a lot, considering we knew virtually nothing about him.

If it was Holmgren sitting there or Bill Parcells, it might have worked. Trust you? Sure, we know your track record. We see your Super Bowl rings. We're on board.

But Reid?

Sorry, big guy, we need a little more proof.

We talk about people winning a press conference. They show a little personality, maybe a sense of humor. They smile. They shake hands. They make nice. Reid did none of that. He was brusque and uptight.

Sports radio WIP carried the press conference live. When it ended, host Jody McDonald said, "I thought I was listening to Rich Kotite." Ouch. In Philadelphia, you could not get a more damning review.

Lurie talked about how Reid blew him away in his interview. He showed up with a binder six inches thick detailing all the things he would do when he was head coach. He started taking notes when he was a graduate assistant at Brigham Young—how to run a training camp, how to run a practice, how to build a coaching staff, and so forth—and he added page after page until it looked like the collected works of James Michener.

"It was obvious to me, Andy had prepared for this opportunity," Lurie said. "He's an organizer and a planner. He covers every detail."

It is one thing to have a plan; it is another to have the guts to stick to it. Reid demonstrated early that he was a stick-to-it kind of guy.

Many Eagles fans wanted the team to use its top draft pick to select Ricky Williams. Reid was planning to install a West Coast–style offense, so he had no desire to draft a running back. His plan was to build around a stud quarterback, and he was all in on Donovan McNabb, the Syracuse All-American.

Ed Rendell was one of those people calling for the Eagles to draft Williams. As the mayor of Philadelphia, he had more visibility than the average fan, and he wasn't shy about using it. He went on Angelo Cataldi's radio show and urged the fans to flood the Eagles' office with calls for the team to draft Williams. The response was so great that it crashed the Eagles' switchboard.

On the morning of the draft, WIP chartered a bus, and Cataldi, with thirty of his loyal listeners—he dubbed them "the Dirty Thirty"—rode to New York City to be there when the Eagles made their selection. They stood in the balcony at the Marriott Marquis, chanting "We want Ricky" as the clock ticked down to the Eagles' choice.

When NFL commissioner Paul Tagliabue announced, "With the second pick in the draft, the Philadelphia Eagles select Donovan McNabb," the Dirty Thirty went ballistic. They booed as McNabb walked on stage to shake the commissioner's hand. It was televised live on ESPN, and, like the snowballs pelting Santa Claus, it became part of the national narrative about Philly fans.

At no time did Reid consider bending to the will of the fans. He had a plan, and he was sticking to it. Not only was it an unpopular decision; it came with enormous risk. Five quarterbacks were drafted in the first round that year—Tim Couch (Cleveland), Donovan McNabb, Akili Smith (Cincinnati), Daunte Culpepper (Minnesota), and Cade McNown (Chicago)—and only McNabb had long-term success. Culpepper fizzled after a good start, and the others were franchise-wrecking disasters.

But drafting McNabb was only part of Reid's plan; the other was to bring him along slowly. He signed Doug Pederson, a seldom-used backup quarterback in Green Bay, to run the offense until McNabb was ready. Reid knew the team would struggle, but he believed that this was the right way to go. If the fans and media wrote him off as a clueless buffoon—and many did—he was willing to take it. He was willing to play the long game in a town with a notoriously short fuse.

The Eagles opened the 1999 season with four consecutive losses. In three of the losses, they failed to score an offensive touchdown. Pederson was overmatched, and the fans screamed for McNabb. Reid never wavered. He stayed with Pederson through nine weeks while the team fell to the division cellar.

Reid didn't help himself with his postgame news conferences. He would step to the podium, clear his throat, and say, "Injuries." Then he would read a list of every bruised thigh and strained ligament coming out of the game. When he had finished, he would raise his head, gaze at the assembled reporters, and growl, "Time's yours."

In other words, *now* I will entertain your questions.

After a bad loss—and there were many that season—Reid would say, "I have to do a better job." OK, but what did that mean? He wouldn't say. Questions about what went wrong on specific plays were dismissed with a curt, "I'm not going to get into that."

His answers were not answers at all; they were deflections or outright stonewalls. His press conferences were as frustrating as the games themselves.

Unlike Vermeil, who was open and honest, Reid was rigid and

guarded. Unlike Buddy Ryan, who was brash and quotable, Reid was a monotone bore. Some reporters stopped going to his press sessions because they were such a waste of time.

No matter how loudly the fans and media howled, Reid stayed the course. Dave Spadaro, the editor of *Eagles Digest*, asked Reid if he would make the move to McNabb to appease the masses. Reid said no, he was sticking with Pederson.

As Spadaro was leaving, Reid said, "Don't worry, Dave. Everything is going to be all right."

"He believed it, too," Spadaro said. "His strength in those times was amazing."

Reid gave McNabb his first start in Week 10, not because he was feeling the heat but because he believed that the rookie was ready. McNabb led the Eagles to a 35–28 win over Washington. He also won the final two games against New England and St. Louis.

It didn't seem like a big deal—what's so great about finishing 5–11?—but Reid saw the wins as important because they gave the young team something to build on.

Going into the 2000 season, most people expected the Eagles to improve largely because McNabb was now the starting quarterback. No one saw them as a playoff contender, however.

That changed in Week 1, when they routed the Cowboys, 41–14. Reid opened the game with an audacious onside kick that the Eagles turned into a quick score. Duce Staley ran for 201 yards and a touchdown. It was clear Reid's young team was growing up in a hurry.

The Eagles went from 5–11 to 11–5, the biggest one-season turnaround in franchise history. Reid was named "Coach of the Year," but he remained the same robotic figure.

People in the organization—coaches, players, trainers—talked about the "other Andy." They said he was warm and funny. They said he wrote poetry and loved books and movies, but he kept that side of himself hidden from the public. OK, but why?

"That's how he wants it," they said.

I heard stories that sounded interesting. For example, he had earned extra money when he was a low-level college coach by driving a limo. He had Loni Anderson, the buxom actress known for the TV series *WKRP in Cincinnati*, as a client. I asked Reid about it one day. He blew me off with a terse, "That was a long time ago."

His wife, Tammy, told a funny story about their first date. Reid had taken her to see the film *Apocalypse Now*, which might be the worst date movie of all time—napalm, severed heads on stakes, wall-to-wall Vietnam carnage. How romantic. I asked Reid about it, hoping he might see the humor. He didn't.

"C'mon, man," he said.

In other words, don't waste my time.

I asked about his conversion to the Mormon faith when he was a student at Brigham Young. He brushed it off with "That's personal."

Assistant coach Brad Childress told me about a 1928 Ford Model A that Reid had inherited from his father and totally rebuilt. I asked Reid about it. I thought I could use it as a metaphor for rebuilding the Eagles.

"I like tinkering around," he said.

You care to talk about it?

"No."

I came to the conclusion that this "other Andy" was a myth. Andy Reid was simply Andy Reid.

In 2002, Steve Sabol had an idea for an NFL Films special. He wanted to do a roundtable with Holmgren and six of his former Green Bay assistants who were now head coaches: Andy Reid, Jon Gruden (Tampa Bay), Dick Jauron (Chicago), Mike Sherman (Green Bay), Steve Mariucci (San Francisco), and Marty Mornhinweg (Detroit).

We set it up for the NFL owners' meetings in Florida. The interview was scheduled for 7 A.M., which gave us an hour before the coaches went off to their various meetings. That meant we had to set up the lights and position the cameras the night before so there would be no wasted time in the morning.

We had four cameras, so we discussed how to best position them. Obviously, one camera would be locked on Holmgren. That left three cameras to cover the other six coaches. We decided to put one camera near Gruden and another near Mariucci. We thought those guys would drive the conversation.

"What about Reid?" Steve asked.

"He's just going to sit there," I said. "He won't say ten words."

The next morning when the cameras started rolling, guess who stole the show?

Right, Andy Reid.

He needled Holmgren mercilessly and told hilarious stories about eating late-night dinners at the Homestead Buffet. He joked about being the buffer between Holmgren and Favre. Poking fun at himself, Reid said, "You can see it required a big buffer."

Reid told a funny story about Holmgren chasing Mariucci's two boys out of the locker room.

"I did not," Holmgren said indignantly.

The other coaches were practically falling out of their chairs laughing.

It was a freewheeling give and take, exactly what we were hoping for, and Reid was the life of the party. Our crew had to reposition one of the cameras just for him. Steve shot me a "What gives?" look. I whispered, "I don't know this guy."

This version of Andy Reid was a revelation. Almost single-handedly, he made *Holmgren's Heroes* one of the best shows of the year. But it irked me because it proved that Reid did have a personality. It meant that all these deadly dull press conferences were a bore because he chose to make them a bore.

If he was just a humorless drone who sat there like a bump on a log, I would've thought, OK, that's him. But to see him turn into this nimble, wise-cracking jokester, a kind of plus-sized Bill Murray, was something else entirely.

Later, I asked Reid why he didn't let people see that side of him more often. It would make him more relatable and buy him a little good will with the fans and the media.

"Reporters are on deadline, they don't have time to waste," he said. "They don't want a comedian up there."

"I think you just want to get out of there quicker," I said.

"Yeah, there's that too," he said with a grin.

Reid's coaching tree has outgrown the Holmgren tree. Of Reid's original staff, seven became head coaches in the NFL. Two of them led teams to the Super Bowl: Ron Rivera with Carolina, John Harbaugh with Baltimore. Three others led teams to the playoffs: Brad Childress and Leslie Frazier with Minnesota, Sean McDermott with Buffalo. Add Steve Spagnuolo (St. Louis) and Pat Shurmur (St. Louis, Eagles, New York Giants), and you have an impressive family portrait.

That staff contributed mightily to Reid's success, especially when you factor in the contribution of defensive coordinator Jim Johnson. It was the best staff I've seen in fifty years of covering the Eagles. He assembled a mix of old-school coaches (Jim Johnson, Tommy Brasher, Ted Williams), guys who had played in the league (Rivera and Frazier won Super Bowl rings with the 1985 Bears), and hungry young guys (McDermott, Shurmur, Spagnuolo) who were willing to work around the clock.

Under Reid, practices were brisk and well organized. There was no time wasted, no standing around. He had a daily schedule and followed it to the letter. It was reminiscent of watching Vermeil's practices in the '70s. You could see something good taking shape.

In the 2000 season, I spent one week embedded with Reid and his coaching staff. He granted NFL Films total access to the team for Week 2 of the regular season. The Eagles were coming off the big opening-day win over Dallas and preparing for the home opener against the Giants. Steve's idea was to have a film crew live with a team for an entire week as it prepared for and then played a game. It would be produced as a thirty-minute ESPN show called *Six Days to Sunday*. Steve assigned me to be the producer.

"Reid knows you," he said. "He'll trust you."

I wasn't so sure about that. It didn't seem to me that Reid trusted anyone in the media. Frankly, I was surprised he went along with the idea. He was so secretive about most things that he seemed like the last person who would allow our cameras to follow him around. I asked why he said yes. First of all, he said, he liked NFL Films. He understood the distinction between NFL Films and other media. "You're like part of the family," he said.

Indeed, Reid already had an assurance from Steve that he would see the film before it went on the air and that if there was something he didn't like, we would take it out. I did not like that arrangement—it smacked of censorship—but I understood that was part of the deal. (As it turned out, Reid only asked for two minor cuts, some mild profanity that he thought might offend his wife, a devout Mormon.)

Reid had another reason for agreeing to do the show, and it was very smart: The Eagles were coming off three straight miserable seasons, and he was looking for ways to raise their self-esteem. The fact that we were there to profile them was evidence that folks around the league were starting to pay attention.

"This is NFL Films, guys," Reid said, introducing our crew at the Monday team meeting. "They could have done this show about any of the thirty-two teams, but they chose *us*. This wouldn't have happened last year or the year before. People are starting to care about the Philadelphia Eagles, and that's a good thing."

I worked the coaches' hours that week. I got to the stadium before 6 A.M. and didn't leave until 10 P.M. I went from meeting room to meeting room, watching the film study and sitting in on strategy sessions. I was more inside the game than I ever was as a news reporter. I came away with two impressions. One, the Vet was wholly inadequate, far worse than I realized. The meeting rooms were too small. The film system was antiquated. The coaches' offices were dark and dreary. I had visited most NFL team facilities, and the Vet was the worst by far. I understood why Lurie and Banner so desperately wanted their own campus.

My other impression was that Reid and his staff knew what they were doing. They still didn't have enough players to challenge the top teams, and the talent level wasn't quite there yet, but I saw what Lurie had seen in his interviews with Reid. The big man had a plan, and he was working it. That week, Reid, Johnson, and the rest of the staff worked eighteen-hour days putting in a carefully drawn game plan, but the Giants rolled them, 33–18. We sat with Reid after the game as he packed up his briefcase.

"They were just better than we were," he said. "That Tiki [Barber], we just couldn't stop him."

But Reid knew the team was on the right path, and it won six of its last seven regular-season games to earn a trip to the playoffs. The Eagles defeated Tampa Bay in the wild-card round before they were eliminated in the divisional playoff game by the Giants, 20–10.

In 2001, the Eagles went all the way to the NFC championship game but lost to the Rams. The next year, they were the number-one seed, and they played for the NFC championship in the final game at Veterans Stadium. What a fitting way to close the Vet; a victory would send the Eagles to Super Bowl XXXVII.

All the stars were aligned. The Eagles were playing Tampa Bay, a team they had defeated earlier in the season. The Bucs had not won a game when the temperature was below forty degrees, and it was freezing that day. Duce Staley scored a touchdown fifty-two seconds into the game. The Vet was rocking. The rout was on—or so we thought.

The Bucs fought back to take the lead, and, with the Eagles trying to mount a late comeback, McNabb threw a pass that Ronde Barber intercepted and returned 92 yards for a touchdown. The Vet, a place famous for its noise, fell silent. It was as if someone hit a mute button. It was so quiet that the NFL Films microphones picked up the sound of Barber's cleats on the squishy turf.

The 66,713 fans left the Vet in a state of shock. On the *Eagles Post-Game Live* show, I compared the emotional wreckage to the 1964 Phillies' collapse. The only difference, I said, was the Phillies' collapse had played out over two weeks. This happened in one afternoon.

The next day at NFL Films, I was assigned to produce the Eagles-Bucs segment for HBO's *Inside the NFL*. When I wrote the script, I borrowed from Stephen Sondheim, writing, "Not since Sweeney Todd had a Barber landed such a lethal blow." Our narrator, Harry Kalas, read the line and gave me a wink.

"It's not often we can work Sweeney Todd into a football game," Kalas said.

The next season, the Eagles came back in a new stadium, and again went to the NFC title game, and again lost to an underdog, the Carolina Panthers. The fans were heartsick over the loss to Tampa Bay, but they were angry over the 14–3 loss to Carolina.

I put much of the blame on Reid. Like most West Coast–offense gurus, he was in love with the forward pass, but Reid took it to extremes. Some weeks, his pass-to-run ratio was a lopsided 70 to 30.

Against Carolina, Reid called 41 pass plays and 26 runs, even though Duce Staley and Correll Buckhalter averaged more than 5 yards a carry. The NFL Films sound camera caught tackle Jon Runyan pleading with Mornhinweg to call more running plays.

"We're *gonna* run it, Jon," Mornhinweg said.

"When?" Runyan barked.

The Eagles never did get around to running the ball, and they lost the game. The Panthers had four interceptions as their secondary bullied the Eagles receivers. It was their third straight loss in the conference final. Even Reid realized something had to change.

In March 2004, the Eagles traded for Terrell Owens, a talented but volatile receiver who had worn out his welcome in San Francisco. He was a four-time Pro Bowler whose 83 touchdown receptions were second only to Jerry Rice in 49ers' history. The Eagles acquired him for a fifth-round draft pick and a backup defensive lineman.

After years of trying to win with the likes of Todd Pinkston, James Thrash, and Torrance Small, Reid finally went all in for an elite receiver. I could not understand why he had waited so long. It didn't make sense to draft a quarterback to be the centerpiece of your team and then surround him with mediocre receivers.

Indianapolis did the opposite with Peyton Manning. Every year, they gave him a shiny new toy to play with—Marvin Harrison, Dallas Clark, Reggie Wayne, Pierre Garcon—and he became the league's most prolific passer. McNabb was trying to compete on the same racetrack with parts better suited for the soap box derby. T. O.'s arrival changed that in a major way.

More than twenty thousand fans drove to Lehigh for the first day of the 2004 training camp. There were so many cars jamming the roads that Reid needed a police escort to get to the field. Owens was smiling, McNabb was smiling, and even Reid was smiling. We knew it probably was too good to last, but for the moment, it sure felt good.

McNabb had his best season in 2004. He established career highs in completion percentage (64 percent), yardage (3,875), and touchdown passes (31). Owens broke the franchise record for touchdown catches with 14 before sitting out the final two games with a fractured tibia.

The Eagles advanced to the NFC title game for the fourth year in a row, but they had to play Atlanta without Owens. The fans felt another gut punch coming. On Friday before the game, I went to a pep rally in Center City. A lady approached me with the forlorn look of someone who had just seen a winning lottery ticket vanish in a gust of wind.

"They're going to break our hearts again, aren't they?" she said.

"I don't know," I said. "This might be their year."

"If it was their year, T. O. wouldn't have gotten hurt," she said.

A foot of snow fell the day before the championship game. The wind chill was near zero as the tailgaters poured into the parking lots at Lincoln Financial Field. With Owens waving a towel to fire up the crowd, the Eagles defeated the Falcons, 27–10. As the final seconds ticked away, Ike Reese and Corey Simon showered the coach with Gatorade.

It was the happiest I had ever seen Reid, walking off the field with one arm around Tammy and the other arm around his son Garrett. He pumped his fist at the cheering crowd before ducking into the tunnel. Jim Johnson wept as he hugged his wife and kids. He had broken into the NFL in 1963 with Buffalo and kicked around the league for years without getting to a Super Bowl. Now he would have that chance.

Super Bowl XXXIX was played in Jacksonville, the smallest city to host the game and the least equipped. There were not enough hotel rooms to handle all the revelers who descended on the city. They brought in cruise ships for additional lodging. Traffic was a nightmare. There weren't enough buses, so hundreds of people were left stranded in the cold, damp weather.

The Eagles fans didn't complain. They took over the city. They came in planes and buses, in vans and sedans, a caravan of green and silver rolling into Jacksonville, filling the streets and bars with "E-A-G-L-E-S" chants. The *Florida Times-Union* had a page 1 story claiming the Eagles fans outnumbered the New England fans 10 to 1.

Glen Macnow and I hosted our Saturday radio show from a tent outside a downtown hotel. The tent was jammed an hour before we went on the air, but people kept coming, squeezing into the aisles and sitting on the floor. We went on the air at 10 A.M., and the chant started.

"E-A-G-L-E-S . . . EAGLES!"

Things quieted down only once, and that was when Timmy Kelly arrived. Timmy was a thirteen-year-old from Huntingdon Valley and the Eagles' unofficial good luck charm. Blind from birth, he was blessed with a beautiful voice.

He sang the national anthem at an Eagles game in 2002, and they won. He sang at another game the following year, and they won again. He sang at the 2004 opener, and they won again. The fans and media began tracking it much like the Flyers did with Kate Smith in the Stanley Cup years.

When the Eagles played Atlanta in the NFC title game, Timmy again sang the national anthem. When the Eagles won that game, the fans were convinced it was no coincidence. They wanted the Eagles to insist that he sing the anthem in Jacksonville.

The NFL had already booked the combined choirs of the three service academies, so there was no way they could change. Besides, it would have been seen as giving an edge to the Eagles, which would have surely angered the Patriots.

But when Timmy walked into the tent that morning, Glen and I looked at each other. We had the same thought.

"Let's do it," he said.

He asked Timmy to sing the national anthem. The game was more than twenty-four hours away, but maybe the magic would still work.

When the blind boy in his Eagles jersey sang an a capella rendition of "The Star-Spangled Banner," the emotion he brought to the song had dozens of burly Eagles fans wiping away tears.

I was going to pick the Eagles to win the game anyway, but with Timmy's anthem now in play, I was certain they would beat the Patriots. I was confident Owens would return from his injury and lead the Eagles to victory.

Owens played brilliantly, catching 9 passes for 122 yards, but the Eagles turned the ball over four times. They trailed 24–14 with 5 minutes and 40 seconds left and went on an agonizingly slow 13-play, 79-yard drive that consumed almost 4 minutes. Even though it ended with a touchdown pass to Greg Lewis, it left them with too little time to score again.

In his book *Education of a Coach*, David Halberstam described Patriots coach Bill Belichick watching the Eagles on that drive—huddling after every play, walking to the line of scrimmage, wasting precious time. He asked his coaches upstairs, "Have I got the score right? We're up 10 [points], right?"

Told the scoreboard was correct, Belichick asked, "Then what the hell are they trying to do?"[1]

Thousands of Eagles fans were asking the same thing.

Why didn't Reid go to a hurry-up offense? They needed *two* scores. They got one touchdown on the pass to Lewis, but even though the defense got a quick three and out, the offense got the ball back at its own 5-yard line with 42 seconds left and no time outs. In full desperation mode, McNabb threw his third interception to end the game.

In his press conference, Reid was asked about the long drive. His answer was a cryptic, "We were trying to hurry up. It was the way things worked out."

I believe that Reid was afraid that if he tried to move faster, his offense—which had been mistake-prone all day—would turn the ball over again, and that would have ended the game. I also don't think he trusted McNabb to run the no huddle in that situation. Reid wanted to call the plays himself, but with his nose buried deep in his play chart, he lost track of time.

It was all part of the Reid narrative: He has trouble with game management. He is very good at planning, but he can't adjust on the fly. He butchers the clock, he wastes time outs, and he calls the wrong plays. He let games get away from him when he was coaching the Eagles, and it was true in Kansas City as well. Good coach, the critics said, but he can't win the big one.

Reid may have finally put it to rest when he led the Chiefs to victory in Super Bowl LIV. The look on his face when the game ended, equal parts joy and relief, spoke volumes. He was seventh on the list of the NFL's all-time winningest coaches and surely on his way to the Pro Football Hall of Fame, but he needed *that* win to complete his resume.

But if that Super Bowl was the highlight of his career, then Super Bowl XXXIX was the low point. It was an excruciating loss, a game the Eagles could have won but let slip away. Again, Reid was guilty of abandoning the run. He called 55 pass plays and just 17 runs, so it was easy for the New England defense to tee off on McNabb.

I had made that point all season, but never as loudly as on Super Bowl Sunday. On the postgame show, I said Reid was more to blame for the loss than McNabb, who was being vilified by the fans.

"Andy," I said, "this one is on you."

I didn't see Reid after the game, but I know he heard my comments, because when we crossed paths back in Philadelphia, he gave me a cold stare.

"I hear you like running the football," he said.

"More than you do, obviously," I replied.

Reid told me to check the stats. The Eagles had gained 45 yards on their 17 rushing attempts, a 2.6-yard average. He said the Patriots had changed their defense to a stunting 4–3 front that made it hard to block.

I said with just 17 rushing attempts, how would he know? If he had stayed with it longer, it might have worked.

I knew Reid was upset with me. We didn't talk much after that Super Bowl.

Then something happened that allowed me to see a different side of him.

In October 2009, my mother died. It wasn't a shock—she had cancer for more than a year—but it was still very sad. As an only child, I was close to my mother. My father was in the Air Force Reserves, so he was away a lot. Mom and I spent many hours at home, just the two of us. She was a great lady, smart and beautiful.

When she passed less than a year after my father, I was left with nothing but memories of our time together. I wouldn't be getting those phone calls on my birthday. I wouldn't get any more handwritten notes in her beautiful Catholic-school penmanship. I felt a huge sense of loss when I went to Florida and began making arrangements for her funeral.

I was at her desk, going through her papers, when my wife called from Philadelphia.

"You're not going to believe who just called the house," she said.

"Who?"

"Andy Reid," she said.

"You're kidding."

"I'm not kidding," she said.

He had never called our house before. Why would he? We weren't exactly friends. But he had seen Mom's death notice in the paper that morning.

The obituary was written by Jack Morrison, an old friend from the *Bulletin*. He wrote a lovely piece about Mom and her devotion to the Eagles. The headline identified her as "Eagles Fan Supreme." Yes, she was all of that.

My parents moved to Florida after my father's retirement, but they refused to adopt the Florida teams. They remained loyal to the Eagles, Phillies, Flyers, and Sixers. They loved their new life in Sarasota, but there was that part of them that never left Southwest Philly.

"Andy called to say he was sorry about your mother," Maria said. "He wants to talk to you."

I called Reid's office. His secretary, Carol Cullen, answered. It was a Tuesday in October. For the coaches, it is the busiest day of the week. It is game-plan day, when they begin preparing for the next opponent. They are in meetings all day. They eat cold cuts at their desks and sleep on the couch.

I told Cullen I had gotten the message that Reid had called.

"I don't want to bother him, I know he's busy," I said. "Just tell him I called."

"He wants to talk to you," she said. "Hold on. I'll put you through."

A moment later, Reid was on the phone. The tone of his voice was different. I almost didn't recognize it.

"How are you doing?" he asked.

He sounded like an old friend calling to express his sympathy.

"I read the piece about your mother," he said. "It sounds like she was a great lady. Big time Eagles fan, huh?"

"The biggest," I said. "She never missed a game."

Reid began talking about his mother. Her name was Elizabeth. She was a radiologist and rabid sports fan. She was the one who took him to Dodgers games. She was the one who signed him up for the punt, pass, and kick competition in junior high. His father, Walter, was a set designer in Hollywood. He was a casual sports fan, but Elizabeth lived it every day.

I told Reid about my mother buying a "Joe Must Go" button and wearing it into Franklin Field. I told him about how she stitched up the holes in my football jersey. He said his mother did the same for him.

He said she had a gift for always saying the right thing when he was feeling down. The same was true of my mother. I told him about the time I took a called third strike in a Little League game with the tying run on third. I was in tears when I got in the car.

"That pitch was a foot outside," she said.

She was lying, of course, but at that moment it helped immensely.

I couldn't believe it when I looked at the clock. We had talked for almost 40 minutes. Surely, his staff was down the hall waiting for him—it was game-plan day, after all. I apologized for taking up so much time.

"I have time," he said. "It's your Mom. It's hard. I know."

The Eagles were playing the Bucs that week. My mother was excited about that. She lived just an hour's drive from Tampa, so she could see the game on TV. She was sure the Eagles would cream the Bucs. In one of our last conversations, she asked, "Is Westbrook playing?" She knew the injury list better than I did most weeks.

"Yeah, Westbrook's playing," I said.

"Good," she said. "He'll run all over the Bucs."

The Eagles routed the Buccaneers, 33–14. My mother would have enjoyed that. It would have given her bragging rights over her neighbors, who were all Bucs fans. Sadly, she wouldn't have that chance now.

"My mother was such a fan," I said. "She got mad at me when I criticized you. I was her son, but you were her coach."

Reid laughed.

"I'm sorry I never got to meet her," he said.

"I'm sorry too," I said.

I thanked Reid for his kindness. I was surprised he took the time. It was a different side of him, that's for sure.

"I just wanted you to know I was thinking of you," he said.

I could tell he meant it. I've always appreciated that.

We talked so much about family that day that it pained me to see what he went through with his own sons, Garrett and Britt. The boys became addicted to drugs and wound up in jail. Because they were the sons of the Eagles' coach, the story was on the front page of the papers and led the TV news.

There were photos of the boys being led into court in handcuffs. It became the number-one topic on sports talk radio. Reid took a five-week leave of absence to support his wife and the other three children.

"How could this happen?" people asked.

No one had the answer to that question. Tragedy can strike any family. Rich or poor, famous or faceless, it doesn't matter.

Years earlier, at NFL Films, I did a feature on the Reid family. One

Saturday, I went with Reid to see Garrett play football at Harriton High School. He sat in the bleachers, watching his son and cheering like every other parent.

"This is when I can really enjoy football," he said.

Twelve years later, Garrett was dead, the victim of a drug overdose. He was out of prison and working with the Eagles' training staff. He was found in a dormitory room at training camp early on a Sunday morning. He was twenty-nine years old.

Two days later, Reid walked out of the tunnel at Lincoln Financial Field for the Eagles' first preseason game. The fans, many of whom were booing Reid the previous year when the team finished 8–8, gave him a standing ovation.

Some people wondered how Reid could return to the sideline so quickly after his son's death. It wasn't because he thought the team needed him; it was the other way around. He needed the team. There was comfort in the routine. Coaching was his life; now it was his refuge.

When Reid met reporters after the game, he began his remarks by addressing the situation.

"I just know that coming back and coaching is the right thing to do," Reid said. "I know my son wouldn't have wanted it any other way. With that, I'll move on and talk about the injuries. . . ."

He was back to business as usual.

I asked Derek Boyko, the team's publicist, if I could get a few minutes alone with Reid. We met in a hallway outside the locker room. Reid had reached out to me after my mother's death. I wanted to do the same for him.

I said all the usual things: how sorry I was for his loss, how I wished the best for his family. He was his stoic self. His emotions were in check. He said he loved his son and would always love him.

"Garrett had a huge heart," Reid said. "He just got caught up in a terrible situation. He fought it, but he lost. At least he's not suffering anymore. I'm grateful for that."

That season, the Eagles fell apart. They finished with a 4–12 record, and Reid was fired after fourteen years in Philadelphia. He admitted it probably was time. He needed a fresh start elsewhere, and he got it in Kansas City, where he enjoyed immediate success.

How much did Garrett's death contribute to the Eagles' collapse in 2012? It is impossible to say, but there is no doubt it took an enormous toll on his father.

"You have to handle what life throws at you," Reid said, "but this. . . ."
He shook his head. He didn't finish the thought. He didn't have to.

"I'm really sorry, Andy," I said.

He thanked me for the good wishes and asked if I could do him one favor.

"Say a prayer for Garrett tonight," he said.

I did.

17

Tommy and Me

I STOOD IN THE BACK of the Plays and Players Theatre, watching the audience file in. I couldn't believe it—all these people coming to see our story.
Who could have imagined such a thing?

Tommy McDonald was in the front row with his
wife, Patty, and their four children. People were coming
up to shake his hand and pose for selfies. He was loving the attention.

Stage manager Jessica DeStefano walked to the microphone and
said, "Welcome to *Tommy and Me* by Ray Didinger."

The audience applauded, the actors appeared, and I wondered, "Is
this really happening?"

I thought back to how it all started.

_____

IT WAS 1957 IN HERSHEY, PENNSYLVANIA, long before Hershey became a vacation destination. At the time, Hershey Park consisted of
a carousel, a miniature railroad, a fun house, and one roller coaster.
It was a far cry from the 120-acre colossus that now draws more than
three million visitors in a typical year.

I didn't care about the roller coaster or any of the other kid stuff. I
was a ten-year-old boy infatuated with the game of football. All I knew
about Hershey was that the Eagles trained there. That's why our family
went there every year on summer vacation.

We checked into the Cocoa Inn—everything in Hershey revolved around the chocolate plant—and spent two weeks watching the team practice. Our neighbors all went to the Jersey Shore. I felt sorry for them. Who wants to sit on the beach when you can watch the Eagles practice?

Today, NFL training camps draw big crowds. In the 1950s, it was just a handful of people. The Eagles practiced on an open field next to the high school stadium. Some families would spread a blanket on the grass and have a picnic. Not us. My parents were all business. During practice, my father would jot down notes on the Cocoa Inn stationary.

I started memorizing the Eagles' roster when I was old enough to read. I wasn't reading the Hardy Boys, that's for sure. I was reading football magazines. One of my favorites was *Stanley Woodward's Football Annual.*

The *Woodward Annual* was *the* definitive college football preview. In 1956, Oklahoma's Tommy McDonald was on the cover. I read the profile of McDonald, a record-setting, triple-threat halfback who looked so small and out of place on a football field. At 5'9" and 170 pounds, he described himself as "a mackerel among sharks."[1]

The story made him sound like a fun-loving cutup who enjoyed goofing around almost as much as he enjoyed playing football. He was the best player on an Oklahoma team with the longest winning streak in college football history, forty-seven games in a row. He went through his entire college career without losing a game.

I became a Tommy McDonald fan. He won the Maxwell Award as College Football Player of the Year. When the Eagles selected him in the third round of the draft, I was elated. I knew I would have the opportunity to see him and perhaps even meet him when we went to Hershey.

That summer, I parked myself outside the locker room and waited. When he came out, I was amazed at how young he looked. He had cropped blond hair and the face of a teenager. He was twenty-two, but he looked sixteen. He was wearing the same number 25 he wore in college, but the jersey was kelly green, not Oklahoma crimson.

I asked him to sign my autograph book.

"Sure," he said, "but you'll have to walk with me. Here, you want to carry my helmet?"

I couldn't believe it. Tommy McDonald was handing me his helmet.

"Really?" I said. "I can carry your helmet?"

"Sure, if it's not too heavy for you," he said.

"Oh no, it's OK," I said.

The helmet was brand new, and it gleamed in the summer sun. I turned it over and over in my hands, studying it as if it were the Hope diamond. I was an altar boy, so I carried religious stuff at church all the time. I once carried holy water for the archbishop of Philadelphia. But Tommy McDonald's helmet? I felt like I should genuflect or something.

It was a three-block walk from the locker room to the practice field. I still remember the sound Tommy's cleats made scraping on the hot gravel. He was walking fast, as he signed my book. I told him my family spent two weeks every summer watching practice.

"In this heat?" he said. "Your folks must really love football."

I told him about my grandfather's bar, the chartered bus, the whole Sunday ritual.

"I thought Oklahoma fans took their football seriously," he said. "I think you have 'em beat."

When we got to the field, he handed back the autograph book.

"See you tomorrow," he said dashing off to join his teammates.

I was waiting at the locker room door the next day and the next day, every day for two weeks. I peppered Tommy with questions about growing up in Roy, New Mexico; about convincing his high school coach to let him play (the coach thought he was too small); about going to Oklahoma (his mother wanted him to go to Notre Dame); and about almost winning the Heisman Trophy (he finished third in the voting).

"Paul Hornung won that year," I said.

"How did you know that?" he asked.

"I have a whole scrapbook about you. You're my favorite player."

He laughed and rubbed my head. He began calling me "Little Brother." One day, he gave me a ride around Hershey in his cherry red convertible. His name was on the door in big block letters along with a Phillies cigar logo. He got the use of the car plus $200 a week just for saying nice things about Phillies cigars. It broke my heart when I had to tell him we were heading home.

"I'll see you next summer," he said.

At Franklin Field, whenever Tommy made a big play, the guys from Ray's Tavern would look at me and shout, "That's your boy." I know it was just in my mind, but I did feel as though we were friends. The "Little Brother" thing felt real to me.

When we went back to Hershey the next year, Tommy put his arm around me.

"I was wondering when you'd show up," he said, handing me his helmet.

We repeated this every summer for seven years. I went from a sixth grader to a senior in high school. He went from a rookie to an All-Pro.

I was at Franklin Field when he caught the touchdown pass from Norm Van Brocklin that put the Eagles ahead in the 1960 NFL championship game against Green Bay. He made the catch right in front of us.

"Your boy," my uncle Jack said, pounding me on the back. "Your boy."

I read every story in the *Bulletin* the next day. There was one account from the Green Bay locker room quoting coach Vince Lombardi, who said, "If I had eleven Tommy McDonalds, I'd win the championship every year." Tommy later said it was the greatest compliment he ever received.[2]

Van Brocklin retired after that season. Tommy told reporters, "Don't worry, I'll make Sonny [Jurgensen] as great as I made Van Brocklin." He was joking when he said it, but he proved to be right. In 1961, Jurgensen took over at quarterback and set a club record with 32 touchdown passes. Tommy led the league with 1,144 receiving yards and 13 touchdowns. He had another great year in 1962, with 58 receptions for 1,146 yards and 10 touchdowns.

Sports Illustrated put Tommy on the cover with the caption "Football's Best Hands." I had the cover framed and hanging in my bedroom. The article itself was titled "The Magnificent Squirt." It focused on Tommy's size and his daredevil antics, such as crawling on the roof of a moving car and hanging by one hand from a hotel balcony.[3]

He was called flaky and goofy; I preferred to think of him as colorful.

I assumed that Tommy would play his entire career in Philadelphia. Why would a team trade an All-Pro player with such a huge fan following? I didn't count on Joe Kuharich coming in and blowing up the team. When Tommy was traded to Dallas, I sat at the kitchen table with tears in my eyes. For me, it was like losing a family member. All those summers, all those walks—it was over, just like that.

It was the first time I realized how powerless you are as a fan. You think your favorite team hears you and respects your feelings, but when it comes right down to it, your feelings don't matter. Kuharich called the trade "a business decision." Gee, here I thought football was a game. A part of me—the fan part—died that day.

I followed Tommy from afar as he played in Dallas, Los Angeles, Atlanta, and finally Cleveland, where he finished his career in 1968. When he retired, he was sixth all-time in catches (495), fourth in receiving yards (8,410), and second in touchdowns (84). The only player with more touchdown catches was Don Hutson, who played for Green Bay in the 1930s.

I thought Tommy was a cinch for the Pro Football Hall of Fame, but he was passed over in his first year of eligibility, then the second, and then the third. I couldn't understand it. How could they ignore a player who had the second-most touchdown catches of all time?

I started covering the Eagles in 1970, so I bumped into Tommy at various events around town. He didn't recognize me. Why would he? The last time he had seen me was the summer of 1963. I was still in high school.

I thought about mentioning our time in Hershey, but I decided against it. I was afraid he might not remember. I wanted to believe that Tommy still remembered that kid at the locker room door, even if he didn't know it was me. Rather than risk being disappointed, I swallowed hard and said nothing.

Tommy had done very well after football. He started an oil portrait business that was quite successful. He was happily married with four children, living in King of Prussia. His oldest son, Chris, was a star football player at the University of Delaware.

Our paths crossed again in 1985, when I was assigned to write a twenty-fifth-anniversary piece on the 1960 championship team. I traveled the country, interviewing members of that team. I visited Don Burroughs, Timmy Brown, and Chuck Weber in California. I found J. D. Smith on a ranch in Texas and Billy Barnes on a construction site in Georgia. Chuck Bednarik was still in the Philadelphia area, as were Pete Retzlaff, Tom Brookshier, Riley Gunnels, and Dick Lucas. Marion Campbell was coaching the Eagles.

I saved the interview with Tommy for last. We met at his house on a warm summer day. We talked for three hours by the pool. He teared up several times while talking about the Dutchman, Van Brocklin, who had died two years earlier. Again, I didn't mention our history. It would have been easy to do—we talked at length about Hershey and Franklin Field—but I resisted opening that door.

I asked if he had any regrets. He said he had always hoped he would make it into the Pro Football Hall of Fame, but now he had given up. He had been retired for sixteen years and never made the final ballot. He couldn't understand it, but he had more or less accepted it.

"Some things aren't meant to be, I guess," he said.

It just so happened that I was appointed to the hall's board of selectors that year, which put me in a position to work on Tommy's behalf. I sent a letter listing his accomplishments to the other voters. It must have worked, because that year for the first time, he was one of the fifteen finalists. He was elated.

I warned him it was no sure thing. He would need 80 percent of the vote for election. There were two other receivers on the ballot—Fred Biletnikoff and Don Maynard—which could split the vote. I was the one making the case for Tommy in the selection meeting. All his hopes were riding on me.

I thought my presentation went well. Everyone seemed to listen. Dave Anderson, the Pulitzer Prize–winning columnist from the *New York Times*, nudged me and said, "Great job." I felt good about Tommy's chances.

Then the votes were cast. He didn't make it. My heart sank.

I thought about calling him, but I didn't know what to say. I called Chris instead.

"How's your dad?" I asked.

"I've never seen him so depressed," Chris said. "You know him, Mr. Happy-Go-Lucky. Not this time. He took it really hard."

"Tell your dad it's not over," I said. "I'll keep trying."

I did keep trying, year after year, for the next ten years. Tommy kept falling short. In 1997, I left the paper to join NFL Films, which made me a league employee. That meant I could no longer serve on the board of selectors. I feared that closed the book on Tommy's chances.

But the next year, he caught a break. Jimmy Johnson, the great 49ers cornerback, was elected to the Hall of Fame. At his press conference, Johnson was asked to name the best receiver he had played against in his seventeen seasons. Without hesitation, he said, "Tommy McDonald." It was a powerful endorsement that put Tommy back in the Hall of Fame discussion.

I no longer had a vote, but I could petition the board of selectors, which I did. I also wrote to a dozen former coaches and players, asking them to write letters of support for Tommy. I knew their words would carry more weight than mine. Everyone responded. Raymond Berry, who set receiving records while playing with Johnny Unitas in Baltimore, wrote the following:

> Two summers ago I was asked by the Hall of Fame to give my recommendations on a list of senior candidates. There was no question in my mind that Tommy and Lou Creekmur [Detroit tackle] were the most worthy candidates, strongly so. Tommy's stats, es-

pecially his touchdowns, speak for themselves. I spoke strongly for Tommy that day so maybe [this] second time will help.[4]

Jurgensen, Tommy's teammate with the Eagles, wrote, "Tommy had a great love and passion for the game and an energy level that was infectious. He also had a great work ethic. In the seven years that I played with Tommy, I don't remember seeing him drop a catchable pass. I played with some great receivers throughout my career and no one caught the ball as well."[5]

The day of the vote—January 24, 1998—I was at home, staring at the clock. The selectors were in San Diego, the site of the Super Bowl, casting their ballots. I had built a strong case for Tommy—especially with the letters from Berry, Jurgensen, Tom Landry, and Don Shula— but I had made a strong case before and wound up disappointed.

Mike Rathet, the *Daily News* sports editor, took my place as the Philadelphia voter. He would make the presentation. I felt good about that. Rathet covered pro football for the Associated Press in the 1960s and served as the Miami Dolphins' publicity director during their Super Bowl seasons. The other voters knew and respected him. I was sure he would make a strong pitch.

Hours passed. Maria kept searching the Internet for the announcement. Finally, I heard her say, "Here it is."

She clicked on the link and got a huge smile on her face.

"He's in," she said.

Before I could say a word, the phone rang. It was Tommy.

"August 1, Canton, Ohio, baby," he shouted. He was laughing and crying at the same time.

"Tommy, I'm so happy for you," I said.

"I just wanted to say thanks," he said. "This never would have happened if it wasn't for you. Look, I gotta go. I gotta call my mother."

"Please tell me you didn't call me before you called your mother," I said.

"You're like family," he said. "I love you, man."

Maria gave me a hug. She knew what this meant to me. I had helped my boyhood hero realize his dream. I thought about the first time I met Tommy at the locker room door. I thought about the first time he handed me his helmet. Here we were, forty years later, sharing this moment. What a journey.

A week later, Tommy visited me at NFL Films. He walked into my office, carrying a briefcase. He was still bubbling from the news of his election. He wanted to show me what he had planned for the trip to Canton. He opened the briefcase and pulled out a boom box and what looked like a script.

"Is this your speech?" I asked.

"I'm not doing a speech," he said. "I want to do something different. Read it. It's all in there."

I read the first line: "Move over Ronald McDonald, there's a new McDonald in town."

"Tommy, what's this?" I asked.

"What's it look like?" he said. "I'm gonna start off with a few jokes."

He wasn't kidding. He had written down a half dozen jokes, each one worse than the one before.

"Then I'll toss my bust in the air," he said, "catch it and say, 'See, I still have great hands.'"

"What if you drop it?" I said. "Those things weigh a ton."

"I won't drop it," he said. "Football's best hands, remember?"

"I'm almost afraid to ask," I said, "but what's with the boom box?"

"After I toss my bust, I'll get my boom box and do a dance," he said.

He hit the "Play" button and, suddenly, the Bee Gees were singing, "Stayin' Alive." Tommy began dancing around my office. My jaw was on the floor.

"Then I'll call up the other inductees, and we'll do a dance," he said.

"You're gonna dance?" I said. "With Mike Singletary?"

"Then I'll high five 'em," he said, "then I'll chest bump 'em. . . ."

"Chest bump?"

I clicked off the boom box.

"Tommy, you can't do this," I said.

"Why not?" he asked.

The obvious answer was because it was lunacy. Hall of Fame inductions are like a coronation—solemn and respectful. Tommy's idea was sure to offend some people. I also pointed out that the ceremony was televised live on ESPN, which meant that playing "Stayin' Alive" would invite a lawsuit from the Bee Gees.

"Do you really think the Bee Gees watch the Hall of Fame inductions?" Tommy asked.

"No, but their lawyers might," I said.

"Aw, that's not gonna happen," he said.

I was still trying to collect my thoughts when Tommy hit me with another bombshell. He wanted me to be his presenter.

I was speechless.

I expected him to ask one of his teammates, most likely Jurgensen. They were one of the most dynamic passing combinations in NFL history. They were training camp roommates for seven years, and Jurgensen was the best man at Tommy and Patty's wedding. They even had their own TV show: *Jurgensen to McDonald.* Jurgensen was the logical choice to present Tommy for induction.

I was honored that Tommy asked me, but I didn't feel right about it.

"I don't belong on that stage, Tommy," I said. "That's for the players and coaches."

"But I want you there with me," he said.

He dropped to his knees and clasped his hands.

"Pleeeezzzzzzee," he said.

How could I say no?

I agreed to be his presenter, but I urged him to reconsider the jokes, the dancing, and the other craziness. It would be better if he went with a traditional speech. He said he had never written a speech. I offered to write one, which I did that very night.

We spoke dozens of times over the next six months. Each time, I tried to convince him to do a speech. He refused. He wouldn't even read the speech I had written. He was determined to do it his way. I asked him what Patty and the kids thought.

"I didn't tell them," he said. "I know they'd try to talk me out of it."

"So I'm the only one who knows?" I said.

"That's right," he said, "and you better not tell anybody."

It was a whirlwind three days in Canton. In addition to Tommy, the Class of 1998 included Mike Singletary, the middle linebacker on Chicago's Super Bowl team; Anthony Munoz, the great offensive tackle for Cincinnati; Paul Krause, the NFL's all-time interception leader; and Dwight Stephenson, the All-Pro center for the Miami Dolphins.

On Friday, at a gala dinner at the Canton Convention Center, the new Hall of Famers received their gold jackets. When Tommy was introduced, he scooped up the Festival Queen and carried her down the aisle. I was seated next to Shula, Stephenson's presenter.

"Tommy is crazy," Shula said, laughing.

"You have no idea," I said. "Wait until tomorrow."

"What do you mean?" he asked.

"You'll see," I said.

On Saturday, we rode in the parade before the enshrinement ceremony. There were twenty-three marching bands in front of us, twenty-one floats behind us, and a quarter of a million people lining the streets. Here I was, riding in an open convertible with my boyhood hero on our way to the Hall of Fame. My heart was pounding the whole way.

One day, I'm a ten-year-old kid sitting twenty-four rows up in Section EE at Franklin Field, cheering for my football hero; the next, I'm presenting him for induction into the Hall of Fame. If that's not the definition of dreams coming true, I don't know what is.

Still, I was concerned about what Tommy had planned. What if the crowd disapproved? What if people started booing? Tommy's big day could turn into an embarrassment. I knew I had to make one last attempt to talk him out of it.

I had the speech I wrote for him in my pocket. All I had to do was convince him to read it. But how could I do that? I had tried for six months. Why would he listen now?

I decided to break down and tell him about Hershey. Maybe I could get through to him that way. It was worth a try. Frankly, it was all I had left.

"Tommy, there's something I should tell you," I said.

I stumbled around trying to find the words. How could I explain this? The enshrinement ceremony was about to start. I looked at the briefcase in his hand. I knew what was in there. I couldn't let this happen.

"When I was a kid, I was your biggest fan," I said.

"Really?" he said.

"Every summer, I came to Hershey with my parents," I said. "I waited for you outside the locker room and. . . ."

His eyes lit up.

"Wait a minute," he said.

A look of disbelief crossed his face, followed by a huge smile.

"You were that kid," he said. "You were 'Little Brother.'"

"That's me," I said.

"Why the heck didn't you say something?" he said. "All this time we spent together."

"I thought you wouldn't remember," I said.

"How could I forget you?" he said. "You carried my helmet every day. You've been beating my drum all these years. I can never repay you for what you've done."

I saw my opening, so I took it.

"You really want to do something for me?" I said.

I pulled the speech from my pocket.

"Take this speech and read it," I said.

"I can't do that," he said.

"It's all right here," I said. "All you have to do is read it."

"We already talked about this," he said. "We're gonna have fun. I'm gonna tell jokes, I'm gonna toss my bust. . . ."

"Tommy, no one has ever done anything like this," I said. "Please, here. . . ."

I made another attempt to hand him the speech. He pushed it away and kept talking.

"I'm gonna dance, I'm gonna chest bump the other guys. . . ."

"Tommy," I shouted, "you're going to look like an idiot!"

It hurt me to say it, but it seemed like the only way to reach him. In another five minutes, we would be on the stage, and it would be too late.

"What's so hard about reading a speech?" I said.

"I'm afraid," he said. "You want the truth? I'm afraid."

"Afraid of what?"

"I'm afraid of breaking down out there," he said.

He told me that if he read my speech, he would start thinking about his late father, and he would think of Van Brocklin and other teammates who were gone, and he would be overcome with emotion. In his career, he took pride in being the toughest guy on the field, the little guy who took all those hits and never backed down. He did not want to get all weepy on the steps at the Hall of Fame.

"Lots of guys cry out there," I said. "Even Ray Nitschke cried."

"I'm not crying all over TV, no way," he said. "Look at those guys out there. Bart Starr, [Paul] Hornung, Otto Graham, [Gale] Sayers, Gino Marchetti. What will they think if I start bawling?"

"It's OK," I said.

"No, it's not, not for me," he replied. "The only way I can get through this is to have fun with it. Trust me. I can do this."

Moments later, the five enshrinees and their presenters went on stage. I was up first. I was under strict orders to keep my speech under four minutes. It was probably the most nervous I've ever been in my life, standing at the podium surrounded by the greatest players of all time. My knees were shaking as I began.

"Tommy McDonald is here today for one reason. He followed his heart. . . ."

My speech was interrupted twice by applause, once for noting that Tommy was the smallest player enshrined in the Hall of Fame and later for this line: "If I had one wish for the NFL today in this era of billion-dollar TV deals and million-dollar contracts, it would be that more players played the game the way Tommy McDonald played it—that they gave as much, cared as much, and loved it as much as he did. We'd all have a lot more fun."

Out of the corner of my eye, I saw NFL commissioner Paul Tagliabue applauding.

I finished my speech just as the button on the podium flashed from yellow to red, indicating I had hit the four-minute mark. I gave Tommy a hug and wished him luck. He did a Charlie Chaplin shuffle to the podium and began with a loud "Ho boy, ho boy, I feel so good, soooo good. . . ."

I saw people in the audience looking around, like, "What the heck is going on?"

I cringed when Tommy told the first joke and the second. I held my breath when he tossed his bust once and then again. Thankfully, he caught it both times.

Shula looked at me and laughed. He recalled what I had said the night before. I looked across the aisle and saw Tagliabue laughing. When Tommy pulled out the boom box and began to dance, the crowd cheered. To my amazement, they were eating it up. Tommy finished by calling out the other enshrinees and chest bumping each one. He bounced off Krause and fell flat on his back, but he jumped right up and shouted, "Thank you, Canton, I love it!" He ran off the stage to a standing ovation.

Canton Repository columnist Steve Doerschuk wrote, "Tommy McDonald's speech was the darndest display of unbridled shared joy any Hall of Fame has ever seen."[6] *Sports Illustrated*'s Gerry Callahan wrote, "Thank you, Tommy, for reminding us sports is meant to be fun."[7]

Kansas City Chiefs owner Lamar Hunt asked John Bankert, the hall's executive director, "Can we induct Tommy McDonald every year? He's a riot."

"See?" Tommy said. "And you didn't think it would work."

In the weeks that followed, I went to his house several times. He was still fielding calls from friends and former teammates congratulating him on his induction. Now that he knew me as Little Brother, he found the whole thing even more amazing.

"It's like a fairy tale," he said.

"You should write a book about it," Patty said.

I agreed it was a great story, a story worth sharing, but I thought it might work better as a play. There was only one problem: I had never written a play. I called Gene Collier, a sportswriter friend in Pittsburgh. He had written a play about Steelers owner Art Rooney, *The Chief*, that had a successful run at the Pittsburgh Public Theatre. I told him the story of Tommy and me. He encouraged me to start working on a script.

"I had never written a play before either," Collier said. "But that doesn't matter. If you have a good story, it will tell itself."

It took a year to complete the first draft of *Tommy and Me*. I brought it to Joe Canuso, the founding artistic director of Theatre Exile. As a football fan, he loved the story, but he felt the script needed polishing. He put me in touch with Bruce Graham, an award-winning Philadelphia playwright, who helped me take the story from the page to the stage.

We worked for six months, taking the story apart and putting it back together, moving pieces around like we were playing with Lego. Joe scheduled a reading at Plays and Players Theater to see how a live audience would respond to the story. If it bombed—and readings sometimes do—*Tommy and Me* would have been buried right then and there.

But the reading went well, and when Matt Pfeiffer, the actor playing the adult Ray, read my Hall of Fame presentation speech, Tommy—the real Tommy—jumped out of his seat and ran to the stage. He pumped his fists in the air and led the crowd in an "E-A-G-L-E-S" chant. It brought the house down.

"I think we have something here," Joe said with a smile.

We began shaping *Tommy and Me* into a full production with video highlights and music. Joe assembled an outstanding cast. Tom Teti, a veteran local actor, played the older Tommy. Pfeiffer was the adult Ray. Simon Kiley, Joe's precocious ten-year-old grandson, was young Ray. Ned Pryce was young Tommy.

Opening night was terrifying. The FringeArts theater was sold out. There were professional theater critics in the house. What if they tore the play to shreds? I saw Bobby Rydell, the Philly rock 'n' roll legend, in the audience, wearing an Eagles cap. There was a buzz in the theater as people took their seats. My stomach was in knots.

Bruce Graham had suggested putting a laugh line early in the show. He said it helps the audience settle into the play and allows the actors to relax.

"But what if they don't laugh?" I asked.

"It's your job to see that they *do* laugh," Bruce said.

My laugh line was on the first page. Tommy sees a photo of Connie Mack Stadium in Ray's office. He sighs and says, "Connie Mack Stadium." Then he shakes his head and says, "What a dump." The shift in tone from wistful to sardonic, delivered with impeccable timing by Teti, got a big laugh. I breathed a sigh of relief.

Opening night was a success. The audience gave the cast a well-deserved standing ovation, and the reviews were overwhelmingly positive.

"Funny and heartwarming. Philadelphia Eagles fans will love it," wrote Tim Dunleavy of *DC Metro Arts*.

"Lovely and elegiac," wrote Neal Zoren of the *Delaware County Daily Times*.

"A supremely touching tale," wrote Steve Cohen of the *Cultural Critic*.

"A lovely story about childhood heroes and love of the game brings an unexpected tear to the eye," wrote Mark Cofta of the *Broad Street Review*.

"The sweet, affecting play is as Philadelphian as cheesesteaks," wrote Howard Shapiro of *NewsWorks*.

"An exquisitely crafted tale that earnestly illustrates the power of sports heroes in our lives," wrote Candis McLean of the *Philly Influencer*.

"Pfeiffer's earnestness effuses like any fan's in the presence of a childhood idol and Teti endears as the older nearly forgotten athlete," wrote Jim Rutter of the *Philadelphia Inquirer*.

"There is a moment when older Tommy recalls a particular play he made, Teti's face is transformed and Pfeiffer watches him silently. It's poignant and wonderful," wrote David Fox in *Philadelphia Magazine*.

The best review was the one we received at the first Saturday matinee. That was the performance Tommy attended with his children and grandchildren. They filled an entire row of the theater. He was smiling from ear to ear. Every so often during the performance, he would nudge his son Chris and point at the stage, as if to say, "Yeah, that's right."

When the play ended, Tommy took a bow along with the cast. In the Q&A, he was asked what he thought of the play.

"S-U-P-E-R," he said.

He stayed around for a full hour, shaking hands and signing autographs. At eighty-three, he loved hearing the cheers again. As he was leaving, he hugged me and said, "Thanks. You let me be Tommy McDonald again."

Tommy and Me ran for three weeks and sold out every performance. The company brought it back to FringeArts for another three-week run the following year. The Media Theatre booked it the next summer, and again it sold out.

Broadway World, the theater website, selected *Tommy and Me* as the outstanding regional theater production of 2018. It named Tom Teti outstanding actor and Frank Nardi Jr., who took over the role of young Tommy, outstanding supporting actor.

Over the years, many former coaches and players came to see *Tommy and Me*. Dick Vermeil came twice, as did Seth Joyner and Vai Sikahema. Harold Carmichael, Bill Bergey, Mike Quick, and Ron Jaworski all came to see it. Former Oakland Raiders quarterback Rich Gannon came to see it as well. Gannon had played with Chris McDonald at the University of Delaware.

Eagles owner Jeff Lurie came to the play with his wife, Tina, in 2019, joining the cast on stage for the post-show Q&A. He said, "In Philadelphia with the fans, it always starts with the heart. That's what this play is about. It's all about the heart. That's what Tommy McDonald was. He was all heart."

Sadly, like many former players, Tommy began showing signs of dementia. He had chronic traumatic encephalopathy, a neurological condition brought about by years of taking blows to the head. I was with Tommy at a dinner in 2018 when Mike Mamula, a former Eagle, asked him what he remembered about his playing career. He replied, "Nothing."

There was a time when Tommy could recount entire games in detail, but in his later years, it was a blank. He did not even remember the 1960 championship game. He knew the Eagles had won, because he still wore the championship ring, but he didn't remember anything about the game itself. He didn't even remember his touchdown. He stopped going to the Hall of Fame reunions because he could not remember people's names.

In 2019, I talked to his son as we were rehearsing for the August run of *Tommy and Me*. Chris said there was no way his father would make it to the theater. Patty had passed away, and Tommy was in a nursing home. He didn't even know where he was. When I visited, we spent most of the time watching game shows on TV.

One day, Chris sent an email to let me know that Tommy was failing. "If you want to see Dad," he said, "you better come soon."

Tommy was in hospice care at the home of his daughter Sherry. The kids wanted him to be surrounded by family and loved ones.

When I came to visit, Chris and Sherry walked me to his room. Tommy was in bed, wearing a green Eagles jersey, number 25.

"I thought you'd want to remember him this way," Sherry said.

Tommy woke up when he heard my voice. He smiled, and his eyes brightened.

"He can't talk," Chris said, "but he knows what you're saying."

Chris and Sherry left the room so Tommy and I could be alone. I sat on the edge of the bed and took his hand. I told him about the play, how we had just finished another successful run. I told him Vermeil and his wife, Carol, had come to the play and loved it. He smiled.

Tommy pointed at the collage that Sherry and Tish, his younger daughter, had put together for him. There were photos from his playing days going back to Oklahoma. There was a photo of Tommy and Patty as glamorous newlyweds, riding in a convertible. There was the famous *Sports Illustrated* cover, "Football's Best Hands."

I squeezed his hands and said, "You still got 'em." He laughed softly and mouthed the word, "Yes."

He closed his eyes, and I hugged him until he drifted off to sleep. I sat there for a while, knowing it was the last time we would be together. I looked at him there in his green jersey and thought about all the times he had referred to himself as "old number two-five."

Sherry was right. This is how I would remember him.

Two days later, I received another email from Chris.

"I just wanted you to know we lost our best buddy this morning," he wrote. "He's in heaven now with Patty and Norm the Dutchman."

Tears filled my eyes as I read the final line.

"You know how much he loved you," Chris wrote.

Of course I know. I was his Little Brother.

18

The Philly Special

IT IS A TERM we all use but don't fully understand: team chemistry.

What is it, really? How do you define it? How do you measure it?

Darned if I know.

Supreme Court Justice Potter Stewart once was asked to rule on a case of alleged pornography. Justice Stewart said he could not define pornography, but "I know it when I see it."

That's how it is with team chemistry: I can't define it, but I know it when I see it.

I saw it in the 2017 Philadelphia Eagles. It was real, and it was powerful, and it helped carry the Eagles to their first Super Bowl championship.

It is a mysterious thing. You can't point to a particular day and say it started here. You can't cite one event that created it. It is a feeling that grows over the course of a season, a sense of confidence and purpose shared by an entire team. When it is there, you see it. You feel it when you walk into the room.

The Eagles' chemistry in 2017 was palpable. It allowed them to overcome obstacles that seemed insurmountable. They assumed the role of underdogs, complete with dog masks, and rode that emotion all the way to the Super Bowl.

What was most surprising was how it seemed to come out of nowhere. There was no trace of team chemistry at the end of the 2015 season. Chip Kelly had destroyed it. Once Jeff Lurie gave him control of the roster, Kelly stripped it down and rebuilt it with sullen mercenaries— Sam Bradford, Byron Maxwell, DeMarco Murray, Ryan Matthews, Kiko Alonso—who never connected with the city or each other.

Doug Pederson replaced Kelly, and in his first year, the team went 7–9 behind rookie quarterback Carson Wentz. They finished last in the NFC East, so while Wentz showed promise, no one was projecting great things for 2017. Yet somewhere, they found that magic.

Injuries sidelined running back Darren Sproles, tackle Jason Peters, linebacker Jordan Hicks, and cornerback Ronald Darby, yet they won ten of their first twelve games. I believe that is where the chemistry began to develop. It was like watching cement harden.

With each new injury, Pederson invoked the mantra, "Next man up." Another player would step into the void, and the team would win another game. Their resilience became their identity, and vice versa.

Pederson had outstanding leadership among his veterans, notably safety Malcolm Jenkins, tight end Brent Celek, center Jason Kelce, and defensive end Chris Long. Jenkins provided a rallying cry—"We all we got; we all we need"—and the team kept winning. But then Wentz— who was playing at an MVP level—suffered a knee injury in December.

The next morning, a caller to Angelo Cataldi's radio show broke down sobbing: "I really thought this was our year. It's like we're cursed in this city."

When Pederson met the press that day, he made it clear he was not giving up.

"I hate it for Carson Wentz," Pederson said. "He was the MVP in my opinion. He's a heckuva player and a great leader for this football team. But we've been taking a next-man-up approach all year, and that's how we'll approach it now.

"There are a lot of great football players in that room," he said, "and they helped put us in this position. They aren't giving up, so there's no reason for anyone else to give up. We're going forward with Nick, and we're going to keep playing."

Pederson was referring to Nick Foles, the backup quarterback who had led the team to the playoffs as the starter under Kelly in 2013. He threw 27 touchdown passes and just 2 interceptions that season, but he was injured the next year, and Kelly traded him to St. Louis, where he was benched and released. He was so dispirited, he considered quitting football.

Andy Reid, the man who drafted him for the Eagles in 2012, convinced Foles to join him in Kansas City. Foles spent one year there and then returned to the Eagles to be the backup for Wentz. His 2013 Pro Bowl season was a distant memory. The idea that he could pick up where Wentz left off and lead the team to the Super Bowl seemed like a fantasy.

Pederson, however, sent a clear message that nothing had changed. At 11–2, the Eagles still controlled the NFC.

"Everything we hoped to achieve is still in front of us," Pederson said. "I believe in these guys; I believe in Nick. No one is saying, 'Woe is me.' This is the NFL. We're going back to work."

It was a great example of leadership. It reminded me of Dick Vermeil when he was coaching the Rams in 1999 and lost quarterback Trent Green in the preseason. Vermeil tearfully but forcefully sent a similar message, vowing, "We'll rally around Kurt Warner, and we'll play good football."

Warner was unknown and unproven, a refugee from the Arena Football League, but he led the NFL in passing that season and won the Super Bowl. Vermeil adjusted his offense to fit the skills of his new quarterback; he also kept his team focused and believing.

Pederson did the same with the Eagles. He lifted a few pages from the Kelly playbook and brought back the run-pass option plays that Foles executed successfully in 2013. It allowed Foles to feel more confident, and he turned that confidence into a memorable postseason run.

Team chemistry was the constant; that was the fiber. When Wentz went down, what was already tight became tighter. The more people doubted the Eagles, the more fiercely they fought.

In the week leading up to the playoff game against Atlanta, the locker room TVs played a nonstop loop of TV pundits picking the Falcons. The Eagles were the first number-one seed to be an underdog to a wild-card team. On a cold night in South Philadelphia, the defense came up with a goal-line stand at the end of the game to preserve a 15–10 victory.

The next week, the Eagles crushed Minnesota, 38–7, scoring 31 unanswered points against the NFL's top-ranked defense. Foles passed for 352 yards as Pederson called a masterful game, including a flea-flicker touchdown pass from Foles to Torrey Smith. Foles had not thrown one of those since high school.

Pederson's aggressive play calling instilled confidence in the team. During the regular season, he went for it on fourth down 26 times, the most in the league, and made it 17 times. It became part of the team's personality: the coach's willingness to trust his players and the players' embrace of that trust.

I became a Pederson believer, which was surprising, considering that I had literally laughed at the idea of him as a head coach just two years earlier.

Glen Macnow and I were on the radio, talking about the Eagles' search for Kelly's successor. Seven teams, including the Eagles, were looking for a head coach. Adam Gase and Ben McAdoo were hot names. Tom Coughlin, with his two Super Bowl rings, was available. I heard Jon Gruden was getting the itch to coach again. There were a lot of candidates.

Late in the show, a caller from Kansas City said he had the name of the Eagles' next coach.

"Doug Pederson," he said.

I laughed. I really thought he was kidding.

The caller insisted he was serious. He said that after the Kelly misfire, Lurie would seek a return to the Andy Reid way of doing things. To Lurie, Pederson was Reid 2.0.

I understood the Reid connection, but it seemed like a real stretch. Tennessee, Miami, Tampa Bay, Cleveland, the Giants, and the 49ers all were in the market for a coach, and none of them had expressed the slightest interest in Pederson.

"Can you imagine the reaction in the city if the Eagles hired Doug Pederson?" Glen said.

One week later, Pederson was introduced as the Eagles' new coach. Somewhere in Kansas City, I'm sure that caller was laughing at us.

It was not a popular decision in Philadelphia. The fans remembered Pederson as the journeyman backup who played ahead of McNabb in 1999. The Eagles won just two of his nine starts. It was ugly. Pederson spent four years as a mid-level assistant coach with the Eagles after retiring as a player.

He rejoined Reid in Kansas City and was promoted to offensive coordinator. He was fresh off a 27–20 playoff loss to New England in which poor clock management—a recurring theme with Reid—played a major role. When asked about it at his first press conference as the Eagles' coach, he fumbled around for an explanation and left reporters scratching their heads.

Wrote Bob Brookover in the *Inquirer*, "Nothing [Pederson] said or did during his introductory news conference assured us that he was the right man for the job."[1]

USA Today rated the seven new coaching hires. Pederson came in seventh. The headline: "Ranking the Seven New Coaching Hires (Sorry, Eagles Fans)." The story read, "I guess just wanting to come to Philadelphia and sign a contract was pretty much the prerequisite."[2]

Pederson's only head coaching experience was the four years he had spent at Calvary Baptist Academy in Shreveport, Louisiana. By all accounts, he did a fine job. The team made the playoffs all four seasons. The kids and their parents loved him. But how did that qualify him to be the head coach of the Eagles?

Mike Lombardi, a former general manager and scout, wrote an online column saying Pederson was overmatched as an NFL head coach.

"Everybody knows Pederson isn't a head coach," Lombardi wrote. "He might be less qualified to coach a team than anyone I've seen in my 30-plus years in the NFL."[3]

I was peppered with questions about why Lurie hired Pederson. I urged the fans to give Pederson a chance, although I had my doubts too.

Shortly after the hiring, I ran into Ron Jaworski. He had accompanied Lurie, club president Don Smolenski, and general manager Howie Roseman on the coaching search.

"Doug Pederson?" I asked.

"He's the guy," Jaworski said.

"Seriously?"

"I'm telling you, he's the guy."

I've known Jaworski since he came to Philadelphia in 1977. He was always honest with me, and he was fully confident in the decision to hire Pederson.

"Doug gets it," he said. "You'll see."

A few weeks later, I was going through my files and came across a *Daily News* profile of Reid when he was hired as the Eagles' coach in 1999. There was a sidebar in which Reid answered a variety of questions. One of them was "What current player will one day be a successful NFL head coach?" Reid's answer was Doug Pederson.[4]

When Lurie hired Pederson, he used such terms as "genuineness" and "emotional intelligence" to describe him. He had found Kelly lacking in those areas. Kelly won ten games during each of his first two seasons, but he lost five of seven games down the stretch in 2015, and

Lurie believed that the coach no longer had the support of the players. The Eagles had allowed an average of 37 points in the five losses; they looked like a team that had quit on its coach.

By then, Kelly had alienated almost everyone in the organization. He was chilly and dismissive, even with his own coaching staff. In Lurie's view, Kelly's presence had become corrosive, so he fired him with one week left in the season. In his search for a new coach, Lurie wanted someone who would rebuild the morale within the Nova Care Complex. He believed that Pederson had those qualities.

Pederson's brand of leadership was low-key but effective. Unlike Kelly, he engaged with everyone in the building. He wasn't a control freak. He invited input. He brought Roseman, who had been exiled by Kelly, back into the football operation.

More than anyone else, Pederson was responsible for the winning chemistry. The players bought into it, but he created it. He made it a point to walk through the locker room every day to take the pulse of the team. It was one way in which Pederson differed from Reid. Reid rarely went into the locker room. He saw that as the players' space. But Pederson found it helpful to make the rounds. Even if it was just chit chat—"Did you see that game last night?"—it was a bonding thing.

The 2017 season did not start in auspicious fashion. The Eagles won the opener in Washington and then lost the following week to Reid's Kansas City Chiefs. The next week, in their home opener, the Eagles blew a 14–0 lead against the Giants and appeared on their way to a disheartening loss when rookie Jake Elliott kicked a 61-yard field goal on the final play to win the game.

Elliott had been with the team one week. He didn't even have a place to live; he was crashing on a friend's couch in Northern Liberties. Most of the Eagles didn't even know his name, yet he kicked the longest field goal in franchise history to win the game. Linebackers Mychal Kendricks and Kamu Grugier-Hill scooped him up and carried him off the field on their shoulders.

I watched it from the *Eagles Post-Game Live* set. When the ball cleared the uprights, my broadcast partner Seth Joyner said, "Shit like that don't just happen. It happens for a reason."

Seth believed that something special was going on with the Eagles. He had lived it himself when he went to Super Bowls with Green Bay and Denver in back-to-back years.

"This might just be the Eagles' year," he said.

"It's Week 3, Seth," I said. "There's a long way to go."

"I'm just sayin'," he replied.

The Elliott game was the start of a nine-game winning streak, tying a club record set in 1949 and tied in 1960. Both of those seasons ended with the Eagles winning the NFL championship, so perhaps Seth was right.

Nelson Agholor, a bust for his first two seasons, suddenly was catching every ball thrown his way. Rookie free agent Corey Clement filled in admirably for Sproles. Halapoulivaati Vaitai took over for All-Pro tackle Jason Peters and played better than he had ever played before. Foles replaced Wentz and played superbly. It wasn't one or two players overachieving—this was an entire team overachieving.

"When a team is winning the way this team is winning now, no one wants to be the guy who lets the group down," Seth said. "You play over your head because you know everyone is counting on you. You draw strength from the other guys. That's what we're seeing here."

The Eagles got stronger with each postseason game. The win over Atlanta went down to the final play, a pass from quarterback Matt Ryan that skipped through the All-Pro hands of Julio Jones. It could have gone the other way, but it didn't.

Minnesota scored on its first possession in the NFC title game, but then Patrick Robinson, a journeyman defensive back picked up off the scrapheap prior to the season, intercepted a pass and returned it for a touchdown. The Eagles blew away the Vikings, 38–7.

Lurie met the media after the victory. He was informed that Las Vegas already had the Eagles as underdogs to New England in Super Bowl LII. Lurie smiled and said, "Great. We wouldn't have it any other way."

On the Thursday before the Super Bowl, I made my weekly appearance on the WIP morning show with Angelo Cataldi. I had my usual stack of statistics, and almost all of them favored the Patriots. I went over them point by point, spelling out all the reasons why the Patriots were the better team. By the time I finished, Angelo was facedown on the desk.

Then I said, "But I think the Eagles are going to win."

Angelo jumped out of his chair, grabbed his head, and let out a howl that probably startled the carriage horses in Independence Mall.

"After all that," he said, "you're picking the Eagles?"

"I just have a feeling about this team," I said.

It was vague and unscientific and probably not very convincing to anyone outside the Philadelphia area, but that's how I felt. I believed in the Eagles. I had picked them to beat Atlanta, I had picked them to beat the Vikings, and even though they were underdogs again, I was confident they would beat the Patriots.

I don't always buy into the team-of-destiny thing, but I believed it with the Eagles. I believed it because I could tell *they* believed it.

In the conference championship round, the AFC game was played first. The Patriots hosted Jacksonville. The Jaguars went ahead in the first half and extended their lead to 20–10 early in the fourth quarter. We were watching the game in the studio. The producers and cameramen were cheering for Jacksonville; they felt the Jags would be an easier opponent in the Super Bowl.

I was rooting the other way. I wanted the Patriots.

To me, it would have been a letdown to get to the Super Bowl and face the Jaguars. If you are the Eagles, a team that never won a Super Bowl, do you really want the first win to come against the Jacksonville Jaguars? Where's the glory in that? You would finally have the chance to tell that big mouth Cowboys fan at the office that your team won the Super Bowl, and his reply would be, "Big deal, you beat the Jaguars."

I also didn't like the fact that Jacksonville brought back painful memories of Super Bowl XXXIX. The Eagles had lost to the Patriots in that stadium. If the Eagles were on their way to Super Bowl LII—and I felt certain they were—I didn't want any trace of Jacksonville.

Also, I was certain the Eagles would be favored over the Jaguars, and that would mess up the underdog karma. The Eagles had become so comfortable in that role and Pederson had become so good at playing it that it would have flipped the script at the worst possible time. Better to be the underdog, especially against the Patriots.

Besides, who goes to the Super Bowl hoping for a soft touch? It's supposed to be about beating the best, right? Well, the Patriots were the best. They proved it again by storming back to beat the Jaguars, 24–20, on two Brady touchdown passes in the fourth quarter.

The Eagles took care of the Vikings, so the matchup was set for Super Bowl LII in Minnesota.

The NFL set up shop at the Mall of America, a ninety-six-acre complex of stores, restaurants, and amusement parks, all under one roof. The Eagles were in an adjoining hotel, which meant their coaches and players spent the week in the mall, mingling with fans and buying souvenirs. You couldn't walk ten steps without bumping into a player, usually with his entire family. They were incredibly loose and having a really good time, which I thought was a good sign.

My biggest concern going into the game was the Patriots' advantage in Super Bowl experience. They had won the previous year with many of the same players. They had played in seven Super Bowls under Belichick, so they knew the event inside and out.

The Eagles had just five players with Super Bowl experience: Chris Long (Rams), Malcolm Jenkins (Saints), Torrey Smith and Tim Jernigan (Ravens), and LeGarrette Blount, who was with the Patriots the previous year. For the rest of the team, it would be their first Super Bowl. Could they keep their emotions in check?

I've seen teams lose Super Bowls long before they play the game. Some are blinded by the bright lights, and others have so much fun partying that they show up for the game exhausted.

The 1980 Eagles looked out of sync the whole week. Emotionally spent after the big win over Dallas, they appeared overwhelmed by the craziness in New Orleans. The Raiders had been through it before, which surely was a factor in their 27–10 victory.

I wondered whether these Eagles would fall victim to the same thing. Like the '80 Eagles, they were the new kids on the block. Like the '80 Raiders, the Patriots had done this dance before. But these Eagles didn't appear fazed at all. I mentioned it to Seth when I caught up with him in Minneapolis.

"These guys can't wait to play this game," he said. "They aren't nervous, not even a little bit."

On Saturday, I called home. My wife said, "I have to tell you something. You're not going to believe it."

She said there was an eagle flying over our house. It circled long enough that she had time to get the binoculars for a better view. Yes, she said, it was definitely an eagle, majestic and unmistakable, right above our house. At one point, it actually landed on our garage.

In the thirty-two years we had lived there, we had seen every kind of bird but never an eagle. So why now? Why on Super Bowl eve?

"I know it sounds crazy," Maria said, "but I think it's the spirit of your mother and father."

"I do too," I said.

Just for the record: We never saw the eagle again. That was the one and only time. Scoff all you want; I think it meant something.

That afternoon, NBC Sports Philadelphia rented out a bar in Minneapolis for an Eagles pep rally. When we arrived, the place was packed, and there was a long line of fans hoping to get in.

It was just like the Super Bowl in Jacksonville. The town was overrun with people dressed in green, and thanks to social media, they found their way to the pep rally. Michael Barkann and Barrett Brooks were onstage, leading an Eagles chant.

"Tomorrow is the day," Michael shouted. "You have to bring it all day. Make this stadium sound like the Linc. Can you do it?"

A cheer went up, followed by another Eagles chant.

"You think the Eagles are going to win?" asked Michelle Murray, the NBC Sports Philadelphia news director.

"Yeah, I do," I said, shouting over the crowd noise.

"You sound like you're really sure," she said.

"I am," I replied.

Game day dawned brutally cold. The wind chill was twenty-five below when we arrived at the U.S. Bank Stadium. We parked two blocks away, which doesn't sound very far, but by the time we got to the media entrance, my face was frozen.

NBC Sports had two separate crews covering the game: NBC Sports Philadelphia and NBC Sports Boston. They had a trailer parked outside the stadium; that was where we would watch the game. It was an awkward arrangement—two crews from rival cities jammed into one trailer, watching the Super Bowl on TV.

Michelle said there would be two separate pregame shows. One would be our usual Eagles pregame. The other would be a sixty-minute special: Philly versus Boston, a no-holds-barred, back-and-forth debate, our panel against the Boston guys.

I didn't want to do it. I had no desire to be part of a TV shout-fest with a lot of name calling. Michelle said the format was already set. There was no getting out of it.

"You're on for one segment," she said. "Just do the best you can."

The plan called for four segments: Michael with Boston talker Mike Felger, Seth with former Patriot Ty Law, Barrett with former Patriot Troy Brown, and me with Felger and NFL Network reporter Albert Breer.

When it was my turn, Felger started in on the Philadelphia fans. He talked about "an undercurrent of violence" at sporting events in Philadelphia. He said it was the only place where he thought he might "get a metal chair in the back of my head."

I thought it was a silly and irresponsible thing to say. I couldn't let it go unchallenged.

"How many games did you see at Schaefer Stadium?" I said, referring to the original Foxboro stadium where the Patriots played in the '70s and I once had a beer poured on my head. "You want to talk about bad fans? You want to talk about thug fans? The fans at Schaefer Stadium were the worst in the NFL."

"Yeah, that was bad," Felger said, "but the Boston fans evolved, unlike the Philadelphia fans."

What happened in Boston had nothing to do with evolving, I said. It had everything to do with winning.

"For years, the Boston fans didn't even know there was a football team in Foxboro," I said.

It was true: Boston fans were all about the Red Sox, Celtics, and Bruins. They didn't pay any attention to the Patriots when they were losing. Bill Simmons, a Boston native who became a national voice on ESPN, compared the Patriots to Fredo, the weakling brother who was shoved to the back row of the Corleone family portrait in *The Godfather*.

"But then they started winning, and all of a sudden everyone got happy," I said. "Boston fans started to care about the Patriots. Hey, it's the easiest thing in the world to jump on a bandwagon. The Philly fans haven't seen a championship in more than fifty years, but look at how many of those people are here today."

Felger shot back, "You're talking about Boston fans forty years ago. . . ."

"And Philly fans are still hearing about throwing snowballs at Santa Claus, and that was *more* than forty years ago," I said. "I'm tired of that stuff. The Philly fans are the best fans in the NFL. They've waited a long time to celebrate, but I think that wait ends tonight."

"Hear, hear," said Michael as he wrapped the segment.

We returned to the trailer to watch the game. As I suspected, there was no semblance of neutrality. The Philly crew was rooting for the Eagles; the Boston crew was rooting for the Patriots. We were jammed in shoulder to shoulder, which made for a lot of lively back and forth, but it got a little edgy when the Eagles opened a 15–6 lead in the second quarter.

This was not what the Boston guys had expected. They were supremely confident. They had Belichick and Brady, the most dynamic coach-quarterback tandem in history. The Eagles had Pederson and Foles, a second-year coach and a backup quarterback. What's to discuss? This would be a blowout.

But unlike other teams that had faced New England, the Eagles were not in awe. As Seth noted earlier, the Eagles couldn't wait to play them. They wouldn't play scared, and Pederson wasn't going to coach scared. They were going to be the same aggressive, go-for-it team they had been all season.

You don't beat the Patriots by playing conservatively. You don't beat them by playing by the book because they know the book too well. Your best chance is to throw some things at them that they haven't seen before. I knew the Eagles would do that.

Boy, did they ever.

With thirty-eight seconds left in the first half, the Eagles had fourth down at the Patriots' 1-yard line. They led 15–12, and a field goal here would send them into the locker room with a 6-point lead. It looked like an easy call. For most coaches, it would be, except there was Pederson, waving his kicking team off the field.

"What the hell is he doing?" asked the Boston guy next to me. "He's gotta kick the field goal."

Pederson and Foles were in deep discussion at the Eagles' bench.

"They're not kicking a field goal," I said.

"Whaddya mean? They gotta take the 3 points," the guy said.

"How many times have you seen the Eagles this season?" I asked.

"Three or four times," he said.

"Well, I've seen them every week," I said, "and I'm telling you, they are not kicking a field goal."

Foles trotted back onto the field. They were going for it on fourth down. This was what the Eagles had done all season. It was a big reason why they were even in this game. To the Boston guys, it was sheer madness. To me, it was Pederson again trusting his gut and trusting his players.

The Eagles lined up in a pistol formation, with Clement directly behind Foles. As the quarterback called signals, he moved to his right, as though he wanted to make sure tackle Lane Johnson could hear him. He called out "Kill, kill," which normally indicated that he was changing the play. He then called out "Lane, Lane," which was the signal for Kelce to snap the ball.

Kelce sent the direct snap to Clement, who ran to his left. He lateraled to tight end Trey Burton, who was coming across the formation to the right. Foles, meanwhile, slipped unnoticed into the end zone. Burton, a former high school quarterback, floated a pass to Foles, who caught it for an easy touchdown.

We knew Pederson was capable of surprises, but *that*? In the Super Bowl? The Boston guy was shaking his head.

"Nah, nah, that can't be legal," he said. "There's gotta be something wrong with that."

There was nothing wrong. It was perfectly legal and downright inspired. NBC's Al Michaels called it "the all-time trick play." Color analyst Cris Collinsworth called it "the greatest play call in Super Bowl history."

We know it now as "the Philly Special."

On a day when the teams combined for an NFL record 1,131 yards, it might seem silly to focus so much on 1 yard. It is like talking about one grain of sand on the beach, one note in a symphony, or one line in a Broadway play. But it was 1 yard that said everything about the 2017 Eagles and their improbable drive to the NFL championship. It didn't win Super Bowl LII, but it will forever define it.

The Patriots came back in the second half and actually took a 33–32 lead in the fourth quarter. The Eagles fought back, converting a key fourth down when Foles hit tight end Zach Ertz, and seven plays later, Foles hit Ertz again with an 11-yard pass for the winning touchdown.

By then, we had left the trailer and moved into the stadium. There was a booth on the mezzanine level where we would do the postgame show. The final play—Brady's desperation pass into the end zone—happened right in front of us.

When I saw the ball hit the ground, I looked at the scoreboard and saw Eagles 41, Patriots 33. I thought about the eagle on our garage, I thought about my parents, I thought about Ray's Tavern. It was a blur of images and emotions, all of them bathed in green and silver confetti.

Unlike other games, we did not come on the air immediately. We knew the viewers back home would want to watch the trophy presentation and the interviews with Lurie, Pederson, and Foles, the game's MVP. We would begin our show when the ceremony on the field ended.

It gave us a chance to sit back and enjoy the scene. Governor Ed Rendell joined us, wearing an Eagles jacket and a smile that stretched across the Twin Cities. In his life, he had celebrated many things—two elections as district attorney, two landslide elections as the city's mayor, two other elections to the office of governor—but he said this was even better. He had to work for the others; this was pure fun.

"What a game," he said. "What a game."

The Patriots finished with 613 yards, and the Eagles finished with 538. Brady threw for a career-high 505 yards, a Super Bowl record, and still lost. Foles, who almost retired a year earlier and started the season on the bench, accounted for 4 touchdowns, 3 on passes he threw and 1 that he caught.

I was watching the players celebrate, making snow angels in the confetti and hoisting their children onto their shoulders. Seth and Barrett were wearing their Super Bowl rings; it was the first time they had worn them all season. They saved them for special occasions. This was a special occasion.

Barrett won his Super Bowl with the Pittsburgh Steelers in 2006. Seth won his with Denver in 1999. For Seth, it was the last game of his brilliant career. What a way to go out. He doesn't smile often, but he was smiling as he watched Foles raise the Lombardi Trophy.

"What's that like, that moment?" I asked.

"There are no words," he said.

I understood.

When we went on the air, it was every bit as festive as you would imagine. Seth smiled throughout the two-hour show. Michael kept things humming along. Reporter Derrick Gunn was downstairs, getting interviews with the coaches and players. There were dozens of Philadelphia fans outside our broadcast location, so we had an "E-A-G-L-E-S" chant going the whole time.

When my son, David, arrived after packing up his NFL Films gear, Michael brought him onto the set. I tried to hold back the tears, but when we hugged, I lost it. I had started the day with an on-camera screaming match and finished the day with an on-camera cry. It was the full range of emotions, but when you win a Super Bowl, stuff just happens.

During a commercial break, David told me, "You know that trick play? Foles called that play."

"What do you mean?" I said.

"It was his idea," David said. "Foles suggested it, and Pederson said OK. I heard the whole thing."

Foles was one of several players wired for sound that day. A cameraman is assigned to each of those players; his job is to keep the camera on his player for the entire day, from pregame warmups right through the postgame handshakes.

As one of NFL Films' top cameramen, David was assigned to Foles, so he heard every word, every signal call, every hit for the entire day. He listened in on every sideline conversation, including the one we all remember. He watched through his viewfinder as Foles approached Pederson on the sideline. Pederson was studying his chart, looking for just the right play to call on fourth and goal.

Foles said, "You want Philly Philly?"

He had the wrong terminology but the right idea. The play was called "the Philly Special," and it was the kind of goofy razzle-dazzle you might run in a schoolyard, but Foles had a hunch it would work here.

Pederson thought a moment and said, "Yeah, let's do it."

Clearly, Pederson had something else in mind, but whatever he saw in Foles's eyes made him decide to trust his quarterback. If Foles felt good about the play, if that's what he wanted to run with the game on the line, Pederson was willing to go with it.

The result was arguably the greatest 1-yard touchdown pass in NFL history, and we only know the full story because we heard the conversation. That's the beauty of NFL Films. Without the wire, we would have assumed Pederson called the play, and Foles executed it, and it was a slick piece of trickery that left the Patriots befuddled. That would have been fine. We still would have celebrated it.

But to see it in its full context—to hear the confidence in Foles's voice, to see Pederson opt to roll the dice, to see how spontaneous and draw-it-up-in-the-dirt crazy it truly was—made it even better. Who would have thought a 1-yard pass play could have such a dramatic arc?

The fact that my son was the cameraman who got the shot made it the perfect ending to a perfect day. I told him he was now part of football history.

"Fifty years from now, your shot will still be playing at the Hall of Fame," I said. "Thanks to you, people will always know about 'the Philly Special.'"

"I'm just glad the Eagles won," David said.

Four days later, the city celebrated the championship with a parade and a rally on the steps of the Art Museum. In freezing temperatures, thousands of fans lined the streets to cheer the Eagles as their bus rolled through Center City. People were hanging from light poles and standing on mailboxes to get a better view. They brought urns with the ashes of their loved ones to share in the moment.

I had a window seat on the press bus, so I was able to take in the whole scene. As we made the turn off Broad Street onto the Benjamin Franklin Parkway, it was a sea of green all the way to Eakins Oval. Our bus could hardly squeeze through the mass of humanity. A little boy caught my eye. He was wearing a Zach Ertz jersey and holding up a small homemade sign that read simply: "It's Ours."

Yes, I thought, it is.

Epilogue

——————

One of my favorite plays is *Our Town,* Thornton Wilder's timeless masterpiece about life in a small New Hampshire village. There is a character called the Stage Manager who guides the audience through this humble place called Grover's Corner.

There is a scene in the third act when Emily, who died in childbirth, is offered a chance to come back to Earth for one day and relive it. She chooses her thirteenth birthday. However, when she returns, she finds the day mired in routine and her parents busy and mostly distracted.

Deeply disappointed, Emily asks the Stage Manager, "Do any human beings ever realize their life while they live it—every, every minute?"

"No," the Stage Manager replies. "The saints and poets maybe, they do some."

I'm neither a saint nor a poet, but I can honestly say I have appreciated my life every day.

It has been a wonderful experience, and that's one of the reasons I wrote this book: I wanted to share those experiences. I also wanted to relive it myself. I wanted to have all those memories swirling around me, glistening like flakes in a snow globe.

I still recall walking through the gates at Connie Mack Stadium for the first time and seeing Byrum Saam, the Phillies radio and TV broad-

322 • Ray Didinger

caster, pass right in front of me. I still remember the sight of him in his gray suit and soft hat, carrying his briefcase and heading for the press elevator.

I stood there taking in the whole ballpark experience—smelling the hot dogs, hearing the distant sounds of batting practice and vendors calling, "Hey, getcha scorecard and lineup here"—thinking it was the most magical place on earth. Connie Mack Stadium, Franklin Field, even the clunky old Arena, that was my Disneyland. And other than Disney, who gets to live his life in Disneyland?

Well, I did.

You don't take that sort of blessing for granted.

I cherish my press box conversations with giants like Jimmy Cannon, Red Smith, Dave Anderson, and Jim Murray. It was a thrill just to sit next to them, hear their stories, and absorb their wisdom. I felt the same working with Sandy Grady, Stan Hochman, and George Kiseda in Philadelphia, true masters of their craft.

I had an advantage by growing up in Philadelphia. The other columnists in town migrated here. Stan Hochman, Bill Conlin, Frank Dolson, and Larry Merchant were from New York. Bill Lyon and Tom Cushman were from Illinois. George Kiseda was from Pittsburgh. Sandy Grady and Mark Whicker were from North Carolina. They were superb columnists, but they had to learn Philly. I had it in my bones.

I came into the business in the late '60s, when newspapers were king. There was no cable TV or sports talk radio. People still ran out to buy the morning paper to read what had happened in the big game. Now they watch the highlights on their cell phones before they go to bed.

Working conditions were certainly different. The first time I went on the road with the Eagles, I wrote my story on a portable typewriter in my hotel room and then hailed a cab to go off and find a Western Union office that was open at 2 A.M. I found one, but the operator was asleep. He was not happy when I handed him four pages of copy.

"I send telegrams, four or five words," he said. "What the hell is this?"

"It's my column for the newspaper," I said, "and it has to be there in an hour."

The operator put on his reading glasses and punched my column into his keyboard. I made deadline—just barely—and when the *Bulletin* rolled off the presses that afternoon, it had my story about Eagles quarterback Norm Snead, which in retrospect probably wasn't worth all the effort.

In the '80s came the transition to computers, and writers went on the road with bulky PCs to file their stories. It required writers like me who are helpless with any sort of technology to live with the 24/7 dread of something going wrong.

I once finished a profile on track star Edwin Moses, and when I hit the send button, there was a zapping sound, and the screen went blank. The entire story—two thousand words at least—was gone, poof, just like that. I called the office in a panic and asked the editor what I should do.

"Write it again," he said, adding, "You have one hour."

Technology improved; the computers got smaller and more reliable. But even as that was happening, newspapers were losing their influence. People started getting their news from TV.

Newspapers lost circulation, and flagship papers, such as the *Bulletin*, the *Chicago Daily News*, the *Houston Post*, the *Dallas Times Herald*, and the *Los Angeles Herald-Examiner*, went out of business. Other papers saw their staffs slashed, and talented journalists wound up on the street.

I don't envy sportswriters today. They live in a world where players are tweeting their every thought twenty-four hours a day, so the news cycle is endless. If you are a writer assigned to the Sixers, every time Joel Embiid starts tweeting, you are back on the clock.

It is no longer as simple as going to a game and talking to players in the locker room. With text messaging and Facebook, they are making news all the time, and you have to keep up with it, frivolous or not.

I don't think I could do it. I don't have a cell phone, for one thing, and I don't have any desire to own one. If I were still in the business, of course, I wouldn't have a choice. I'd have to get one, but I would not be happy about it. I would feel the phone in my pocket, and I would feel as though I never left the office. It would drive me crazy.

But while the business has changed greatly, the fact is that people still crave information. And whether you are pounding it out on a typewriter or tapping it out with your thumbs, it is a tough job, but there is nothing I would have rather done. How many people can say they walked Merion East with Jack Nicklaus, shot pool with Mean Joe Greene, or sat with Joe Namath on the deck of his Florida home and listened to him recount Super Bowl III while he rocked his baby daughter to sleep? I'll have those memories forever.

I had the pleasure of writing TV scripts for the likes of James Coburn, Liev Schreiber, Gary Busey, Gene Hackman, Tom Selleck, and Ed Harris. They are all accomplished actors—Oscar winners, in some cases—but they were genuinely excited to be narrating for NFL Films. They grew up watching our shows, and adding their voices to the game's historical archive was a thrill. I remember Bruce Willis stopping in the middle of a sentence and saying, "Man, this is *sooooo* cool. . ."

I knew exactly what he meant.

In 1995, I won the Dick McCann Award from the Professional Football Writers of America. The award goes to one writer each year for what they describe as "long and distinguished reporting on professional football." The winner's name is added to the writer's honor roll at the Pro Football Hall of Fame in Canton, Ohio.

You receive the award during enshrinement weekend. In effect, you are part of the induction class. You don't get a gold jacket or a bust, but your name goes on the gallery wall, so you are in the same room with Johnny Unitas, Dick Butkus, and Joe Montana. You are there forever.

I invited Jack Wilson and his wife, Pat, to Canton to share in the celebration. I wanted him there since he was the editor who gave me the chance to write about sports at the *Bulletin*. Unfortunately, he was in poor health and could not make the trip, but he sent me this lovely letter:

> I wish I could be in Canton whooping it up to let everybody know how proud I am of you. Maybe I figured you'd be in the Hall of Fame when I first met you in that Temple journalism class about 35 years ago. Remember? It was a lucky day for me.
>
> I used to tell people I would have hired you if you were the meanest guy in town because you had so much talent and I also told them that I would have hired you if you had no talent because you might have been the nicest guy in town.
>
> The only thing that could possibly make this even better would be if we were all tooling along the turnpike with your grandfather in his merry old DeSoto. I'm sure he had a big part in you becoming the writer and the person you are.
>
> Pat joins me in our prayers and best wishes.[1]

I made the trip to Canton with my wife, Maria, and our two children, David and Kathleen. My parents met us there.

I received my award at the Mayor's Breakfast at the Canton Civic Center on Friday, the day before the enshrinement ceremony. I stepped to the microphone and looked around. Some of the greatest players of all time—Otto Graham, Bob Lilly, Bart Starr, Deacon Jones, Roger Staubach, Paul Hornung, Gale Sayers—were on the stage, all of them looking at me.

I took a deep breath to calm myself. I had my speech written out on index cards. It was short, simple, and straight from the heart. Here is what I said:

> I'm sure when this year's inductees speak tomorrow at the Hall of Fame, they will thank the coaches and teammates who helped them get there. Going in the Hall of Fame may be a singular honor, but, like most things in football, it is the product of a team effort.
>
> I am similarly grateful, and I'm delighted that my team can be here to share in this very special weekend—my wife, Maria; our children, David and Kathleen; and my parents, who came all the way from Florida after celebrating their fiftieth wedding anniversary last month.
>
> My family loves football, and they passed that love on to me. It was truly a wonderful gift.
>
> I feel both lucky and privileged to have been part of the greatest sport in the world. I'm thrilled beyond words to be here with these men whose eloquence on the playing field far surpassed anything I could ever hope to put on paper.
>
> I'd like to congratulate each of the inductees and thank them for giving us so much to write about over the years. It has been a joy, and if as this award says I contributed even a little bit to the game of professional football, then this is the greatest honor I've ever received.
>
> I'd like to thank the Pro Football Writers of America for this award, and I'd like to thank the staff at the Pro Football Hall of Fame and all the people here in Canton for giving me and my family a weekend we will never forget. Thank you very much.

When I returned home, there was a stack of cards and letters waiting for me. They were from friends and colleagues congratulating me on the McCann Award.

I also had a telephone message. It was from Ed Gebhart, the sports editor of the *Delaware County Daily Times*. In the one year I worked there, I had made a few extra bucks covering high school football on the weekends.

As the editor, Gebhart made the assignments. He gave the best games to his three full-time sports reporters. Since I was a news reporter and, in Gebhart's view, not a sports guy, I was assigned to the B-list games.

After a month or so, I was itching to cover a big game. Ridley High School was the reigning football power of Delaware County. The coach, Phil Marion, played on the same Fordham team as Vince Lombardi and Alex Wojciechowicz.

One day, I summoned up the courage to walk over to Gebhart's desk and ask if I could cover the Ridley game that week. He peered at me over his glasses.

"You aren't ready for Ridley," he said.

When I came home from Canton and checked my phone messages, I smiled when I heard Gebhart's voice.

"OK, Didinger," he said, "you're ready for Ridley."

Notes

This book is mostly a collection of stories, interviews, and memories gathered over the course of my fifty years in the business. The majority of the quotes come from interviews I did with various athletes and coaches, front-office executives, and league officials over the years.

I saved hundreds of notebooks—you should see my office—so, thankfully, I had a lot of material at my fingertips.

I used other sources, including books, newspaper and magazine articles, and interviews done for various projects at NFL Films. I did many of those interviews myself, but there were other interviews done by other NFL Films producers, and those are identified here.

I also quote directly from several of my columns for the *Bulletin* and the *Daily News*. They are noted here.

CHAPTER 1

1. Brent Musburger, "Bizarre Protest by Smith, Carlos Tarnishes Medals," *Chicago American*, October 17, 1968.
2. Nancy Armour, "Finally, Civil Rights Icons Honored," *USA Today*, September 24, 2019, 2C.
3. Deacon Jones, NFL Films interview, August 7, 1997.
4. Steve Sabol, NFL Films interview, June 16, 1997.
5. Larry Merchant, NFL Films interview, June 2, 1997.
6. Gary Pettigrew, NFL Films interview, August 25, 1997.

CHAPTER 2

1. Jay Greenberg, *Full Spectrum: The Complete History of the Philadelphia Flyers Hockey Club* (Chicago: Triumph Books, 1996), 8.

CHAPTER 4

1. Les Bowen, "The Champions," *Philadelphia Daily News*, January 17, 1992, H-5.
2. Jack Chevalier, *The Broad Street Bullies: The Incredible Story of the Philadelphia Flyers* (New York: Collier Books, 1974), 156.
3. Ibid., 172.
4. Tom Fox, "America Singing Again," *Philadelphia Daily News*, May 21, 1974.
5. Bowen, "The Champions," H-25.

CHAPTER 5

1. Tom Cushman, "Sir Wilbert of Camelot," *Philadelphia Daily News*, January 12, 1981, 75.

CHAPTER 6

1. Dave Anderson, "The Big Doolies of the World," *New York Times*, February 25, 1980.
2. E. M. Swift, "Miracle, the Sequel, Takes the Author Back to 1980," *Sports Illustrated*, February 9, 2004.

CHAPTER 7

1. Thomas Boswell, "Littlest Phillie Is Taking Wing," *Washington Post*, August 17, 1978.
2. Ray Didinger, "Phillies Are Rose-Less and Red-Faced," *Philadelphia Bulletin*, December 1, 1978, 53.
3. Larry Bowa and Barry Bloom, *I Still Hate to Lose* (Champaign, IL: Sports Publishing LLC, 2004).
4. Ray Didinger, "Bowa's Actions Typify What the Phils Have Become," *Philadelphia Bulletin*, August 11, 1978, 34.
5. Boswell, "Littlest Phillie Is Taking Wing."

CHAPTER 8

1. Ray Didinger, "A Sense of Perspective," *Philadelphia Daily News*, March 31, 1981.
2. Ibid.

CHAPTER 9

1. Sam Procopio, NFL Films interview, October 30, 1998.
2. Ibid.
3. John Spagnola, NFL Films interview, August 10, 1998.
4. Jim Murray, NFL Films interview, October 9, 1998.
5. Herbert Freudenberger, with Geraldine Richelson, *Burn-Out: The High Cost of High Achievement* (Garden City, NY: Anchor Press, 1980).
6. Jack Edelstein, NFL Films interview, November 11, 1998.
7. Ray Didinger, "Thanks Leonard but No Thanks," *Philadelphia Daily News*, December 17, 1984, 103.

8. Ray Didinger, "NFL Should Sack Tose," *Philadelphia Daily News*, December 19, 1984.

9. Ray Didinger, "Leonard's Legacy Is Not What He Intended," *Philadelphia Daily News*, March 13, 1985.

10. Frank Litsky, "Leonard Tose Dead at 88," *New York Times*, April 16, 2003.

11. Stan Hochman, "He Lost a Lot but He Loved the Game," *Philadelphia Daily News*, April 16, 2003.

CHAPTER 10

1. Ray Didinger, "A Man with a Mission," *Clearwater Sun*, July 26, 1985, 1B.

CHAPTER 11

1. Jack McCallum, "Doc across America," *Sports Illustrated*, May 4, 1987, 74.

2. Frank Deford, "A Star's Legacy," *Sports Illustrated*, May 4, 1987, 83.

3. Marty Bell, "Dr. J, Awesome Again," *Sport Magazine*, November 1979, 81.

4. Dave Wohl, "Man-Child in the NBA," *Sports Illustrated*, April 11, 1988, 80.

5. Ibid., 84.

6. Ibid., 80.

7. McCallum, "Doc across America," 75.

8. John Schulian, "The Ball Is in Bird's Court," *Philadelphia Daily News*, December 12, 1984, 105.

9. Phil Jasner, "Erving Is on a Peace Mission," *Philadelphia Daily News*, December 12, 1984, 106.

10. Stan Hochman, "Calling the Doctor," *Philadelphia Daily News*, May 10, 1993, 89.

CHAPTER 12

1. Ray Didinger, "The 500 Club," *Philadelphia Daily News*, April 20, 1987, S-24.

2. Roger Kahn, *The Boys of Summer* (New York: Harper and Rowe, 1972).

CHAPTER 13

1. Mark Kram Jr., *Smokin' Joe: The Life of Joe Frazier* (New York: HarperCollins, 2019), 188.

2. Stan Hochman, "A Fight to Cherish," *Philadelphia Daily News*, March 9, 1971.

3. Thomas Sowell, "Thoughts from Wise Thinkers," *New York Post*, July 23, 2013, 23.

4. Vincent Canby, "Robert De Niro in Raging Bull," *New York Times*, November 14, 1980.

CHAPTER 14

1. Gerald Eskenazi, "A Pool Finds a New Life as a Wine Cellar," *New York Times*, May 2, 1990, C12.

2. Stan Hochman, "Norm's Fire Might Just Go up in Smoke," *Philadelphia Daily News*, March 25, 1993, 99.

3. Stan Hochman, "Sweet Dreams about a Lemon," *Philadelphia Daily News*, March 13, 1985, 107.

4. Associated Press, "Discrepancies in NFL Revenue," *New York Times*, July 2, 1992.

5. Stan Hochman, "He's the Boss," *Philadelphia Daily News*, September 5, 1986, F-6.

6. Howard Balzer, "Raiders Set League Standard for Signing Rookies," *Pro Football Weekly*, August 9, 1992, 7.

7. Rich Hofmann, "Braman Became Own Worst Enemy," *Philadelphia Daily News*, April 7, 1994, 91.

8. Phil Sheridan, "What Makes Ray Run?" *Philadelphia Inquirer*, August 28, 1997.

CHAPTER 16

1. David Halberstam, *The Education of a Coach* (New York: Hachette Books, 2005).

CHAPTER 17

1. Tommy McDonald and Tex Maule, "The Monsters and Me," *Sports Illustrated*, July 27, 1964.

2. Amy Killian, "Compliment from Lombardi Was Highlight of a Stellar Career," *Columbus Free Press*, July 26, 1998, A9.

3. John Underwood, "The Magnificent Squirt," *Sports Illustrated*, October 8, 1962.

4. Letter, Raymond Berry to author, June 15, 1997.

5. Letter, Sonny Jurgensen to author, July 17, 1997.

6. Steve Doerschuk, "McDonald's Speech Belongs in the Hall," *Canton Repository*, August 2, 1998.

7. Gerry Callahan, "Hall of Famer McDonald Has a New Fan," *Sports Illustrated*, August 8, 1998.

CHAPTER 18

1. Bob Brookover, "A Disturbing Sign on Clock Management," *Philadelphia Inquirer*, January 20, 2016, D1.

2. Chris Chase, "Ranking the New NFL Coaches," *USA Today*, January 19, 2016.

3. Mike Lombardi, *The Ringer*, September 3, 2017.

4. NFL Interview, "The Reid File," *Philadelphia Daily News*, September 9, 1999, E-3.

EPILOGUE

1. Letter, Jack Wilson to author, July 19, 1995.

Index

Page numbers in italics indicate a photograph.

Ray Didinger was the first print journalist inducted into the Philadelphia Sports Hall of Fame. As a columnist for the *Philadelphia Bulletin* and the *Philadelphia Daily News,* he was named Pennsylvania Sportswriter of the Year five times. In 1995, he won the Dick McCann Award for long and distinguished reporting on pro football, and his name was added to the writers' honor roll at the Pro Football Hall of Fame. He also won six Emmy Awards as a writer and producer for NFL Films. He has authored or coauthored eleven books, including *The Eagles Encyclopedia, One Last Read: The Collected Works of the World's Slowest Sportswriter* (both Temple), and *The Ultimate Book of Sports Movies.* His play, *Tommy and Me,* which is about his friendship with Eagles Hall of Famer Tommy McDonald, was produced by Theatre Exile in Philadelphia and premiered in 2016. He is a talk show host on 94WIP Sports Radio and a football analyst for NBC Sports Philadelphia.